Research-Based Strategies for Improving Outcomes in Behavior

Kathleen Lynne Lane
University of Kansas

Bryan G. Cook
University of Hawaii

Melody Tankersley
Kent State University

PEARSON

Boston   Columbus   Indianapolis   New York   San Francisco   Upper Saddle River
Amsterdam   Cape Town   Dubai   London   Madrid   Milan   Munich   Paris   Montreal   Toronto
Delhi   Mexico City   São Paulo   Sydney   Hong Kong   Seoul   Singapore   Taipei   Tokyo

Vice President and Editorial Director: Jeffery W. Johnston
Executive Editor: Ann Castel Davis
Editorial Assistant: Andrea Hall
Vice President, Director of Marketing: Margaret Waples
Marketing Manager: Joanna Sabella
Senior Managing Editor: Pamela D. Bennett
Project Manager: Sheryl Glicker Langner
Senior Operations Supervisor: Matthew Ottenweller
Senior Art Director: Diane C. Lorenzo

Cover Designer: Candace Rowley
Cover Art: Background: © Lora liu/Shutterstock;
Image: © Nailia Schwarz/Shutterstock
Full-Service Project Management: S4Carlisle
Publishing Services
Composition: S4Carlisle Publishing Services
Printer/Binder: Edwards Brothers Malloy
Cover Printer: Lehigh-Phoenix Color/Hagerstown
Text Font: Times LT Std

Credits and acknowledgments for material borrowed from other sources and reproduced, with permission, in this textbook appear on the appropriate page within the text.

Photo Credits: Chapter-opening photo: © Nailia Schwarz/Shutterstock. Design images (from left to right): © Orange Line Media/Shutterstock; © kali9/iStockphoto; © Nailia Schwarz/Shutterstock; © iofoto/Shutterstock; © Jaren Jai Wicklund/Shutterstock.

Every effort has been made to provide accurate and current Internet information in this book. However, the Internet and information posted on it are constantly changing, so it is inevitable that some of the Internet addresses listed in this textbook will change.

Library of Congress Cataloging-in-Publication Data is available upon request.

10 9 8 7 6 5 4 3 2 1

ISBN 10:   0-13-702878-4
ISBN 13: 978-0-13-702878-8

Dedication

We dedicate this to our families, who help us remember what life is really about.

To Craig, Nathan, and Katie. – KLL

To Lysandra, Zoe, and Ben. – BC

To Bebe and Jackson. – MT

Preface

Research-Based Strategies for Improving Outcomes in Behavior was born of discussions over many years between special education practitioners and researchers regarding the need for a reliable and practical guide to highly effective, research-based practices in special education. Providing this type of information is a primary focus of the Council for Exceptional Children's Division for Research (CEC-DR), which the Division has pursued in many ways—sometimes with considerable success, sometimes with disappointment. At a meeting of the Executive Board of CEC-DR, then President Dr. Robin A. McWilliam suggested that the division consider producing a textbook to meet this need that would be unique in its emphasis on research-based practices. And so began concrete discussions that led to the book you are now reading.

You have probably read or heard something about the research-to-practice gap in special education—when practice is not based on research and, although less often emphasized in the professional literature, when research is not relevant to practice. This gap is not unique to special education; it occurs in general education and many other professional fields, including medicine. It is unlikely that the gap between research and practice will ever disappear entirely; indeed, it may not be desirable to thoroughly commingle the worlds of special education research and practice. However, when the gap between research and practice becomes a chasm, with practice being dictated more by tradition and personal trial-and-error than reliable research, the outcomes and opportunities of students suffer unnecessarily. Simply stated, special educators need to use the most effective instructional practices so that students with disabilities can reach their potentials; all too often, that does not occur.

We believe that this text is made all the more timely and important given the recent explosion of information on the Internet. The wealth of information available on the Internet (as well as from other, more traditional sources of recommendations on instructional practices such as professional development trainings, textbooks, and journals) can be an important asset in helping to determine what works. However, much of the information on the Internet and other sources is not research based and therefore is often inaccurate. Thus, although having thousands of pieces of information about various teaching techniques at one's fingertips may seem wonderful, it often has a stultifying effect, leaving educators drowning in a sea of information overload, without the time or necessary information (i.e., research findings) to determine what is truly credible and what is not. Rather than unsubstantiated promotion of scores of techniques, special educators need in-depth information on the practices shown by reliable research to be most effective for improving important outcomes of learners with disabilities, which is our aim in this text. By focusing on practices with solid research support, such as those featured in this text, special educators can feel confident that they are implementing approaches that are most likely to work for learners with disabilities.

It is important to realize, though, that research support is not an iron-clad guarantee of effectiveness for each and every student. Even the most effective, research-based practices do not work for everyone (there are nonresponders to every practice); and contextual factors (e.g., school and classroom environments, student characteristics) found in practice seldom align perfectly with the research studies supporting most practices. Therefore, teachers will have to rely on their professional wisdom to select and adapt the research-based practices targeted in this text to make them work in their classrooms, for their students. Nonetheless, having practices identified as effective on the basis of sound research, knowing what the research says about those practices, and understanding how those practices work are the critical first steps in achieving effective special education practice.

We believe that *Research-Based Strategies for Improving Outcomes in Behavior* will be counted as one of the considerable successes of CEC-DR because it provides researchers, teacher trainers, policy makers, practitioners, family members, and other stakeholders information about research-based practices shown to generally produce desirable outcomes in the core area of behavior. Moreover, this text provides readers with sufficient information about the practices and their research support to make informed decisions about practices that are right for them and their learners, and whether and how they might adapt the practices to fit their setting.

Acknowledgments

Very little is accomplished in isolation, and that was certainly true for this text. It is important for us to acknowledge the many professionals whose hard work is responsible for this text. We first acknowledge the chapter authors. We were fortunate to have the participation of the foremost authorities in the topics of focus in this work. We thank them for sharing their expertise and working so diligently and agreeably with us throughout the entire process. We thank Ann Davis, our editor at Pearson, for her unflagging support and insightful assistance. We also express our appreciation to Dr. Christine Balan, Dr. Lysandra Cook, Luanne Dreyer Elliott, and Norine Strang for their excellent and professional editing. Thank you to our reviewers: Mary E. Cronin, University of New Orleans, and E. Paula Crowley, Illinois State University. And most importantly, we acknowledge our families, without whose support and forbearance this work could not have been accomplished.

Kathleen Lynne Lane
University of Kansas

Bryan G. Cook
University of Hawaii

Melody Tankersley
Kent State University

Contents

8 Research-Based Practices for Social Behavior: *Social Skills Training, Replacement Behavior Training, and Positive Peer Reporting*

Frank M. Gresham, Lisa Libster, and Keri Menesses

CHAPTER 1

Introduction to Research-Based Practices for Increasing Behavioral Outcomes

Bryan G. Cook | *University of Hawaii*

Melody Tankersley | *Kent State University*

This is not a typical introductory textbook in special education that provides brief overviews of a large number of student characteristics and instructional practices. Textbooks with this focus serve important purposes. For example, individuals who are just beginning to explore the field of special education need to understand the breadth of student needs and corresponding instructional techniques that have been and are being used to teach students with disabilities. This text addresses a different need—the need for extensive information on selected, highly effective practices in special education. Stakeholders such as advanced pre-service special educators, practicing special education and inclusive teachers, administrators, parents, and many teacher-educators are more directly involved with the instruction and learning of children and youth with disabilities and as a result need in-depth treatments of the most effective practices that they can use to meaningfully impact and improve the educational experiences of children and youth with and at risk for disabilities.

In this textbook we provide extensive (rather than cursory) information on selected, highly effective practices (rather than on many practices, some of which may be less than effective) in special education. This endeavor begs an important question: What are the most highly effective practices identified in special education?

That is, how do we tell "what works" for children and youth with and at risk for disabilities?

Traditionally, special educators have relied on sources such as personal experience, colleagues, tradition, and experts to guide their instructional decision making (e.g., Cook & Smith, 2012). These resources have served teachers well in many ways. Special education teachers are skilled professionals who learn from their personal experiences and refine their teaching accordingly. Traditions and custom represent the accumulated personal experiences of whole groups and cultures and therefore can be imbued with great wisdom. And experts most often know of which they speak (and write) and make many valid recommendations. Yet, just as in other aspects of life, the personal experiences that lie at the root of these sources of knowing are prone to error and can lead special educators to false conclusions about which practices work and should be implemented with students with disabilities.

Limitations of Traditional Methods for Determining What Works

Chabris and Simons (2010) described five everyday illusions documented in the psychological literature (i.e., illusions of attention, memory, confidence, knowledge, and cause) that cast doubt on whether teachers can use personal experiences (their own, or those of their colleagues) to determine reliably whether practices work for their students. Chabris and Simons noted that although people assume that they attend to everything within their perceptual field, in reality many stimuli—especially those that contrast with one's expectations—"often go completely unnoticed" (p. 7). That is, people tend to focus their attention on what they expect to happen. Moreover, even when people actively attend to phenomena, their memories are unlikely to be wholly accurate and also are biased by their preconceptions. "We cannot play back our memories like a DVD—each time we recall a memory, we integrate whatever details we do remember with our expectations for what we should remember" (p. 49). Moreover, people tend to hold false illusions of confidence (e.g., most people think of themselves as above-average drivers) and knowledge (e.g., people tend to falsely believe that they know how familiar tools and systems work). Finally, "Our minds are built to detect meaning in patterns, to infer causal relationships from coincidences, and to believe that earlier events cause later ones" (p. 153), even though many patterns are meaningless, many associations are coincidental, and earlier events often simply precede rather than cause later occurrences.

Special education teachers—just like other people in their professional and day-to-day lives—may, then, not attend to events in a classroom that they do not expect (e.g., when using preferred practices, teachers may be more likely to focus on students who are doing well but not recognize struggling students); may construct memories of teaching experiences that are influenced by their preconceptions of whether a practice is likely to work; may be more confident than warranted that a favored instructional approach works when they use it; may believe that they fully understand why and how a practice works when they do not; and may believe that a practice causes positive changes in student outcomes when it does not. We are not suggesting that special educators are more gullible or error prone than anyone else. Nonetheless, these documented illusions show that using one's perceptions of personal experiences is an error-prone method for establishing whether instructional practices cause improved student outcomes.

Traditional wisdom shares many important traits with scientific research (e.g., refining understanding based on empirical input over time; Arunachalam, 2001). Indeed, many traditional practices are shown to be valid when examined scientifically (Dickson, 2003). Yet, tradition and custom often are based on incomplete science or consist of inaccurate superstition and folklore. History is replete with examples of traditional thinking that science subsequently has shown to be incorrect—from the flat-earth and geocentric models of the solar system to the direct inheritability of intelligence and ineducability of individuals with various disabilities. Accordingly, although many traditional instructional practices for students with disabilities may be effective, others have been passed down through generations of teachers even though they do not have a consistently positive effect on student outcomes. Basing instruction on the individual learning styles of students with disabilities, for example, is an accepted, traditional teaching practice despite the lack of supporting evidence (see Landrum & McDuffie, 2010).

As with personal experience and tradition, expert opinion is often faulty. Indeed, a common logical fallacy is the appeal to authority, in which one argues that a statement is true based on the authority of who said it. Not surprisingly, so-called authorities such as new-age gurus and celebrities often support less than effective products. But experts more commonly considered credible, such as textbook authors, also frequently provide inaccurate guidance. "The fact is, expert wisdom usually turns out to be at best highly contested and ephemeral, and at worst flat-out wrong" (Freedman, 2010, p. 7). In special education, "experts" have a long history of advocating for ineffective practices such as avoiding immunizations, facilitated communication, colored glasses or prism lenses, and patterning (e.g., Mostert, 2010; Mostert & Crockett, 2000). Thus, special educators need to be wary of basing instructional decisions on unverified expert recommendation.

Unlike their nondisabled peers, who often experience success in school while receiving mediocre or even poor instruction, students with disabilities require the most effective instruction to succeed (Dammann & Vaughn, 2001). As Malouf and Schiller (1995) noted, special education serves "students and families who are especially dependent on receiving effective services and who are especially vulnerable to fraudulent treatment claims" (p. 223). It appears, then, that those who teach and work with students with disabilities need a more reliable and trustworthy method for determining what works than personal experience, tradition, or expert opinion. Scientific research can provide a meaningful guide to special educators and other stakeholders when making decisions about what and how to teach learners with disabilities.

Benefits of Using Research to Determine What Works

It is the professional and ethical duty of special educators to implement the instructional techniques most likely to benefit the students they serve. Indeed, the Council for Exceptional Children's (CEC) standards for well-prepared special education teachers specify that special educators should keep abreast of research findings and implement

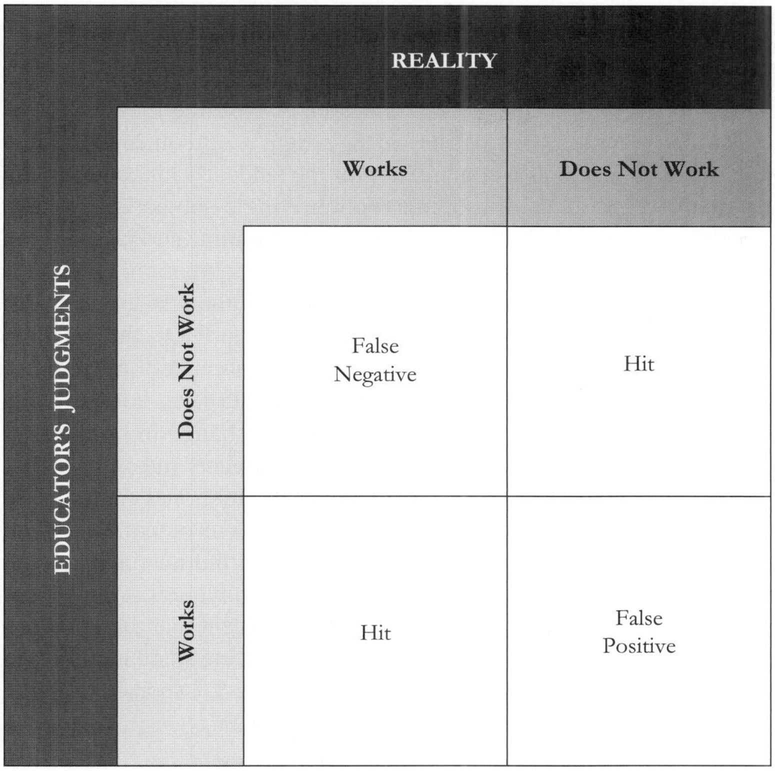

Figure 1.1 Relation between educator's judgments and reality regarding the effectiveness of instructional practices.

research-based practices with their students (CEC, 2009). Moreover, the No Child Left Behind Act and the Individuals with Disabilities Education Act of 2004 both place considerable emphasis on practices that are supported by scientifically based research (e.g., Hess & Petrilli, 2006; A. Smith, 2003; H. R. Turnbull, 2005). Using research as the preferred method to determine what and how to teach makes sense because research can address many of the shortcomings of other traditional approaches for identifying what works.

False Positives and False Negatives

When examining a practice's effectiveness, four possibilities exist to represent the relation between reality (Does the practice actually work for the children in question?) and educators' judgments (Do I believe that the practice works?) (see Figure 1.1). Educators can be right, or hit, in two ways: they can conclude that the practice (a) works, and it actually does, or (b) does not work, and it actually does not. They can also be wrong, or miss, in two ways. First, educators can commit a false positive by concluding that the practice works when it actually *is not* effective. Second, educators can commit a false negative by concluding that the practice does not work, when it actually *is* effective. The goal of any approach to determining what works is to maximize the number of hits while minimizing the likelihood of false positives and false negatives.

As discussed in the previous section, using personal experience, colleagues, tradition, and expert opinion leaves the door open to false positives and false negatives, which results in ineffective teaching and suboptimal outcomes for students with disabilities. Sound scientific research reduces the likelihood of false positives and false negatives in a number of ways, such as (a) using credible measures of student performance, (b) involving large and representative samples, (c) using research designs that rule out alternative explanations for change in student performance, and (d) engaging in the open and iterative nature of science (Lloyd, Pullen, Tankersley, & Lloyd, 2006).

Safeguards in Scientific Research

Credible Measures

Teachers' perceptions of students' behavior and academic performance are often based on subjective perceptions and unreliable measures and therefore do not correspond strictly with actual student behavior and performance (e.g., Madelaine & Wheldall, 2005). In contrast, sound scientific research uses trustworthy methods for measuring phenomena. Whether using direct observations of behavior, formal assessments, curriculum-based measures, or standardized rating scales, high-quality research utilizes procedures and instruments that are both reliable (i.e., consistent) and valid (i.e., meaningful) to accurately gauge student behavior and performance.

Large and Representative Samples

Educators typically interact with a limited number of students, whose performance and behavior may differ meaningfully from other students. Consequently, personal experience (as well as the experiences of colleagues or experts) may not generalize to other students. That is, just because a practice worked for a few students does not mean that it will work for most others. In contrast, research studies typically involve relatively large and often representative samples of student participants across multiple environments and educators. When research has shown that a practice has been effective for the vast majority of a very large number of students, the results are likely to generalize to others in the same population. It is true, however, that most single-subject research studies and some group experimental studies involve a relatively small number of participants. In these cases, confidence in research findings is obtained across a body of research, when multiple studies with convergent findings show that an intervention works for a substantial number of students within a population.

Ruling Out Alternative Explanations

When educators informally examine whether a practice works, they might implement the technique and observe whether students' outcomes subsequently improve. If outcomes do improve, it might seem reasonable to conclude that the intervention worked. However, this conclusion might be a false positive. The students may have improved because of their own development, or something else (e.g., a new educational assistant, a change in class schedule) may be responsible for improved outcomes. Group experimental and single-subject research studies are designed to rule out explanations for improved student outcomes other than the intervention being examined. In other words, causality (i.e., an intervention generally *causes* improved outcomes) can be inferred reasonably from these designs (B. G. Cook, Tankersley, Cook, & Landrum, 2008).

Group experimental research incorporates a control group (to which participants are randomly assigned in true experiments) that is as similar as possible to the experimental group. Ideally, the control and experimental groups comprise functionally equivalent participants and the only differences in their experiences are that the experimental group receives the intervention whereas the control group does not. Under these conditions, if the experimental group improves more than the control group, those improved

outcomes must logically be ascribed to the intervention (e.g., L. Cook, Cook, Landrum, & Tankersley, 2008).

In single-subject research studies, individuals provide their own control condition. A baseline measure (e.g., typical instruction) of a student's outcomes over time serves as a comparison for the student's outcomes in the presence of the intervention. Single-subject researchers strive to make conditions in the baseline and intervention phases equivalent, except for the intervention. Of course, it is possible that the student's outcomes improved in the presence of the intervention relative to the outcome trend during baseline because of a number of phenomena outside the control of the researcher (i.e., not the intervention; e.g., new medication, a change in home life). Accordingly, single-subject researchers must provide at least three demonstrations of a functional relationship between the intervention and student outcomes. When the intervention is introduced or withdrawn and student outcomes change in the predicted direction at least three times, educators can then be confident that the intervention was responsible for changes in the student outcomes (e.g., Tankersley, Harjusola-Webb, & Landrum, 2008).

Open and Iterative Nature of Science

Although many safeguards exist at the level of individual studies to protect against false positives and false negatives, scientific research is inevitably an imperfect enterprise. No study is ideal, and it is impossible for researchers to control for all possible factors that may influence student outcomes in the real world of schools. Furthermore, researchers can and sometimes do make mistakes, which may result in reporting misleading findings. The more general process and nature of scientific research protects against spurious findings in at least two additional ways: public examination of research and recognizing that knowledge is an iterative process.

When reporting a study, researchers must describe their research (e.g., sample, procedures, instruments) in detail. Additionally, before being published in a peer-reviewed journal (the most common outlet for research studies), research studies are evaluated by the journal editors and blind-reviewed (the reviewers' and authors' identities are confidential) by a number of experts in the relevant field. Authors also must provide contact information, which readers can use to make queries about the study or request the data for reevaluation. These processes necessitate that published research undergoes multiple layers of scrutiny, which are likely to (a) weed out most studies with serious errors before being published and (b) identify errors that do exist in published studies.

Finally, it is critical to recognize that research is an iterative process in which greater confidence in a practice is accrued as findings from multiple studies converge in its support. Even with the safeguard of peer review and public scrutiny of research, published studies do sometimes report inaccurate findings. However, the iterative nature of science suggests that conclusions are best examined across entire bodies of research literature made up of multiple studies. For truly effective practices, the possible erroneous conclusions of one or two studies will be shown to be incorrect by a far larger number of studies with accurate findings. Thus, in contrast to relying on personal experience or on expert opinions, science has built-in self-correction mechanisms for identifying spurious results (Sagan, 1996; Shermer, 2002).

Caveats

Research-based practices represent powerful tools for improving the educational outcomes of students with disabilities, yet special educators need to understand a number of associated caveats and limitations. Specifically, research-based practices (a) will not work for everyone, (b) need to be implemented in concert with effective teaching practices, (c) must be selected carefully to match the needs of targeted students, and (d) should be adapted to maximize their impact.

Special educators cannot assume that a practice shown by research to be *generally* effective will be automatically effective for *all* of their students. No number of research participants or studies translates into a guarantee that a practice will work for each and every student, especially for students with disabilities who have unique learning characteristics and needs. Nonresponders, or treatment resistors, will exist for even the most effective instructional approaches. Therefore, although research-based practices are highly likely to be effective and special educators should therefore prioritize these practices, special educators should also always systematically evaluate the effects of these practices through progress monitoring (e.g., Deno, 2006).

Furthermore, research-based practices do not constitute good teaching but represent one important component of effective instruction. Research on effective teaching indicates that effective instruction is characterized by a collection of teacher behaviors, such as pacing instruction appropriately, emphasizing academic instruction, previewing instruction and reviewing previous instruction, monitoring student performance, circulating around and scanning the instructional environment to identify learner needs, recognizing appropriate student behavior, exhibiting enthusiasm, displaying "withitness" (an awareness of what is happening throughout the classroom), and using wait time after asking questions (Brophy & Good, 1986; Doyle, 1986). When educators implement research-based practices in the context of generally *ineffective* instruction—instruction

that occurs in the absence of these hallmarks of effective teaching—the practices are unlikely to produce desired outcomes. As such, research-based practices cannot take the place of and should always be applied in the context of good teaching (B. G. Cook, Tankersley, & Harjusola-Webb, 2008).

Another important caveat is that a practice demonstrated by research studies to be effective for one group may not work for others. It is therefore important that special educators are aware of the student group for which a practice has been demonstrated to be effective when selecting instructional and assessment practices to use with their students. For example, although a practice may have been shown by research studies to be effective for elementary students with learning disabilities, it may not work or even be appropriate for high school students with autism. However, highly effective practices tend to be powerful and their effects robust, and as such, they typically work for more than one specific group of children. For example, the use of mnemonic strategies has been shown to be effective for nondisabled students, students with learning disabilities, students with emotional and behavioral disorders, and students with intellectual impairments at a variety of grade levels (Scruggs & Mastropieri, 2000). Therefore, when reading about a practice that has been validated by research as effective with, for example, students with learning disabilities, special educators working with children and youth with other disabilities should not simply assume that the practice will be similarly effective for their students. But neither should they automatically assume that the practice will be ineffective. Rather, we recommend that special educators use their unique insights and knowledge of their students to evaluate the supporting research, underlying theory, and critical elements of a practice to determine the likelihood that a research-based practice will work for them.

Furthermore, special educators will need to consider whether and how to adapt research-based practices to meet the unique needs of their students. Although implementing a practice as designed is important (e.g., if a practice is not implemented correctly, one cannot expect it to be as effective as it was in the supporting research), recent research has indicated that overly rigid adherence to research-based practices may actually reduce their effectiveness (e.g., Hogue et al., 2008). It appears that teachers should adapt research-based practices to match the unique learning needs of their students and make the practice their own (McMaster et al., 2010). Yet they must do so in a way that preserves the integrity of the essential elements of the research-based practice to avoid rendering it ineffective.

These caveats notwithstanding, because of its many safeguards protecting against false-positive and false-negative conclusions regarding what works, scientific research is the best method available for special educators to identify effective instructional practices. By making decisions about how to teach on the basis of collective bodies of peer-reviewed research studies, special educators can identify with confidence practices that are likely to work for their students.

The Research-to-Practice Gap in Special Education

"Educational research could and should be a vital resource to teachers, particularly when they work with diverse learners—students with disabilities, children of poverty, limited-English speaking students. It is not" (Carnine, 1997, p. 513). The research-to-practice gap describes the commonplace occurrence of children and youth being taught with unproven practices while practices supported through research are not implemented. It is a complex phenomenon with many underlying causes that defies simple solutions. Kauffman (1996) suggested that the research-to-practice gap may be particularly extreme in special education, illustrating that an inverse relationship may actually exist between research support and degree of implementation for instructional practices in special education.

Despite reforms and legislation supporting the role of research in education, research findings indicate that the gap between research and practice continues to persist. For example, special educators reported using research-based practices no more often than ineffective practices (Burns & Ysseldyke, 2009; Jones, 2009). Jones also observed that some special education teachers over-reported their use of research-based practices, suggesting that the actual implementation rate of research-based practices may be even lower than reported. To make matters worse, when special educators do implement research-based practices, they often do so with low levels of fidelity (or not as designed; e.g., B. G. Cook & Schirmer, 2006)—potentially rendering the practices ineffective. Furthermore, many special educators report that they do not trust research or researchers (Boardman, Arguelles, Vaughn, Hughes, & Klingner, 2005) and find information from other teachers more trustworthy and usable (Landrum, Cook, Tankersley, & Fitzgerald, 2002, 2007).

The research-to-practice gap has clear and direct implications for the educational outcomes of students with disabilities. Using practices shown to have reliable and positive effects on student outcomes is the most likely way to improve student performance. Using research-based practices should, therefore, be a professional and ethical imperative for educators. This is true for all teachers. But as Dammann and Vaughn (2001) noted, whereas nondisabled students may perform adequately even in the presence of less than optimal instruction, students

with disabilities require that their teachers use the most effective instructional practices to reach their potentials and attain successful school outcomes.

This Textbook and Addressing the Research-to-Practice Gap

Bridging the research-to-practice gap in special education represents a significant challenge. Many issues will have to be addressed, such as improving teachers' attitudes toward research, providing ongoing supports for teachers to adopt and maintain research-based practices, and conducting high-quality research that is relevant to special education teachers (see B. G. Cook, Landrum, Tankersley, & Kauffman, 2003). But perhaps the most fundamental issues for bridging the research-to-practice gap are (a) *identifying* those practices that are research-based in critical areas of special education and (b) *providing the relevant information* (e.g., supporting theory, critical elements of the research-based practices, specific information on the supporting research studies) necessary to guide special educators in deciding whether the practice is right for them and their students and how to implement it. Without these critical first steps of identifying and providing special educators relevant information about research-based practices, the field of special education is unlikely to make significant progress in bridging the gap between research and practice.

Turning to original reports of research is an unsatisfactory alternative for the vast majority of special educators. Most teachers do not have the training to critically analyze technical research reports that often are geared for audiences with advanced training in statistics and research (Greenwood & Abbott, 2001). And even for those educators with advanced training in these areas, their full-time teaching jobs should and typically do occupy their time. It is simply not realistic for teachers to read through, synthesize, and critically analyze entire bodies of research literature for every instructional decision with which they are faced.

Textbooks focused on methods of instruction and assessment seem an ideal place to provide educators with useful information on research-based practices that can be used to bridge the research-to-practice gap. Unfortunately, much of teacher education—both pre-service and in-service—is based on expert opinion and the personal experiences of those conducting the training or writing the training materials (e.g., textbooks). For example, textbook authors frequently recommend practices with little justification. Discussion of supporting research, if provided at all, is often too brief and incomplete for educators to make informed decisions about the appropriateness of the recommended practice for their classrooms. For example, Dacy, Nihalani, Cestone, and Robinson (2011) analyzed the content of three teaching methods textbooks and found that when prescriptive recommendations for using practices were supported by citations, authors predominantly cited secondary sources (e.g., books, position papers) rather than provide discussions of original research from which their readers might arrive at meaningful conclusions regarding the effectiveness of the practices.

To address special educators' need for trustworthy, detailed, and teacher-friendly summaries of the research literature regarding what works in special education, the chapters in the complete, four-part text (Cook & Tankersley, 2013) provide thorough synopses of the research literature supporting research-based practices in core areas of special education: academics, behavior, assessment, and targeted groups of learners. Specifically, in this text on improving the behavioral outcomes of students with disabilities, chapter authors, who are documented experts on the topics of focus, address how to improve the outcomes of students with disabilities in critical areas and facets of behavior: school-wide behavior and positive behavioral supports, preventing problem behavior, academic engagement, compliance, internalizing behavioral problems, aggressive behavior, and social behavior. Chapter authors discuss this and recommend practices and approaches based on supporting research. Chapter authors also provide readers with descriptions of the underlying theory supporting the practices; supporting research studies, including information such as the research designs, the number and type of participants, and the degree to which the recommended practices positively affected student outcomes; and the critical elements of each research-based practice. Using this information, special educators can (a) make informed decisions about which research-based practices best fit their needs and (b) begin to implement the practices and improve the behavioral outcomes of their students with disabilities.

Conclusion

Special educators clearly want to use the most effective practices to enhance the educational outcomes and opportunities of the students they teach. However, given traditional methods for determining what works and the rapid proliferation of information on teaching techniques on the Internet (Landrum & Tankersley, 2004), much of which is misleading, it is increasingly difficult and complicated to know what works, what doesn't, and how to know the difference. Research is the most trustworthy method for determining what works in special education. This text provides readers with a wealth of information on specific research-based practices for behavioral outcomes in special education.

CHAPTER 2

Positive Behavior Support: *A Framework for Preventing and Responding to Learning and Behavior Problems*

Kathleen Lynne Lane | *University of North Carolina, Chapel Hill*

Holly Mariah Menzies | *California State University, Los Angeles*

Wendy P. Oakes and **Jemma Robertson Kalberg** | *Vanderbilt University*

Teachers, administrators, and support staff working in K–12 school systems are confronted with a number of responsibilities. For example, they are expected to teach highly rigorous content; ensure that all students make adequate yearly progress academically; serve an increasingly diverse student population; support students with exceptionalities in inclusive environments; and teach social and behavioral competencies necessary to maintain a safe, positive climate (Kauffman, 2010; Lane, Kalberg, & Menzies, 2009; MacMillan, Gresham, & Forness, 1996; No Child Left Behind Act, 2001). The last objective is particularly formidable, given the rise of antisocial behavior among our nation's youth, which is reflective of the growing incivility of society as a whole (H. M. Walker, 2003). For example, a national survey on school crime and safety found that violent incidents were reported by 75.5% ($n = 62,600$) of schools surveyed, with a total of 1,332,400 violent acts in one school year (Neiman & DeVoe, 2009). Further, 20,260 acts were student threats of physical attack with a weapon. In 2007, students ages 12 to 18 were more likely to become a victim of a nonfatal crime at school (1.5 million) than

away from school (1.1 million; Dinkes, Kemp, & Baum, 2009). It is not surprising that many school-site personnel feel overwhelmed and challenged, particularly when it comes to managing student behavior (Lane, Menzies, Bruhn, & Crnobori, 2011).

National estimates suggest that between 3% and 6% of school-age students have emotional and behavioral disorders (EBDs), with less than 1% of students meeting the inclusionary criteria necessary to qualify for services under the Individuals with Disabilities Education Act (IDEA, 2004). Consequently, it is the job of the general education community to identify and support students with and at risk for EBD. Students with EBD include individuals with externalizing (e.g., aggression, coercion, noncompliance, delinquency), internalizing (e.g., anxiety, social withdrawal, depression), and comorbid conditions. Clearly, teachers are more apt to notice students with externalizing behaviors, because their behavior patterns often impose safety concerns and impede the teacher's ability to deliver instruction—posing significant challenges to the educational environment (Kauffman & Brigham, 2009; H. M. Walker, Ramsey, & Gresham, 2004). For example, in a recent national survey, 34% of teachers reported that student behavior interfered with their teaching (Dinkes et al., 2009). In fact, such challenging behavior is a major determinant in teachers' decisions to leave the field of education (Brouwers & Tomic, 2000; L. Harris, 1991; Martin, Linfoot, & Stephenson, 1999).

Not only does student behavior affect instruction, but teachers themselves are victims of student violence. Teachers of secondary (8%) and elementary (7%) schools report being victims of violent threats, whereas elementary teachers are more often (6%) attacked by students than are secondary teachers (2%; Dinkes et al., 2009). Many schools have increased safety procedures to address such trends. For example, 99% of schools require visitors to sign in, 90% maintain locked and monitored facilities, 43% have electronic procedures for alerting the building and community of a threat, 55% monitor safety with security cameras, and 55% require adults to wear security badges with photos. These procedures also serve as daily reminders of the potential safety threats to students and teachers. Thus, concerns surrounding school safety are warranted, and attempts to address these concerns are evident. Although teachers and support staff may not have expected that they would be responsible for addressing social and behavioral considerations in addition to academics, this is clearly the case (Lane, Kalberg, & Menzies, 2009).

During the last 10 years, a number of legal and legislative mandates have been established that require schools to establish safe, nonviolent environments. For example, Title IV of Improving America's Schools Act of 1994, The Safe and Drug-Free Schools and Communities Act (1994), called for states and local educational agencies (LEAs) to design school-wide violence and drug abuse prevention programs (A. Turnbull et al., 2002). Title IV may have also prompted the zero-tolerance policy for drugs and weapons that was also included in the IDEA (1997). In addition, the White House issued a charge calling for systemic changes to guarantee a safe, nonviolent environment for all students (Dwyer, Osher, & Warger, 1998; Kern & Manz, 2004). To this end, the Surgeon General's *Report on Youth Violence* offered the following recommendations to address antisocial behavior that occurs in schools: (a) eliminate antisocial networks, (b) boost students' academic performance, (c) establish prosocial school climates, and (d) adopt a primary prevention agenda that focuses on designing, implementing, and evaluating prevention efforts (Satcher, 2001). IDEA (2004) includes parallel language specifying "incentives for whole-school approaches, scientifically based early reading programs, positive behavior interventions and supports, and early intervening services to reduce the need to label children as disabled in order to address the learning and

behavioral needs of such children" (p. 4). Thus, the expectation is clear: schools need to establish safe, nonviolent environments to facilitate both instruction and the personal safety of all individuals (students, faculty, and staff; American Psychological Association [APA] Board of Educational Affairs Task Force on Classroom Violence Directed Against Teachers, 2011).

To meet this charge, many school sites and districts across the country have adopted three-tiered models of prevention that are grounded in systemic change and data-based decision making to better meet students' academic, behavioral, and social needs. A variety of models have been developed such as (a) positive behavior support (PBS) models (Lewis & Sugai, 1999; Sugai & Horner, 2002), which, initially, focused predominantly (if not solely) on behavior; (b) Response to Intervention (RtI; Gresham, 2002b; Sugai, Horner, & Gresham, 2002) models, which focus mainly on meeting students' academic needs and providing alternative methods of identifying students for special education services under the specific learning disabilities category; and (c) integrated, comprehensive, three-tiered (CI3T) models that include features of PBS and RtI models, with a goal of supporting students' combined academic, behavioral, and social needs. We contend that integrated models pose particular benefit, given that academic and behavioral concerns do not appear in isolation, but rather interact to influence one another—a transactional relation mediated by many other variables (e.g., teacher–student interactions [see Chapters 4 and 5, this volume], social competence [see Chapter 8, this volume], and instructional techniques [see Chard, Cook, & Tankersley, 2013; Lane & Wehby, 2002]).

The concept of three-tiered models is not new; they originated in the mental health industry and were adapted to provide a new delivery of instructional and behavioral support in the educational system (Lane, 2007). One of the main theoretical benefits of such models, particularly for students with and at risk for EBD, is that they ideally provide a seamless delivery of increasingly intensive supports (a) to prevent the development of learning and behavioral problems through the use of primary prevention (Tier 1) supports and (b) to respond to existing learning and behavioral problems through the use of secondary (Tier 2) and tertiary (Tier 3) supports. No longer are learning and behavioral challenges viewed solely as within-child problems. Instead of traditional models that require students to fail before supports can be offered, three-tiered models subscribe to a proactive, instructional approach to provide the necessary level of supports based on individual student needs within this larger prevention framework (Horner & Sugai, 2000; Lane, Robertson, & Graham-Bailey, 2006). Ideally, school-wide data collected as part of regular school practices are used to determine which students may benefit from secondary and tertiary efforts. These decisions are made by leadership teams who meet regularly to engage in this data-based decision-making process.

In this chapter we write to both practitioner and researcher audiences. We begin by describing an integrated, comprehensive three-tier model of prevention that includes key features of PBS and RtI models, *not* with an emphasis on identifying students for special education services, but with a focus on meeting the academic, behavioral, and social needs of students. Specifically, we describe each level of prevention—primary, secondary, and tertiary—with an emphasis on primary prevention efforts. We conclude the chapter by offering a summary of the strengths of the model as well as areas for improvement in future inquiry.

Primary Prevention: Building a Comprehensive Base Program

At the base of a three-tiered model is the primary prevention component, which can be referred to as school-wide, universal, or Tier-1 prevention. Tier 1 has no screening or eligibility determinations: *all* students participate just by virtue of attending school (Lane, Kalberg, & Edwards, 2008). The intent of Tier-1 support is to *prevent harm* from occurring by providing a support that is accessed by all students (H. M. Walker & Severson, 2002). This same logic is evident in a medical model. For example, in a medical model, parents may elect to have their children receive a vaccination for the flu. The intent of receiving the vaccine is to *prevent* their children from getting the virus.

Ideally, in a school-based model, prevention would include three core components: academic, behavioral, and social. Specifically, the school-site leadership team would construct a primary prevention plan that addresses each of these three components. For example, an elementary-level team may select the Scott Foresman reading program (see www.sfreading.com) as the base curriculum to teach reading and the Second Steps Violence Prevention Program (SSVP; Committee for Children, 2007) as their social skills component. Strong evidence bases support the feasibility and efficacy of each program to increase academic performance and decrease problem behaviors, respectively (e.g., Frey, Hirschstein, & Guzzo, 2000; S. D. McMahon & Washburn, 2003; Wehby, Lane, & Falk, 2005).

The team may decide to design its own school-wide positive behavior support (SW-PBS) program for the behavioral component. This would involve establishing school-wide expectations for behavior (e.g., respect, responsibility, and best effort) that are operationally defined in all relevant settings (e.g., hallways, bathrooms, classrooms, cafeterias, buses, drop-off and pick-up areas; see Table 2.1 for an example of an expectation matrix). We recommend using a data-based method of identifying those expectations that faculty and staff view as essential for students' success (Lane, Kalberg, & Menzies, 2009). One method is to have school-site personnel rate the importance of the 30 social skills items specified on the Social Skills Rating System (SRSS; Gresham & Elliott, 1990). Rather than rating each item for each individual student, teachers and staff rate the extent to which each item is essential for student success in their class (e.g., *listens to instructions*, *makes assistance needs known in an appropriate manner*). Each item is rated on the same 3-point Likert-type scale as specified in the manual: 0 (*not important*), 1 (*important*), or 2 (*critical*). Then, these data can be analyzed using frequency counts to determine which items are rated by the majority (>50%) of faculty and staff as critical for success (rated as a 2). This information is used to construct the teacher-expectation matrix (see Lane, Kalberg, & Menzies, 2009, for additional details on the planning process).

After the expectations are established and all adults (e.g., administrators, teachers, custodians, secretaries) in the building have reached consensus, the next step is to teach these expectations explicitly to students. This can be done through school-wide lessons and other instructional activities (e.g., posting of expectations, videos, assemblies). Then, students should be afforded opportunities to practice and receive reinforcement for meeting these expectations. The reinforcement typically occurs by allocating PBS tickets that are delivered intermittently in response to students exhibiting target behaviors and are paired with behavior specific praise (J. O. Cooper, Heron, & Heward, 2007). Students then exchange these tickets for secondary reinforcers that allow students to access (positive reinforcement) or avoid (negative reinforcement) attention (e.g., lunch with a teacher); activities, tasks, or tangibles (e.g., homework pass); and sensory experiences (e.g., listen to music during independent seat work; Lane, Kalberg, & Menzies, 2009; Umbreit, Ferro, Liaupsin, & Lane, 2007).

Assessment Considerations

When implementing such a model, it is important to monitor all aspects of the program including treatment integrity, social validity, and student performance. In the sections that follow, we define each of these constructs and discuss issues of measurement and relevance.

Table 2.1 Sample Expectation Matrix for Use at the Elementary Level

	Settings					
	Classroom	Hallway	Cafeteria	Playground	Bathroom	Bus
Respect	Follow directions. Use kind words and actions. Control your temper. Cooperate with others. Use an inside voice.	Use a quiet voice. Walk on the right side of the hallway. Keep hands to yourself.	Use an inside voice. Use manners. Listen to and follow adult requests.	Respect other peoples' personal space. Follow the rules of the game.	Use the restroom, and then return to class. Stay in your own bathroom stall. Little talking.	Use kind words toward the bus driver and other students. Listen to and follow the bus driver's rules.
Responsibility	Arrive to class on time. Remain in school for the whole day. Bring your required materials. Turn in finished work. Exercise self-control.	Keep hands to yourself. Walk in the hallway. Stay in line with your class.	Make your choices quickly. Eat your own food. Choose a seat, and stick with it. Clean up after yourself.	Play approved games. Use equipment appropriately. Return equipment when you are done. Line up when the bell rings.	Flush toilet. Wash hands with soap. Throw away any trash properly. Report any problems to your teacher.	Talk quietly with others. Listen to and follow the bus drivers' rules. Remain in seat after you enter the bus. Use self-control.
Best Effort	Participate in class activities. Complete work with best effort. Ask for help politely.	Walk quietly. Walk directly to next location.	Use your table manners. Use an inside voice.	Include others in your games. Be active. Follow the rules of the game.	Take care of your business quickly. Keep bathroom tidy.	Listen to and follow the bus drivers' rules. Keep hands and feet to self.

Source: Information from Walker, H. M., Ramsey, E., & Gresham, F. M. (2004). *Antisocial behavior in school: Evidence-based practices* (2nd ed., p. 138). Belmont, CA: Wadsworth.

Treatment Integrity

Treatment integrity refers to the extent to which the plan is implemented as intended (Gresham, 1989; Yeaton & Sechrest, 1981). Treatment integrity is an essential, but often omitted, measure (see Lane, Kalberg, Bruhn, Mahoney, & Driscoll, 2008). If treatment integrity data are not collected, we cannot establish that the plan actually occurred as intended. Consequently, we cannot be certain that the change in students' performance (or absence of changes) was the result of the intervention effort or some other extraneous variables (e.g., the introduction of hall monitors, which was not in the original plan).

Monitoring the integrity of school-wide plans is challenging, particularly in middle and high schools, because the buildings are larger and the number of persons involved (e.g., teachers and students) is greater than

elementary settings. Nonetheless, if a school-site leadership team or research team wants to draw accurate conclusions regarding the effect of primary prevention efforts on student outcomes, treatment integrity must be measured. Some methods of measurement include teacher self-reports using behavioral checklists with intervention components specified; outside observers (e.g., research assistants, behavior specialist, principal) completing behavioral checklists; and teacher self-reports of the same period for which the outside observer is present, with a comparison of the two perspectives used as coaching information (see Lane, Kalberg, Bruhn, et al., 2008, for a detailed explanation of how to collect and use treatment integrity data collected using these perspectives).

Standardized measures such as the School-wide Evaluation Tool (SET; Sugai, Lewis-Palmer, Todd, & Horner, 2001) can also provide treatment integrity data. The SET includes 28 items that make up seven key features of SW-PBS (Horner, Todd, Lewis-Palmer, Irvin, Sugai, & Boland, 2004). Specifically, subscales measure the degree to which the following occur: (a) school-wide behavior expectations are defined; (b) school-wide expectations are taught to all students and rewards are provided for meeting school-wide behavior expectations; (c) a consistently implemented continuum of consequences for problem behavior is utilized; (d) problem behavior patterns are monitored, and the data are used as part of ongoing decision-making; (e) an administrator actively supports and is involved in the SW-PBS program; and (f) the district provides support to the school (e.g., functional policies, staff training opportunities, and data collection; Horner et al., 2004). Each item is scored on a 3-point Likert-type scale ranging from 0 (*not implemented*), to 1 (*partially implemented*), to 2 (*fully implemented*). Subscale summary scores are formed by computing the percentage of possible points for each of the seven key features. An overall summary score is computed by averaging the seven subscale scores. The SET has strong psychometric properties (alpha coefficient of 0.96; Horner et al., 2004).

In addition to assisting with the interpretation of intervention outcomes, data collected using each of these techniques can be used to inform the coaching process. Specifically, treatment integrity data can assist school-site leadership team members in identifying those features of the plan that are and are not being implemented as designed. For example, a core construct of a reinforcement plan is to pair the delivery of the reinforcement (e.g., a ticket) to students with behavior-specific praise that is tied to school-wide expectations. If a leadership team finds, through the use of the SET, that faculty and staff are giving the reinforcer (tickets) but are unable to state the school-wide expectations, the leadership team may want to provide a refresher for faculty on the expectations and provide examples with practice in using behavior-specific praise (e.g., "Sarah, you have earned a ticket for being responsible in remembering your homework today").

One factor that may influence teachers' level of implementation integrity is their perceptions of the plan, or social validity. Namely, if teachers believe that a plan targets meaningful goals, has reasonable procedures, and is likely to "work," they may be more likely to implement the plan as designed—with treatment integrity.

Social Validity

al validity refers to the social significance of the
the acceptability of intervention procedures con-
he plan, and the social importance of the effects

(either expected or actualized; Kazdin, 1977; Lane & Beebe-Frankenberger, 2004; Wolf, 1978). When monitoring the social validity of a primary prevention plan, we recommend administering measures of social validity (either formally or informally) before implementing a school-wide model, and again following each year of implementation. In 2002, the Intervention Rating Profile-15 (Witt & Elliott, 1985) was modified for use with primary-level interventions. In an initial validation study of the modified version, the Primary Intervention Rating Scale (PIRS; Lane, Robertson, & Wehby, 2002) was found to be a one-factor measure with high internal consistency in elementary, middle, and high school settings with alpha coefficients of 0.97, 0.98, and 0.97, respectively (Lane, Kalberg, & Menzies, 2009). Furthermore, site-level mean scores on the PIRS predicted mean levels of treatment integrity (measured using a teacher-completed behavioral checklist) during the first year of implementation ($r = 0.71$, $p = 0.005$), suggesting that high social validity may promote treatment integrity. Additional studies are necessary before using the PIRS on a wide-scale basis.

Social validity data collected before implementation can provide important information that educators can use to identify areas of concern and subsequently modify a plan before implementing it. And (as indicated previously) the data may predict the extent to which the intervention is implemented as intended. Social validity data collected after the first year of implementation can be used to inform revisions. Educators should remain mindful of the fact that primary prevention plans should not be modified during an academic year if the school would like to evaluate the extent to which the plan is associated with changes in student outcome measures. In other words, if the plan continually shifts throughout a school year, it is not possible to evaluate it accurately. Essentially, the plan becomes a moving target. It is more effective to wait until the end of each academic year to collect social validity data from teachers, students, and parents to inform revisions that can occur before the onset of the next academic year (see Lane, Kalberg, & Menzies, 2009, for a more detailed explanation). The intent of each revision is to ensure that the plan is customized to the ever-changing community of students that the school serves, with an overall goal of creating an environment that facilitates learning. This is accomplished by creating a context that is safe for all students (physically, intellectually, and otherwise), so that students are motivated and encouraged to take risks to extend their learning. To determine if these lofty goals are achieved, it is necessary to measure students' performance in order to inform ongoing refinement of the primary prevention plan as well as to monitor each individual student's performance.

Student Performance

To monitor student performance, school-wide data collected as part of regular school practices are used to monitor (a) overall level of performance for the school or grade levels as a whole and (b) how individual students respond over time to identify those students who may need more assistance. Table 2.2 shows a sample assessment schedule that features school-wide data such as curriculum-based measures to monitor academic performance (AIMSweb; Pearson Education, 2008), attendance (unexcused tardies and absences), office discipline referrals (ODR), behavioral screeners (Systematic Screening for Behavior Disorders [SSBD], H. M. Walker & Severson, 1992), and referrals to counseling. When determining which measures to include in an assessment schedule, it is important to attend to issues of reliability, validity, and feasibility. For example, data should be accurate in terms of measurement and practical, given the constraints of the school day.

ODRs, for instance, are a frequently used outcome measure in SW-PBS, in large part due to the feasibility of collecting this data (e.g., takes limited teacher time, already is required by the district; e.g., Clonan, McDougal, Clark, & Davison, 2007; K. McIntosh, Campbell, Carter, & Zumbo, 2009). However, without using specific procedures to ensure the consistency with which ODR and other school-based outcomes are measured, reliability of the data can be problematic; the school's overall level of risk and the identification of students for secondary or tertiary supports therefore may not be accurate (Lane, Kalberg, Bruhn, et al., 2008; Nelson, Benner, Reid, Epstein, & Currin, 2002). For example, use of a system such as the School-Wide Information System (SWIS; S. May et al., 2000) is important to ensure that the procedures are clear for determining which behaviors do and do not warrant an ODR (minor or major offenses). Furthermore, ensuring that such a system is implemented as planned

Table 2.2 Sample Elementary School Assessment Schedule

Measure	Aug	Sept	Oct	Nov	Dec	Jan	Feb	Mar	April	May
Report cards and progress reports		X		X		X			X	
Writing assessment		X			X				X	
Curriculum-based measures (CBMs)	X	X	X	X	X	X	X	X	X	X
State-wide assessment										X
Office discipline referrals (ODRs)	X	X	X	X	X	X	X	X	X	X
Student Risk Screening Scale (SRSS; Drummond, 1994)		X			X				X	
Systematic Screening for Behavior Disorders (SSBD; H. M. Walker & Severson, 1992)		X			X				X	
Attendance	X	X	X	X	X	X	X	X	X	X
Counseling referrals	X	X	X	X	X	X	X	X	X	X
Bullying referrals	X	X	X	X	X	X	X	X	X	X
Social Validity Survey: Primary Intervention Rating Scale (PIRS; Lane, Robertson, & Wehby, 2002)		X							X	
School-wide evaluation tool (SET; Sugai, Lewis-Palmer, Todd, & Horner, 2001)		X							X	
Treatment integrity: self-report and direct observations by an outside observer	X	X	X	X	X	X	X	X	X	X
Rate of access to reinforcement (PBS Tickets)		X							X	
Effective behavior supports (EBS; Sugai, Horner, & Todd, 2000)		X							X	

Source: Information from Lane, K. L., Kalberg, J. R., & Menzies, H. M. (2009). *Developing schoolwide programs to prevent and manage problem behaviors: A step-by-step approach* (p. 105). New York, NY: Guilford Press.

Note: PBS = positive behavior support.

(with procedural fidelity) is also necessary, so that the school-site leadership team can be certain that the data are reliable and that the decisions made based on these data are valid.

Concerns about the reliability and validity of ODR data have prompted some researchers and practitioners to choose validated systematic screening tools such as the SSBD, the Strengths and Difficulties Questionnaire (SDQ; Goodman, 1997), the Student Risk Screening Scale (SRSS; Drummond, 1994), the Behavior and Emotional Screening System (BESS; Kamphaus & Reynolds, 2007), and the Social Skills Improvement System: Classwide Intervention Program (SSiS; Elliott & Gresham, 2007). These measures have strong psychometric properties suggesting that they accurately identify students who do and do not exhibit the characteristics of the behavior pattern of interest (e.g., externalizing or internalizing; SSBD). It is beyond the scope of this chapter to provide a complete discussion of the features, psychometric properties, strengths, and limitations of each screening tool. However, this information is presented elsewhere (see Lane, Menzies, Oakes, & Kalberg, 2012).

These screening tools can be administered at multiple times during an academic school year such as 4 to 6 weeks after the onset of the school year, before winter break, and before year end. Data from these time points within and across school years can be compared to examine how the level of risk shifts over time within a building. Also, these data can be used either in isolation or in conjunction with other data (e.g., curriculum-based measure [CBM] data or course failures) to identify specific students who might benefit from secondary and tertiary supports as provided by the school's three-tiered

model of prevention. For example, consider the SDQ, a factor analytically derived tool with different versions for different age groups and different raters. It is designed to assess students' (ages 3 to 17) strengths and deficits in sociobehavioral domains (Goodman, 2001; Goodman, Meltzer, & Bailey, 1998). The SDQ contains teacher-completed, parent-completed, and self-report forms (ages 11 to 17, only) available at no cost. When teachers complete the SDQ, they complete one page for *each* student in their class, rating each student on the 25 items constituting the SDQ on a 3-point, Likert-type scale (*not true* = 0, *somewhat true* = 1, *certainly true* = 2). These items are equally distributed across five factors: emotional symptoms, conduct problems, hyperactivity, peer problems, and prosocial behavior. Subscale scores range from 0 to 10, with high scores indicating higher degrees of risk for the first four factors, and higher prosocial skills for the final factor (prosocial behavior). The total score ranges from 0 to 40, which includes the first four factors. Each subscale as well as the total score place students into one of three discrete categories: normal, borderline, or abnormal.

Figure 2.1 shows SDQ data from the hyperactivity scale. In Panel A, Fall 2006 and Winter 2007 data are presented for an elementary school serving students in grades K–4 (Lane & Eisner, 2007). When the primary prevention program was initially implemented, 76.80% of the students in the school scored in the normal range on the hyperactivity subscale score, with 3.61% placing in the borderline range, and 19.59% placing in the abnormal range. By the winter SDQ administration (approximately 3 months later), the overall student body showed improvement, as evidenced by an increase in the percentage of students placing in the normal category (82.32%) and a decrease

Figure 2.1   Strength and Difficulties Questionnaire (SDQ) data.

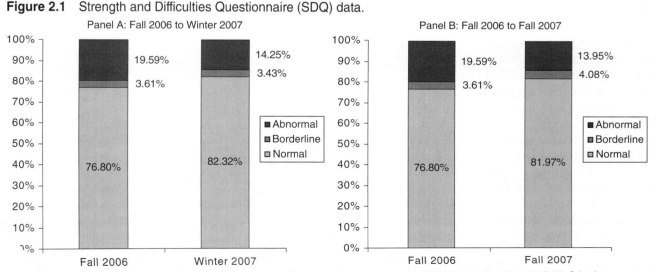

Data from Lane K. L., & Eisner, S. (2007). *Behavior screening at the elementary level.* Paper presented at Metropolitan Nashville Public Schools.

in the students placing in the abnormal category (14.25%). The school-site team can use these data in conjunction with other data (e.g., CBMs) to (a) identify students for secondary interventions, and (b) inform the selection of secondary supports. For example, the students still scoring in the abnormal category on the hyperactivity who also fall below the CBM benchmark for their grade level may benefit from secondary interventions to, for example, improve oral reading fluency (e.g., repeated readings; Chard, Ketterlin-Geller, Baker, Doabler, & Apichataburta, 2009) and academic engagement (e.g., self-monitoring; Mooney, Ryan, Uhing, Reid, & Epstein, 2005).

Behavior screening can also be used to examine the overall level of risk evident in a building over time (Lane, Kalberg, Bruhn, et al., 2008). For example, Figure 2.1, Panel B, illustrates SDQ hyperactivity scores from Fall 2006 to Fall 2007. These data also suggest improvements; however, it is imperative not to draw causal conclusions from such descriptive analyses. This is an important point and is one we will return to when we consider the research that examines the impact of primary prevention efforts.

Supporting Literature

Since the late 1990s, an extensive body of research has been developed that examines the utility of primary prevention efforts that include behavioral supports in elementary, middle, and high school settings. To date, more cases of primary prevention efforts have been documented in elementary settings than in middle and high school settings. However, the standard for SW-PBS was developed in middle schools (Gottfredson, Gottfredson, & Hyble, 1993; Mayer, Butterworth, Nafpaktitis, & Sulzer-Azaroff, 1983). While findings of systematic literature reviews can be found elsewhere, we highlight a few features of the studies conducted to date. See Lane, Kalberg, and Edwards (2008) for a systematic review of primary prevention efforts at the elementary level, and see Lane, Robertson, et al., (2006) for a systematic review of such efforts in middle and high schools.

Methodological Design and Student Outcomes

The vast majority of studies conducted to date have used descriptive rather than experimental procedures. Numerous studies provide illustrations or case studies of implementation over one or more years. Given that the school is the unit of analysis, random assignment should occur at the school level in group design experimental studies. However, very few studies have used random assignment when assigning schools to either treatment or comparison conditions (e.g., T. D. Cook et al., 1999;

Stevens, De Bourdeaudhuij, & Van Oost, 2000). In some instances, school administrators selected treatment and comparison schools (Gottfredson et al., 1993; Sprague et al., 2001), with the lack of a formal experimental comparison acknowledged as a weakness of the study. Similarly, efficacy and scaling up studies of SW-PBS are highly limited. To date Horner and colleagues (Horner et al., 2009) are the only research team to have conducted a randomized, wait-list controlled trial to examine the impact of primary prevention efforts (SW-PBS) at the elementary level. In this study, training and technical assistance in SW-PBS were provided by state personnel over a 3-year period in Hawaii and Illinois. Results suggested that improved use of SW-PBS was functionally related to improvements in the perceptions of school safety and the proportion of third-grade students who met or exceeded state standards for reading performance.

According to studies conducted to date, primary prevention programs have been associated with improved student behavior. For example, at the elementary level, results suggested decreases in ODRs, suspensions, and expulsions (e.g., McCurdy, Manella, & Eldridge, 2003; Nelson, 1996; Nelson, Martella, & Galand, 1998; T. M. Scott & Barrett, 2004; Todd, Haugen, Anderson, & Spriggs, 2002). In addition, evidence indicates improvement in school climate (Netzel & Eber, 2003) and academic skills (Ervin, Schaughency, Goodman, McGlinchey, & Matthews, 2006). Similar findings are noted in middle and high school settings. Specifically, school-wide interventions with primary prevention components that included a behavioral emphasis exhibited decreases in ODRs (Lohrmann-O'Rourke et al., 2000; Metzler, Biglan, Rusby, & Sprague, 2001; Taylor-Greene et al., 1997; Taylor-Greene & Kartub, 2000), detentions (Luiselli, Putnam, & Sunderland, 2002), physical and verbal aggression (Metzler et al., 2001), and noise in hallways during lunch time (Kartub, Taylor-Green, March, & Horner, 2000).

Only a few studies report the use of systemic screening data. This is a concern given that these data can be used to reliably (a) assess the overall index of the level of risk present at a school site over time (Lane, 2007; Lane, Kalberg, Bruhn, et al., 2008; Lane, Kalberg, et al., 2011; Lane & Menzies, 2005) and (b) identify students who may benefit from targeted supports (e.g., secondary or tertiary intervention efforts; Cheney, Blum, & Walker, 2004; Kalberg, Lane, & Menzies, 2010; Kalberg, Lane, & Lambert, 2012; Lane et al., 2003; Lane, Wehby, et al., 2002; B. Walker, Cheney, Stage, & Blum, 2005).

Overall, results of these investigations suggest that primary prevention efforts improve behavior and, to a lesser extent, school climate and academic performance. Although it is very important to avoid drawing causal conclusions from correlational or descriptive research, evidence suggests that primary prevention programs are associated with positive impacts on school climate and students' outcomes.

Treatment Integrity

Another factor to consider when interpreting the research on primary prevention efforts is the presence or absence of treatment integrity. For the reasons we discussed previously, this is a critical feature of all intervention research. In a systematic review of primary prevention at the elementary level (Lane, Kalberg, & Edwards, 2008), only five of the 19 studies reviewed monitored and reported treatment integrity results (Ervin et al., 2006; Leff, Costigan, & Power, 2003; Marr, Aduette, White, Ellis, & Algozzine, 2002; McCurdy et al., 2003; Sprague et al., 2001). Similar findings were noted in a parallel systematic review of primary prevention efforts in middle and high schools. Specifically, only 5 of the 14 studies reviewed measured treatment fidelity; 3 used team or teacher surveys or reports (T. D. Cook et al., 1999; Gottfredson et al., 1993; Sprague et al., 2001), 1 used parent phone interviews (Cook et al., 1999), and 1 used process measures (Metzler et al., 2001). Direct observation techniques rarely have been used to monitor treatment integrity of primary prevention efforts (Lane, Kalberg, Bruhn, et al., 2008; Lane & Menzies, 2002, 2003). It is encouraging to note, however, that several investigators reported the absence of treatment integrity data as a limitation (Colvin, Sugai, Good, & Lee, 1997; Leedy, Bates, & Safran, 2004; Lewis, Powers, Kelk, & Newcomer, 2002; Lewis, Sugai, & Colvin, 1998; Nelson, 1996; Nelson et al., 1998; Nelson, Martella, & Marchand-Martella, 2002; T. M. Scott, 2001; T. M. Scott & Barrett, 2004). Clearly, the field recognizes the importance of treatment integrity and is aware that the absence of this information limits the internal and external validity of findings (Gresham, Gansle, & Noell, 1993; Lane, Kalberg, & Menzies, 2009).

Social Validity

Another noteworthy construct in this literature is social validity. Yet, like treatment integrity, studies infrequently have attended to this construct. A few studies at the elementary level have mentioned and reported social validity from the teacher perspective (Ervin et al., 2006; Leff et al., 2003; McCurdy et al., 2003; Nelson, 1996; Nelson, Martella, et al., 2002; Todd et al., 2002). However, parent and student views were not considered. A few studies implemented in middle and high school settings have attended to social validity from teacher, students, and/or parent view points (e.g., Gottfredson et al., 1993;

Kartub et al., 2000; Metzler, Biglan, Rusby, & Sprague, 2001; Taylor-Green et al., 1997; Taylor-Green & Kartub, 2000). In addition, some studies (e.g., T. D. Cook et al., 1999) have actually measured and reported social validity from all three perspectives.

In sum, this growing body of research points to several important considerations for both practice and research. It appears evident that time and resources spent on designing and implementing primary prevention plans can result in positive outcomes for schools and students. Additionally, primary prevention is appropriate for all levels of schooling, although less evidence supports its utility at the high school level. As new studies are conducted, increased emphasis should be put on random assignment, measuring treatment integrity, and assessing social validity. Improving the methodological rigor of studies will provide more reliable and valid information that enhances the decision-making abilities of school personnel.

Secondary Prevention: Targeted Supports for Students Who Need More

Approximately 80% of the student body is likely to respond to primary prevention efforts (Gresham, Sugai, Horner, Quinn, & McInerney, 1998; Sugai & Horner, 2006). However, such global prevention efforts are not expected to meet all students' needs. Consequently, secondary supports that have the potential to *reverse harm* (H. M. Walker & Severson, 2002) should be in place. In other words, a school site needs to have supports available for students who are identified with low-level concerns but who have not responded adequately to the primary prevention program. Such concerns may pertain to academic performance (e.g., poor oral reading fluency), limited social interactions (e.g., difficulty interacting with peers during unstructured activities), and interfering behavioral problems (e.g., verbal aggression toward peers and adults). Secondary supports typically include small-group, whole-class, or other low-intensity strategies, some of which you will read about in subsequent chapters.

Some secondary supports include services that are currently available at many school sites such as social skills groups led by school counselors, divorce recovery groups led by school psychologists, homework clubs led by paraprofessionals during after-school care, or Tier-2 reading interventions led by the classroom teacher during a regularly scheduled literacy block. Other secondary supports may be more formalized interventions such as the Behavior Education Program (Crone, Horner, & Hawken, 2004; Hawken, MacLeod, & Rawlings, 2007) or high-intensity academic interventions such as self-regulated strategy development for writing (K. R. Harris, Graham, Mason, & Friedlander, 2008). Other secondary supports can address both academic and behavioral domains, such as behavior contracts (Downing, 2002) and self-monitoring strategies (Mooney et al., 2005). Still others may focus on shaping teacher behaviors with an emphasis on low-intensity strategies such as active supervision; effective instructional techniques (e.g., proximity, withitness, appropriate use of praise, providing opportunities to respond, instructive feedback); and use of high-engagement strategies such as offering choice and preferred activities (Lane, Menzies, et al., 2011).

The remaining chapters in this text present a wide range of strategies for secondary prevention. For example, in Chapter 3, Jolivette, Alter, Scott, Josephs, and Swoszowski present three strategies to prevent and respond to problem behaviors that include choice making, precorrection, and self-management. In Chapter 4, Sutherland and Wright introduce three strategies to improve academic engagement: increasing students' opportunities to respond, improving teachers' use of praise, and the Good Behavior Game. Davis and McLaughlin, in Chapter 5, introduce compliance training and high-probability requests to improve students' compliance. And in Chapter 8, Gresham, Libster, and Menesses introduce three strategies to improve students' social competence: social skills training, replacement behavior training, and positive peer reporting. These strategies are designed to reverse harm by providing additional supports (either by shaping teacher behavior or introducing more student-directed practices) to meet students' individualized needs via low-to-moderately intensive procedures.

Secondary support practices should be grounded in research, with the ultimate goal of implementing practices that are evidence based (e.g., Self-Regulated Strategy Instruction Development for Writing; K. R. Harris et al., 2008). Evidence-based practices are those that have been rigorously studied to suggest that they are effective for use with a particular group of students when delivered by a designated professional (or paraprofessional) within a given context; or as Mark Wolery would say, who is doing what to whom and under what conditions (Lane, Wolery, Reichow, & Rogers, 2006).

Recently, much discussion has surfaced in the literature about how to determine whether a practice is evidence based (see Gersten, Fuchs, Compton, Coyne, Greenwood, & Innocenti, 2005, and Horner, Carr, Halle, McGee, Odom, & Wolery, 2005, for a discussion of determining evidence-based practices using group design and single-case methodologies, respectively). To determine whether a practice is evidence based, reviewers evaluate research studies on a practice, examining whether each study meets indicators of methodological quality associated with trustworthy research. Reviewers then determine whether a sufficient number of high-quality research studies support the practice as causing meaningfully improved student outcomes. For example, Horner et al. require that five high-quality single-case studies support a practice as effective for it to be considered evidence based.

In our work with school-site teams interested in designing, implementing, and evaluating three-tiered models of prevention, we encourage schools to develop secondary intervention grids that contain a master list of all secondary supports available at their school site (see Table 2.3). Then, the school-site leadership team (a) describes the service, including who will implement the support, under what conditions, and information regarding "dosage" (i.e., how long and how often the service is implemented); (b) identifies how students will be identified for possible participation; (c) specifies how treatment integrity data will be monitored to ensure implementation; (d) delineates how data will be collected and monitored to determine how secondary support shapes student performance; and (e) states the criteria for terminating the service.

Central to this model is accurate identification of which students may benefit from extra support. For this reason, we highly recommend the use of reliable behavior and academic screening tools to determine which students need support. Table 2.2 includes an example of the various screening measures that were collected at a school site as part of regular school practices. Curriculum-based measures were used to monitor academic performance, and attendance data were collected to look for problems with truancy or tardiness. Other measures were implemented so that the school could collect systematic data on student behavior. For example, although the school kept records of ODRs, they decided to also administer the SSBD (H. M. Walker & Severson, 1992) so that they would have additional, and perhaps more reliable, data about students' individual behavior.

Another benefit of this model is that it provides a forum for conducting scientific inquiry using group (e.g., Lane, Harris, et al., 2011; Kalberg et al., 2012) and single-case research designs (Lane, Wehby, Menzies, et al., 2002, 2003) to examine how well these intervention efforts support students (Lane, 2007). Within the context of this applied research model, the teaching community benefits from on-site supports and the research community benefits from gaining knowledge regarding the effects of interventions in applied contexts. The same benefits apply to the next level of prevention—tertiary supports.

Table 2.3 Secondary Intervention Grid: Elementary Level

Support	Description	School-wide Data: Entry Criteria	Data to Monitor Progress	Exit Criteria
Study Skills Group	Identified students meet 3 days a week during the enrichment block, in which 30-min lessons are taught focusing on study skill strategies. This group can be run by teachers, trained parent volunteers, or paraprofessionals in a designated classroom, an office, or in the school library or cafeteria.	• Report cards: earned a "needs improvement" score on study skills or a C− or lower in any academic content area, or • Below proficient on curriculum-based measures, or • Scored in the bottom quartile on standardized state assessments.	• Weekly grades collected by the teacher (accuracy percentage) • Weekly completion collected by the teacher (percentage of assignments completed)	Complete the program when they: (a) demonstrate mastery of study skills taught on a criterion-referenced assessment, and (b) weekly teacher records reflect a minimum of 80% accuracy and 90% work completion over a 3-week period.
Behavior Education Program (BEP; Crone, Horner, & Hawken, 2004)	The BEP is designed for students with persistent behavior concerns that are not dangerous. The BEP provides a daily check-in/check-out system that helps teachers provide students with (a) immediate feedback on their behavior by completing a Daily Progress Report (DPR) and (b) additional opportunities for positive adult interactions. Parents participate by signing off on daily sheets.	Academic and Behavioral Concerns: *Academic* • Report cards: earned a "needs improvement" score on study skills or a C− or lower in any academic content area, or • Below proficient on curriculum-based measures, or *Behavioral* • Behavioral Student Risk Screening Scale (SRSS) score in the moderate risk range, or • Systematic Screening for Behavior Disorders (SSBD) score exceeding normative criteria on externalizing, or internalizing behavior on Stage-2 rating scales	Daily progress-monitoring forms collected by teacher and viewed by parent might note what is monitored (e.g., an operationally defined target behavior)	Move into the maintenance self-monitoring phase when they meet their goals for 3 consecutive weeks. Self-monitoring phase ends when the next academic reporting period and behavior rating results indicated the absence of risk following the same criteria stated in the inclusion criteria.
Incredible Years Training for Children	This curriculum builds skills in anger management, school success, and interpersonal problem solving. It is delivered as a "pull out" for small groups in a designated classroom or office. (See *Blueprints for Violence Prevention* www.colorado.edu/cspv/index.html for further details.)	• Scored in the moderate risk range on the SRSS with a 2 or higher on item 4 (peer rejection) or 5 (low achievement), or • 2 or more bullying referrals turned in, or • 3 or more major office discipline referrals (ODR)	• Information pertinent to elements of intervention are established, then collected and analyzed (e.g., results of social skills training, academic tutoring) by teacher.	• Students complete the curriculum components and then are assessed and compared to initial inclusionary criteria. • Students exit if they score in the low-risk range on the SRSS during the next systematic screening period and do not receive bullying referrals or ODRs for 3 consecutive weeks during the same rating period.

| Social Skills Group | Identified students meet 3 days/week during the enrichment block for 30-min lessons focused on improving specific social skills deficits. Students meet with school psychologist or interns 2 days/week for 30-min lessons for 10 weeks in the student's specific areas of concerns (see Lane et al., 2003; Miller, Lane, & Wehby, 2005). This group would be held in a designated classroom or office. | Behavioral Concern:

Internalizing Group

- SSBD score exceeding normative criteria on internalizing behavior on Stage-2 rating scales, or

- 1 or more unexcused absences or 3 or more unexcused tardies during the first 6 weeks of school.

Externalizing Group

- SSBD score exceeding normative criteria on externalizing behavior on Stage-2 rating scales, or

- 1 or more office discipline referrals for major offenses during the first 6 weeks of school. | School Psychologist monitor:

Internalizing Group

- Daily attendance patterns

- Daily social interactions on the playground

Externalizing Group

- Daily discipline records

- Daily social interactions on the playground | Concludes the social skills group when (a) teacher-completed SSRS (Gresham & Elliott, 1990) scores indicate average performance on the social skills and problem behavior subscale scores and (b) the SSBD scores collected during the next behavior rating period indicate the absence of risk. |

Source: Information from Lane, K. L., Kalberg, J. R., & Menzies, H. M. (2009). *Developing schoolwide programs to prevent and manage problem behaviors: A step-by-step approach* (pp. 130–131). New York, NY: Guilford Press.

Tertiary Prevention: Increased Intensity

Tertiary supports are the most intensive level of prevention offered within the three-tiered model and are designed to *reduce harm* (H. M. Walker & Severson, 2002). Approximately 3% to 5% of the student body is likely to require tertiary supports because they will have (a) not responded to primary prevention or secondary prevention efforts as measured by school-wide data, (b) been repeatedly exposed to multiple risk factors that place them at heightened risk for school failure, or (c) experienced both these conditions (Kern & Manz, 2004). Such interventions are highly ideographic in nature and must be customized to meet an individual student's comprehensive needs.

Examples of tertiary prevention efforts include both process and programmatic supports such as function-based interventions (Umbreit et al., 2007); the First Step to Success program (see Chapter 7, this volume); the Multisystemic Therapy program (MST; Henggeler, 1998); and highly intensive, individualized reading interventions (e.g., Clarke-Edmands, 2004; Wilson, 2000). Because not all students experience externalizing issues, it is also important to have tertiary supports in place for students who have internalizing issues. To this end, Kern, Hilt-Panahon, and Mukherjee (Chapter 6, this volume) discuss three research-based supports to address internalizing behaviors (i.e., cognitive behavior therapy, anxiety management/relaxation training, and pharmacological intervention) that teachers can use as tertiary interventions.

As with secondary supports, we recommend that school-site teams establish tertiary intervention grids to delineate the supports available for students who require this level of prevention. The same procedures we described for establishing secondary intervention grids should be followed. Again, we contend that it is important to design, implement, and evaluate tertiary supports that are grounded in research. Given the investments that these supports require in terms of personnel and student time, money, effort, and otherwise, it is essential to make wise decisions when establishing the scope of these services at each school site. We encourage the use of *only* evidenced-based practices (as previously described) for tertiary supports to ensure the (a) best possible outcomes for students in the greatest need of intervention and (b) most efficient use of teacher and other school-site personnel's time. Likewise, it is paramount that these supports include the necessary features in terms of intervention design (e.g., control features that ensure that the intervention, and not other variables [e.g., introduction of a student teacher], was responsible for changes in

students' behavior); outcome measures (reliable, valid, clearly defined); treatment integrity; and social validity to ensure that accurate conclusions can be drawn in terms of intervention outcomes (Horner et al., 2005). If the student does respond to the tertiary intervention and attains the desired behavior, then she may return to the primary plan in isolation or perhaps receive a secondary support (e.g., behavioral contract) to promote maintenance of the new behavior. If the student does not respond to the plan, then a different tertiary support may be necessary, or perhaps a referral to determine special education eligibility may be warranted.

Summary: Strengths and Considerations

As we conclude this chapter, we highlight some strengths as well as areas to consider as educators seek to improve comprehensive, three-tiered models of prevention. First, this systemic approach focuses on the school as the unit of change (and the unit of analysis) allowing school-site personnel to establish an integrated approach that addresses school-wide, class-wide, and noninstructional areas of concern, as well as individual student needs (Sugai & Horner, 2006). One benefit of this model is that this approach moves away from viewing problems as "within the child" and instead views concerns from an integrated, systemic approach.

Second, this integrated model includes a continuum of supports based on individual student needs. Central to this model is a data-driven approach to preventing and responding to learning and behavioral challenges. Specifically, it is imperative that educators make accurate decisions about which students may benefit from targeted intervention, whether secondary or tertiary levels of prevention. Movement between these levels of prevention should not be arbitrary and instead should be guided using data-based decision procedures involving reliable, valid measures. For example, rather than making decisions on which students need behavioral supports using ODR data, we recommend using measures with documented reliability such as behavior screening tools. Furthermore, we recommend analyzing data from academic screening tools (e.g., CBM) and behavioral screening tools (e.g., SSBD) in conjunction with one another to obtain a complete view of students' individual needs. A concern we hold is that too often the decision-making process can be incomplete when decisions are made using (a) measures that lack sufficient psychometric properties to yield accurate decisions and (b) data that reflect only one dimension of student functioning (e.g., ODRs in isolation from academic performance data) to obtain a view of students' needs.

Third, we view this model as being particularly beneficial for students with and at risk for EBD (Lane, 2007). While many teachers enter the field of education fully expecting to work with students who struggle to meet academic expectations, teachers often feel less prepared to identify and support students with behavioral challenges (Schumm & Vaughn, 1995). Specifically, some teachers need additional training in a range of strategies that include low-intensity strategies (e.g., choice making and increasing opportunities to respond), moderate-intensity (e.g., behavioral contracts and self-monitoring techniques), and functional assessment-based interventions (Umbreit et al., 2007) to prevent and respond to problem behavior, with an ultimate goal of facilitating instruction (Lane, Menzies, et al., 2011). Teachers need this full continuum of supports in order to adequately, and quickly, meet the needs of students who require more intensive assistance. This integrated three-tiered model provides a structure and context that supports teachers to work with all students—including those with behavioral challenges, who may or may not have academic deficits as well (Lane, 2007).

Fourth, this model also provides an incredibly useful forum for conducting additional scientific inquiry. We are encouraged that the research and teaching communities are beginning to capitalize on this opportunity by conducting scientifically rigorous studies using group and single-case methodologies to examine the additive benefit of academic and behavioral supports when implemented as secondary prevention efforts within the context of three-tiered models of prevention. For example, Karen Harris, Steve Graham, and colleagues have begun to explore the relative benefits of self-regulated strategy development in writing for students with behavior concerns as a secondary support in the elementary school settings (e.g., Sandmel et al., 2009). Jemma Kalberg and colleagues have explored the utility of social skills and conflict resolution strategies for middle school students with low academic performance and combined behavior concerns (Kalberg et al., 2012; Robertson & Lane, 2007).

And Doug Cheney and colleagues have examined the effects of addressing social domains within a three-tiered RtI model for elementary students at risk for developing EBD (Cheney, Flower, & Templeton, 2008). These efforts are particularly encouraging given that until relatively recently the secondary prevention efforts had received somewhat limited attention within the three-tiered model of prevention. Moving forward, it will be important to explore the feasibility and effectiveness of these supports in the absence of university assistance. However, at this time, a strong partnership between school sites and university-supported projects are providing (a) service to the local school systems and (b) a venue for scientific inquiry for university personnel.

Finally, the research community has offered several guidelines for conducting high-quality studies in order to identify evidence-based practices that can support school-personnel in their day-to-day activities (Gersten et al., 2005; Horner et al., 2005). However, too often these standards are not met when conducting applied investigations at the school-site level. Consequently, we encourage research teams to ensure that procedures are clearly articulated, with clear specification of the responsibilities involved for all key parties, for each level of prevention. Furthermore, student performance data should be collected for primary, secondary, and tertiary levels of prevention using reliable, valid measures to monitor the behaviors (academic, social, and behavioral) targeted for change. In addition, treatment integrity and social validity data should be collected and examined to assist in interpreting intervention outcomes so that they may subsequently be used to revise intervention efforts.

In sum, comprehensive, integrated, three-tiered (CI3T) models of prevention have many valuable features. These models provide an important framework for meeting students' multiple needs in a respectful, efficient, data-driven fashion. We encourage the continued exploration of these models, with particular attention to (a) improving the methods by which students are identified for additional supports and (b) the rigor with which we test the utility of secondary supports implemented within the context of this model.

CHAPTER 3

Strategies to Prevent Problem Behavior

Kristine Jolivette | *Georgia State University*

Peter Alter | *Saint Mary's College of California*

Terrance M. Scott | *University of Louisville*

Nikki L. Josephs | *Xavier University of Louisiana*

Nicole C. Swoszowski | *The University of Alabama*

R esearchers and classroom practitioners alike are focusing on changing environmental variables so that student inappropriate behaviors become irrelevant, ineffective, and inefficient (Horner, 2000), while student appropriate behaviors become more relevant, effective, and efficient within their environment. The effects of problem behavior within the classroom, community, and home negatively affect students, peers, and adults. Such effects include (a) increased adult time dealing with inappropriate behavior, (b) lost valuable instructional time for both student and peers, (c) disruption to family routines within the home, and (d) problems assimilating into the community.

The purpose of this chapter is to describe richly, from less to more intrusive, three specific behavioral strategies used to prevent and reduce problem student behavior in school, community, and home settings. These three strategies are pre-correction, choice making, self-management. Each strategy has literature bases ry in their extensiveness to address student prob- vior. We discuss the definitions and theoretical

framework, steps for implementation, brief literature review, and future directions for each strategy.

Pre-Correction

The intervention strategy of pre-correction is perhaps the simplest application of the statement, "If we can predict problem behavior, we can prevent problem behavior." Setting students up to succeed by providing brief reminders of desired behavior can be an effective method to stop challenging behaviors before they start or develop into a pattern. For many adults who work with students who engage in problem behavior, this strategy is one they have used often, even when they did not know what to call it. By being aware of emerging behavior patterns, adults can be in the position to "stop it before it starts." For example, a teacher who notices that a group of students excludes a specific peer during free time may mention right before free time begins, "Don't forget, it is important to play with everyone and to treat each other respectfully." This prompt, in essence, pre-corrects the problem behavior of exclusion by providing a reminder of expectations.

Definition and Theoretical Framework

Pre-correction is defined as "an antecedent instructional event designed to prevent the occurrence of predictable problem behavior and to facilitate the occurrence of more appropriate replacement behavior" (Colvin, Sugai, & Patching, 1993, p. 145). In other words, pre-corrections are brief prompts, often verbal questions, statements, or gestures, directed to a student or group of students just before the students enter a context in which predictable problem behaviors often occur (e.g., "We are about to line up for lunch. What are you going to do with your hands and feet?"). Pre-corrections specify the desired behavior (which is typically incompatible with the problem behavior) in close temporal proximity to environments that are predictive of these problem behaviors. By using pre-correction right before the problem context, teachers can increase the probability of students' success (e.g., student engages in the desired behavior rather than the problem behavior) for two reasons. First, the reminder of appropriate behavior is fresh in the student's mind as he initiates the task. Second, the pre-correction alerts the student that the teacher will be monitoring his behavior.

Grounded in the theoretical underpinnings of a wide range of disciplines including school-wide positive behavior support (SW-PBS; Lewis, Colvin, & Sugai, 2000), prevention science, and applied behavior analysis, pre-correction is one of the least-intrusive prevention strategies available. Moreover, it is efficient. The efficiency of the use of pre-correction is that by preventing the error before it occurs, the step of "unlearning" the wrong way to do something and relearning the right way to do it is simplified through pre-correction. Students are prompted to do it correctly the first time.

Pre-correction has four key features. First, pre-correction is *predicated on accurate prediction*. Clearly, no one can identify all of the contexts that precede problem behavior, but in both theory and process the need for accurate prediction is clear: by anticipating the inappropriate behavior in advance of its occurrence, we can provide prompts that will direct students to use a more appropriate behavior instead. To anticipate the problem behavior, it is helpful to make note of when problem behaviors occur, the environments in which they occur, and the antecedents of the behaviors. Synthesizing such information over time allows us to notice patterns in responding. Once you have established a pattern (e.g., talking loudly in the hallways, touching others when lining up for recess, complaining after being given directions to get out one's math book, entering class late), you can

use pre-correction questions, statements, and/or gestures to proactively prompt the appropriate behavior.

Second, pre-correction is *simple*. It is brief; effective pre-correction does not require long drawn out exchanges between teacher and student. Rather, it is a quick verbal question, brief statement, or succinct gesture that identifies the desired replacement behavior. Fading pre-corrective statements to more subtle forms, such as signals or environmental cues, is an important element to using this process effectively. If a teacher can use a brief gesture (e.g., a finger pressed to the lips to remind the student of the behavioral expectation in the hallways) rather than having to use verbal statements (e.g., "Silence in the hallways"), then pre-correction becomes even more efficient and effective.

Third, pre-correction is used *consistently to enforce rules, routines, and procedures*. The use of pre-correction to model and enforce expectations should be as predictable as the occurrences of the problem behavior. Predictability allows students consistent instruction and, over time, helps in fading the overt prompts to more subtle forms. The brief question of "What are you going to do with your hands and feet when we line up?" asked consistently can soon become the teacher's simply modeling having their hands to their sides until students often reach a point where they say, "I know, I know, keep my hands and feet to myself when we line up." Consistent implementation leads to fading and ultimately self-enforcement of the rule by students.

Fourth, if pre-correction is ineffective in curbing problem behavior, it can certainly be *combined with other more intensive interventions or abandoned*. Action is implicit in the name "pre-correction." If prompting questions, statements, or gestures do not stop or "correct" problem behaviors before they become apparent, then pre-correction has not occurred, and the intervention should be modified or discarded. Steps for implementation capture these four key features and lead to the use of an efficient and effective process.

Steps to Implementing Pre-Correction

Figure 3.1 presents the effective use of pre-correction as a step-by-step process summarized by Colvin et al. (1993). The steps that follow are an expanded version of that checklist and include an example of effective implementation.

First, *identify the predictors within various contexts and environments* that lead the student or students to engage in problem behavior. A number of effective tools for predicting patterns of challenging behavior have been developed largely as a result of work in the area of functional behavior assessment. Although some

Figure 3.1   Essential steps in implementing pre-correction.

1. Identify the predictors within various contexts and environments that lead the student or students to engage in problem behavior.

2. Identify the predictable problem behavior and the desired replacement behavior.

3. Ensure that the desired replacement behavior is in the student's repertoire by teaching and conducting rehearsals.

4. Provide a prompt regarding the appropriate replacement behavior at the appropriate time just before the behavior is warranted.

5. Listen to the student's response and assess accuracy.

6. When the student engages in the appropriate replacement behavior, provide reinforcement to ensure future occurrences of the same behavior.

7. Collect data on the occurrences of desired behaviors and occurrences of problem behavior.

8. When behavior is occurring at an acceptable rate, fade pre-corrects to be less frequent and more subtle.

Source: Information from Colvin, G., Sugai, G., & Patching, B. (1993). Pre-correction: An instructional approach for managing predictable problem behaviors. *Intervention in School and Clinic, 28,* 143–150.

instruments focus only on the function or what environmental events occur *after* the problem behavior, many others also include measures to determine what occurs *before* the problem behavior. These tools include direct observation-recording devices such as scatter plots and Antecedent-Behavior-Consequence (ABC) worksheets, as well as indirect measures such as the Functional Analysis Interview (FAI; O'Neill et al., 1997) and the Functional Assessment Checklist for Teachers and Staff (FACTS; R. March et al., 2000). Predictors of problem behavior may be related to time of day, type of activity (or a specific activity), proximity of specific people (other students and adults,) or just proximity of people in general. For example, based on an analysis a teacher might identify that, "Student pushes, trips, and hits others on the way to lunch line-up each day."

Second, *identify the predictable problem behavior and the desired replacement behavior.* The desired replacement behavior is often a behavior that is incompatible with the problem behavior. That is, the student cannot engage in the problem behavior while performing the desired replacement behavior. Questions to guide what the replacement behavior should look like may include, "What do other students do in this situation?" and "What does the teacher want the process to look like?"

An identified replacement behavior for the pushing, tripping, and hitting problems may be, "Walk to the line and stand with hands and feet to self in single file."

Third, *ensure that the desired replacement behavior is in the student's repertoire by teaching and conducting rehearsals.* Teachers can use modeling, role-plays, and guided practice to ensure that the student understands what behavior the teacher is looking for from the student. This instruction needs to be explicit. Teaching the desired behavior within the context that it occurs (e.g., teach appropriate behavior for clearing lunch trays in the cafeteria rather than the classroom) will increase its salience and therefore its effectiveness. For example, the teacher may talk to students about how to line up and allow practice with feedback. The teacher can instruct students to role-play examples of the appropriate replacement behavior such as keeping hands to yourself and respecting other people's personal space, while the teacher role-plays the problem behavior.

Fourth, *provide a prompt regarding the appropriate replacement behavior* at the appropriate time just before the behavior is warranted, such as asking the student a question about what behavior is expected. Rhode, Jenson, and Reavis (1992) identify a number of variables that will increase compliance when providing these types of prompts including having close proximity to the student, using a quiet voice, and giving the student an opportunity to respond appropriately before repeating the prompt. For example, the prompt may be, "It's almost lunch time. When we line up today, what will you do?"

Fifth, the teacher should *listen to the student's response and assess accuracy.* If the student responds correctly, the teacher has an opportunity to provide positive, specific praise for the appropriate response, such as, "You're right! Keep your hands to yourself when we line up. Good for you!" Also, this statement cues the student that praise will be available again if she engages in the correct behavior (Conroy, Sutherland, Snyder, Al-Hendaawi, & Vo, 2009). Increasing rates of praise is one effective practice teachers may use to increase future occurrences of desired behaviors. If the student does not respond correctly, the teacher should use this as an opportunity to briefly re-teach and emphasize the important characteristics of the desired replacement behavior. Feedback for an incorrect response may be, "Think again. Your hands will be at your sides and kept to yourself. Where are your hands going to be when I give the direction to line up?"

Sixth, when the student engages in the appropriate replacement behavior, it is vital that the teacher *provide reinforcement to ensure future occurrences of the same behavior.* A consideration of function can help in providing the student with equivalent outcomes for the desired appropriate behavior, making the problem behavior inefficient, ineffective, and irrelevant. For example, if the student's goal is to get to lunch quickly, a similar outcome would be that good line-up behavior moves the student to the front of the cafeteria line and poor line-up behavior does not allow the student to be at the front of the line.

Seventh, it is important for teachers to *collect data on the occurrences of desired behaviors and occurrences of problem behavior.* The teacher should bear in mind the number of times the student was in the context that was predictive of problem behavior and view these as opportunities. This number of opportunities becomes the denominator, and the number of either successful or unsuccessful behaviors will become the numerator for calculating the percentage of positive or negative behaviors occurring in relation to the opportunities for response. This way a teacher can systematically determine the effectiveness of the use of pre-correction on the student's behavior. For example, the data may indicate that the *student lines up correctly 95% of the opportunities available,* which may be determined as satisfactory.

Eighth, now that the behavior is occurring at an acceptable rate, the teacher can *fade these pre-corrects* to be less frequent and more subtle. For example, the teacher may give a pre-correction reminder only every other time the behavior should occur or move from verbal questions to a hand gesture or a quick nod. Decreasing the student's need for overt pre-corrects increases student independence and allows an opportunity to be increasingly more self-directed about his behavior. For example, right before lunch time, the teacher makes eye contact with the student and quickly models keeping hands by your side. The teacher then gives the direction to line up for lunch.

Pre-Correction as an Intervention for Students with Problem Behavior

To accurately describe the research base of pre-correction, we need to clarify terminology. *Pre-correction* is the application of an instructional strategy to remediate problem behaviors through prompts. A large body of research supports the use of prompts as a strategy to help strengthen students' ability to discriminate when a response is required to help prevent academic or behavioral errors. In fact, the use of prompts could be described as one of the foundational strategies of applied behavior analysis (see Wolery & Gast, 1984, for a review). Yet, using the term *pre-correction* to describe the use of prompts may make the literature base supporting this practice seem artificially thin. Ultimately, although pre-correction may be broadly considered as the use of prompts to prevent problem behavior, the prescriptive nature with which pre-correction is described in initial

articles including the seven-point checklist (Colvin et al., 1993) may indicate its more specific use and application. Thus, this literature review is restricted only to empirical research articles that use the term *pre-correction* (or *precorrection*) and describe primary research using pre-correction strategies to address problem behaviors. A total of six articles met these criteria. The pre-correction articles are described in terms of participants and settings, level of support, and the effect of the intervention on outcome measures.

Although pre-correction can be implemented for increasing positive behavior or for reducing problem behavior, all six studies reviewed for this chapter described the reduction of problem behaviors as a result of the prescribed intervention package (i.e., pre-correction was one aspect of the package). For example, one study used office discipline referrals (ODRs) as the outcome measure (Haydon & Scott, 2008), while the other five used problem behaviors that are best summarized in the description by Stormont, Smith, and Lewis (2007) as "off-task, oppositional, disruptive, aggressive and other types of externalizing behavior" (p. 283). Most of these studies reported decreases in problem behaviors from baseline to intervention. For example, Haydon and Scott reported decreases from 77 ODRs during baseline to 12 with the use of pre-correction, and Lewis, Sugai, and Colvin (1998) produced a decreasing trend in problem behaviors during transitions using pre-correction (but not an overall meaningful level change for the other settings).

Pre-correction can be effective in a variety of settings. Five of the six studies reviewed occurred in elementary schools, and the sixth (Stormont et al., 2007) was implemented at a Head Start center. Four of the six studies targeted whole schools as the populations for change, with a range of 110 to 475 students, and the pre-correction intervention occurred in a variety of settings including recess (Lewis et al., 2000; Lewis et al., 1998), cafeteria (Lewis et al., 1998), and morning gym (Haydon & Scott, 2008), and in the doorways and hallways during transitions (Colvin, Sugai, Good, & Lee, 1997; Lewis et al., 1998). One study targeted a single sixth-grade classroom ($N = 26$) (Depry & Sugai, 2002), and one study targeted three small-group learning activities with seven or nine students in the group ($N = 25$) (Stormont et al., 2007).

Research has also shown that pre-correction is a relatively easy and efficient intervention to implement. For all reviewed studies, the teachers and other school staff (e.g., paraprofessionals) served as the implementers of the intervention and were trained in relatively short amounts of time, with an average of 2 hours of training. In some examples, pre-correction was included as part of a larger training such as a 2-day workshop on

School-wide Positive Behavior Support (Lewis et al., 1998) and always as one part of a multi-pronged intervention package. For one study, feedback on the use of pre-correction was provided throughout the intervention (Stormont et al., 2007), but for all other studies, researchers simply collected baseline data, provided training for school practitioners, and collected data during the intervention phase. Three of the six studies identified the ease and efficiency of training teachers how to use pre-correction as a strength of the intervention and a rationale for its continued use.

Future Research Directions

Pre-correction is a strategy grounded in research regarding the use of prompts to effectively elicit desired behaviors when initial discriminative stimuli are ineffective at transferring stimulus control. However, as an identified strategy used and applied in classrooms, a dearth of evidence supports the application of this practice alone. Due to this shortage, future research is warranted. Specifically, future research should investigate the effectiveness of pre-correction with students of various ages with specified variables regarding setting, cultural and linguistic diversity, exceptionality, and other demographics. Such information would provide evidence of the robust nature of intervention. Because most studies evaluated its effectiveness on generic problem behavior and ODRs, research focusing on more specific dependent variables is needed. Moreover, future research should investigate the effects of pre-correction as the sole intervention on a variety of problem behaviors, rather than as a part of an intervention package. Such investigations should also evaluate the fidelity of pre-correction implementation (Lewis et al., 2000) as well as the social validity of pre-correction as a school, home, or community strategy to address problem behavior.

Regardless of these future directions, pre-correction has shown to be a promising strategy used to prevent the occurrence of problem behavior. This strategy is cost-effective, easy to implement, and requires minimal training to implement. In addition, in its broad form as a behavioral prompt, it is a common practice that has been used in schools and homes. A second strategy used to address problem behavior, choice making, shares these same characteristics with pre-correction.

Choice Making

The extension of opportunities for students to make choices is a critical aspect of a high-quality education (F. Sigafoos & Dempsey, 1992), especially when students have histories of displaying problematic behaviors. In fact,

some researchers have pointed to choice making as an important aspect of teaching and learning, and Bambara, Koger, Katzer, and Davenport (1995) even stated that "the absence of choice making can have a devastating effect on students' quality of life and emotional development" (p. 185). As intervention, choice-making strategies have demonstrated positive, clinical significance for students across ages, disabilities, and behaviors. As K. M. McCormick, Jolivette, and Ridgely (2003) suggested, "if you provide choices instead of demands, children are more likely to respond in a positive manner" (p. 8).

Shogren, Faggella-Luby, Bae, and Wehmeyer (2004) conducted a meta-analysis of 13 choice-making studies that used either task-order choice (choice of order of task to complete) or either/or choice (choice of two activities) to intervene with student problem behavior. They found that the intervention was effective overall, and the greatest effect was found for younger students (4- to 7-year-olds), for students with emotional and behavioral disorders, and for aggressive behavior.

Although the use of choice making has been shown to be an effective intervention, few studies have attempted to establish the naturally occurring rates of choice-making opportunities for students with and without disabilities typically available in most classroom situations (before manipulations of the number and types of choices provided). For example, during structured activities, Jolivette, Stichter, Sibilsky, Scott, and Ridgely (2002) observed the natural provision of choice-making opportunities provided to 14 students (seven with speech and language disabilities or developmental delay and the other seven at risk for school failure) ages 4 to 5 years old in a university-based preschool program. They found that choice-making opportunities were provided to the students with disabilities at a rate of 0.17 per minute and at a rate of 0.12 for those at risk. In addition, Jolivette, McCormick, McLaren, and Steed (2009) observed naturally occurring choice-making opportunities provided by an interdisciplinary team in two inclusive preschool classrooms with a total of 42 students, ages 2 to 3 years, who were typically developing, had disabilities, or were at risk for disabilities. They found that choices were provided at an overall rate of 0.51 per minute for 26 hours of observations. Differences in the types of choices, areas in the room in which choice was provided, and choice-delivery methods were observed across the interdisciplinary team members. Such differences may be due to the goal/objectives of the learning centers, team member purposefulness of the use and type of choice, and specific classroom conditions.

Establishing the rate of choice-making opportunities within a variety of educational settings and across ages is an important first step in understanding the natural occurrences of choice before intervention. Knowing the rates provides a context in which a researcher, teacher, or parent may manipulate the number, types, and complexity of choice-making opportunities as a means to improve behavior.

Definition and Theoretical Framework

The provision of a choice-making opportunity as a teaching or intervention method is simply the manipulation of existing variables such as items, task demands, situations, and reinforcers. Shevin and Klein (1984) defined choice as "the act of a student's selection of a preferred alternative from among several familiar options" (p. 160). For example, a teacher may say, "After you accurately complete the worksheet, would you like to listen to your CD, draw a picture, or read a book at your desk?" Such options are choices. Choice-making interventions may be conceptualized as a prevention method, as choices are typically provided before the occurrence of problem behavior based on known behavioral patterns. With choice making rooted in behaviorism and applied behavior analysis, choice making is an operant response as students indicate and access a preferred option, thus increasing rates of reinforcement (Morgan, 2006).

Steps to Implementing Choice Making

Most research studies implementing choice making as an intervention follow a similar set of steps, whether implicitly or explicitly stated, as suggested by J. Sigafoos, Roberts, Couzens, and Kerr (1993). The six steps, as summarized in Figure 3.2, include (a) offering, (b) asking, (c) waiting, (d) responding, (e) prompting, and (f) reinforcing.

Figure 3.2   Essential steps in implementing choice making.

1. Offer the student or group of students a choice of at least two options.
2. Ask the student or group of students to make a choice based on the options provided.
3. Wait for the student or group of students to make their choice.
4. The student responds.
5. Prompt the student to make a choice if, after waiting the predetermined amount of time, the student has yet to make a choice.
6. Reinforce the choice option, giving the selected item to the student.

After identifying a student or group of students for the choice-making intervention and selecting an environmental context for implementation, the teacher is ready to begin the first step. First, *offer* the student or group of students a choice of at least two options. An offer of a choice typically is provided through orally verbalizing a statement, signing the statement, or showing the actual options. For example, a teacher may say, sign, or indicate by holding up items in succession, "Do you want a, b, or c?" A combination of the offer method (e.g., verbalizing while holding up the two options) also can be used. The offer method depends on the developmental, cognitive, and communication skills of the students being provided with the choice. Additionally, the number of choice options extended will be influenced by the student's developmental and cognitive abilities as well as the learning objectives/goals within the context.

Second, *ask* the student or group of students to make a choice based on the options provided. The asking must be clear and concise so that the students can unmistakably understand their options. When extending more than two choice options, the specificity of the choice options becomes even more critical. For example, a teacher may provide a choice to a student with attention deficit hyperactivity disorder (ADHD) and say, "Would you like to use a mechanical pencil, a black pen, or blue gel pen (holding just these three in her hand) to write your spelling words?" This example highlights the exact options being offered free of other distractions. A nonexample would be to say, "Mechanical, black, or blue?" That question is not explicit or specific, and the student may not know the context of the statement or that a choice is being offered. In fact, the nonexample may inadvertently become an antecedent to further problem behavior from the student, because it could promote disengagement, discussion, negotiation, or noncompliance, leading to overall increased levels of off-task behaviors.

Third, *wait* for the student or group of students to make their choice. Typically, 5 to 10 seconds of wait time is provided per student to make a choice, although the specific wait time will depend on the student's or group's abilities. If administering choice-making opportunities to a small or large group of students, 5 to 10 seconds may be too intrusive to the learning environment. In this case, the teacher may provide a time construct within step two by adding a specific length of time for the students to respond. Also, teachers may conduct steps one and two with a small group of students to minimize the effects of student wait time on instructional time. For example, when working with a small group of students, the students should be purposefully grouped depending on ability (e.g., all students in the group typically take the same amount of time to respond), the choice offering and asking can be together, and the options the same for each member.

Fourth, the student *responds*. How students respond will vary based on their unique communication characteristics. For example, a student may orally verbalize or sign his selection; or gesture (e.g., nodding, blinking) toward, point to, or touch his selection. To illustrate, for a student with severe disabilities and limited communication skills who has a history of inappropriate behavior during meal times (e.g., food refusal, screaming), the teacher may provide a snack choice using the actual two options as prompts. With the two boxes directly in front of the student, the teacher orally states, "Do you want to have pretzels [while pointing to the pretzels and placing the student's hand on the box] or crackers [while pointing to the crackers and placing the student's hand on the box] for snack [orienting the student's hand in the middle of the two options]?" The teacher may repeat this option several times before removing physical guidance (depending on the student's communication abilities and styles) and waiting for the student to place his hand on one of the items.

Fifth, *prompt* the student to make a choice if, after waiting the predetermined amount of time, the student has yet to make a choice. It is possible that when choice is first introduced to a student, the student may not fully understand that he is permitted to exert control over the situation and make a selection. If a student does not make a choice within 10 seconds, then the teacher should provide steps one and two again. In some cases, it may be necessary to add to step two additional verbal, gestural, model, or physical assistance prompts to the student. For example, if a teacher has offered a choice (e.g., "Would you like to jump like a rabbit, walk like a person, or walk like a robot to lunch?"), asked for a response, waited a specified amount of time, and received no response, the teacher may offer additional assistance. In relation to the previous example, the teacher may also model what each option looks like—hopping, walking naturally, and walking in a stiff manner—before continuing with the steps.

Sixth, *reinforce* the choice option, giving the selected item to the student. This reinforcement should be immediate and match the item selected. As a caveat, some researchers have permitted students to change their minds about their initial choice option selection during the intervention session. If this is an option a teacher would like to extend to the student, then a statement indicating this needs to be part of step two. For example, the teacher might say, "Once you begin the task, if you change your mind and want to select one of these other choices, you may." This may be helpful to students who engage in problem behavior as a means to exert control over their environments. If the option to change one's mind is being offered, then the teacher needs to consider (a) how the student is to indicate this change of mind, (b) the repercussions of accepting partially completed

tasks (e.g., half-completed worksheets), and (c) how many times students may change their minds. Kern and State (2009) contend that even before the six steps to choice-making opportunities are implemented several tasks are necessary for the teacher to prepare the environment for choice:

> (1) create a menu of choices you would be willing to provide your students, (2) look through your choice menu before planning your lesson, (3) decide what types of choices are appropriate for your lesson, (4) decide where choice-making opportunities fit best in your lesson, (5) incorporate the choices you decided as appropriate into your lesson, and (6) provide the planned choices while delivering the lesson. (Kern & State, 2009, p. 5)

Once the steps have been successfully completed, the teacher can evaluate the student's performance across academic and social domains to determine whether choice making has resulted in improved academic or social behavior of the student. For example, a teacher may academically measure student performance on the number of problems attempted/completed, the accuracy of the work product, the time it took to complete the work product, and the overall quality of the product to judge the intervention effectiveness. Socially, the teacher may measure student performance on the percentage of on-task, off-task, disruptive, noncompliant, compliant, or aggressive behaviors and peer interactions. Whether measuring academic and/or social student behavior during and after choice-making opportunities, it is critical to monitor the effectiveness of the choice-making interventions, because some students may not benefit from choice.

Choice-Making Interventions for Students with Problem Behaviors

Choice-making interventions and their effects on student problem behavior as well as academic and social deficits have been more widely investigated than pre-correction. In this section, we review the literature on choice making in relation to the variety of conditions (e.g., types of behavior, disability populations, age groups, and environments) in which it has been studied.

The provision of choice-making opportunities has been investigated across varying types of problem behavior. Investigations include measuring the effects of choice-making opportunities on (a) student task performance, attempted task problems, and problems correct (e.g., Cole & Levinson, 2002; Jolivette, Wehby, Canale, & Massey, 2001; Kern, Mantegna, Vorndran, Bailin, & Hilt, 2001); (b) off-task behavior, disruption, and noncompliance (e.g., Dunlap et al., 1994; Dyer, Dunlap, & Winterling, 1990; Jolivette et al., 2001; Romaniuk et al., 2002); (c) aggression (e.g., Haynes, Derby, McLaughlin, & Weber, 2002; Kern, Mantegna, et al., 2001;

Vaughn & Horner, 1997; see Chapter 7 in this volume for additional strategies to address aggression); (d) self-stimulation (e.g., Dattilo & Rusch, 1985); and (e) spontaneous speech (Dyer, 1987).

For example, Carlson, Luiselli, Slyman, and Markwoski (2008) investigated the effects of two clothing choices provided several times a day to address the disrobing and incontinence behaviors of a 13-year-old female with autism and a 5-year-old male with pervasive developmental disorder. The decision to provide clothing choices was based on the results of a functional behavioral assessment indicating that both students used their inappropriate behavior to gain access to preferred clothing items. Both students demonstrated decreases in their disrobing and incontinence behaviors to near-zero levels when they were provided the opportunity to make choices about what they would wear. In addition, maintenance 6 months afterward for the female remained at near-zero levels.

The provision of choice-making opportunities as an intervention began with students with severe disabilities (e.g., Bambara et al., 1995; Dattilo & Rusch, 1985; Vaughn & Horner, 1997; for a review, see Lancioni, O'Reilly, & Emerson, 1996) to address problem behavior as well as a means to build autonomy and self-determination. Since then, choice-making opportunities have been extended to those with other disabilities such as emotional and behavioral disorders (EBDs; e.g., Dunlap et al., 1994; Jolivette et al., 2001; Kern, Mantegna, et al., 2001) and developmental disabilities (e.g., Carlson et al., 2008; Cole & Levinson, 2002; Kern, Mantegna, et al., 2001; Romaniuk et al., 2002), as well as those with typical development (e.g., Tiger, Hanley, & Hernandez, 2006). For example, for students with EBD, Ramsey et al. (2010) investigated the effects of choice of task sequence on five students, ages 14 to 16 years, with EBD in a residential facility who displayed problematic behavior related to low levels of on-task behavior, task completion, and accuracy during academic tasks. Results suggested that four of the students demonstrated overall increases in on-task behavior and task completion when provided choice in the order of their task completion, but had mixed results on the accuracy of the products.

Additionally, choice-making opportunities have been implemented across various age groups including preschool (e.g., S. M. Peck et al., 1996; Tiger et al., 2006), elementary (e.g., Jolivette et al., 2001; Umbreit & Blair, 1996; Vaughn & Horner, 1997), middle school (e.g., Kern, Bambara, & Fogt, 2002), high school (e.g., Seybert, Dunlap, & Ferro, 1996), and adult (e.g., Bambara et al., 1995) learners as a means to address problem behavior. For example, Seybert et al. investigated task choice on the problem behavior (i.e., self-stimulation, inappropriate use of objects, inappropriate vocalizations, noncompliance, and off-task) of

three high school students, ages 14 to 21 years, with intellectual disabilities during school domestic and vocational tasks. Results suggest that the choice condition resulted in a greater than 50% reduction in problem behavior for all three students when compared to behavior during nonchoice conditions.

Choice-making opportunities also have been implemented in varying environments such as in the school, community (e.g., E. G. Carr & Carlson, 1993), and home (Vaughn & Horner, 1995). The ease of implementation and naturally occurring choice options within each environment makes the provision of choices a flexible and useful intervention amenable to most contexts. For example, Jolivette et al. (2001) studied the effects of choice versus no choice of task sequence in an elementary self-contained math class for three students with EBD. Two of the students decreased their off-task and disruptive behaviors and increased their attempted math problems and correct problems.

Strengths and Future Directions

Multiple strengths to providing choice-making opportunities to students who exhibit problematic academic and social behavior within the school day, out in the community, or in the home setting have been noted in the literature. The provision of choice making is simple and easy without causing additional burden in time and preparation to those providing the choice (Carlson et al., 2008; Kern & State, 2009) and can be embedded within regular routines across environments (Cole & Levinson, 2002). K. M. McCormick et al. (2003) state embedding choice is important because it "supports decision making, social competence, and autonomy" (p. 5) while promoting engagement in tasks/activities selected by the student. Moreover, the provision of choice making requires no special training beyond following the choice-making steps outlined and thinking ahead of time how choice will be implemented within the lesson and classroom (Kern & State, 2009).

Given the mixed yet promising results of choice making as an intervention on reducing student problem behavior and increasing student positive behaviors, many future directions might be fruitfully explored. Future research should continue to investigate the effects of choice-making opportunities on task engagement in terms of the amount of work completed, the time required to complete the work, and the accuracy of the work completed for students who display chronic and persistent problem behavior (von Mizener & Williams, 2009). Research should also investigate the generalizability of the effects of choice making to other problematic behaviors or settings in which problematic behaviors occur (Carlson et al., 2008) as well as the long-term effect of choice-making interventions on student academic and social behaviors after the withdrawal of the intervention. It would also be helpful to know if, once students are exposed to choice-making opportunities, student-initiated choices are recognized and reinforced by teachers. It is also unclear if differential effects result from choice making opportunities based on a student's disability and the severity of the disability (Morgan, 2006) or why choice-making is effective for some participants but not others. These future directions provide a focus for empirical inquiries of choice making as educators seek interventions to reduce and prevent student problem academic and social behaviors.

Even with questions remaining, evidence points to choice making as an effective and efficient prevention-focused intervention strategy. In brief, choice-making opportunities should be consistent, be frequent, range from basic to complex, and be reinforced (Jolivette, Ridgely, & White, 2002). In addition, implications for practice include being realistic when first providing choice-making opportunities, focusing on curricula areas where the student will benefit most, viewing choice-making opportunities on a continuum, and being consistent in presentation and reinforcement of the selection of the choice as a means to prevent problem behavior (Jolivette, Stichter, & McCormick, 2002). Kern and State (2009) contend that the provision of choice-making opportunities "is well worth the time, especially because teachers of students with EBD spend a considerable amount of time dealing with problem behaviors. This time could be used more effectively to prevent problems by planning how to make choices available" (p. 11). Another proactive strategy to address problem behavior that is also well worth the time and effort is self-management.

Self-Management

Teaching students self-management skills shifts the locus of control from teacher-mediated external reinforcement (e.g., teacher praise, tangible rewards) to student-directed intrinsic reinforcement (Fitzpatrick & Knowlton, 2009). Researchers have reported many benefits associated with self-management including (a) increased probability of maintenance of learned behavior because of student implementation, (b) less teacher time and resources required for addressing classroom problems, (c) increased autonomy of students, and (d) a greater sense of ownership of and responsibility for one's actions.

Definition and Theoretical Framework

Self-management is a process through which a student is taught to control her own behavior (McDougall, 1998). Generally, self-management is a procedure with multiple components including self-monitoring, self-instruction, self-assessment/self-evaluation, and self-reinforcement (Mooney, Ryan, Uhing, Reid, & Epstein,

2005); however, no prescribed order of implementation is necessary for success of a self-management intervention (Niesyn, 2009). Self-management is founded on the principles of behaviorism, cognitive theory, and social cognitive theory. The theory of behaviorism (and most specifically operant conditioning), which is founded on the three-tier contingency model of antecedent, behavior, and consequence, perhaps offers the most direct explanation of self-management (Schunk, 2004). Self-management involves a consistent and predictable routine for providing immediate feedback for behavior. Students are not expected to delay gratification but are taught to reinforce their own behavior through self-praise or tangible reinforcement according to a schedule and agreed-upon criteria for reinforcement, which works to increase the likelihood of future desirable behavior. Furthermore, the principles of behaviorism are evident in the antecedent manipulations associated with some self-management interventions. Having students write the steps for completion of a specific academic task such as the steps to complete a multi-step division problem, or a mnemonic for the mathematical order of operations (e.g., *Please Excuse My Dear Aunt Sally* for remembering **p**arentheses, **e**xponentiation, **m**ultiplication, **d**ivision, **a**ddition, **s**ubtraction) are examples of antecedent modifications.

Cognitive theory and social cognitive theory are also apparent in the theoretical foundation of self-management. The concepts of self-talk and self-efficacy are evident when students are taught to manage independently their own behavior. Students cognitively process demonstrations of behavior, communicate and process desired behavior, and evaluate whether they demonstrate the targeted behavior. Furthermore, in line with social cognitive theory, students must feel they are capable of increasing or decreasing the target behavior; that is, they must have a sense of self-efficacy (Bandura, 1979, 1993).

Components to Implementing Self-Management for Students with Problem Behavior

Implementing self-management with students exhibiting problem behavior has four components: self-monitoring, self-instruction, self-evaluation/assessment, and self-reinforcement. Each is described in the following sections, and specific steps for each component are summarized in Figure 3.3.

Self-Monitoring

A major component of self-management is self-monitoring. Self-monitoring includes teaching students two tasks: (a) to realize the absence or presence of a target behavior, and (b) to record the occurrence or nonoccurrence of that

Figure 3.3 Essential steps in implementing self-management.

Self-monitoring

1. Identify the target behavior(s) of concern, and operationally define the behavior(s).

2. Develop a plan for how students will be cued to record their behavior (e.g., tone played on an audio recorder, visual prompt on a form) and a schedule for monitoring.

3. Meet with the student to explain the management plan.

4. Develop a self-monitoring sheet for data collection.

5. Teach the students how to use the self-management plan by first modeling for the student the act of self-recording while verbalizing the steps out loud.

6. Assess for accuracy of recording.

7. Fade the plan.

Self-instruction

1. Identify the problem.

2. Attend to the situation.

3. Plan during the phase.

Self-assessment/evaluation

1. Conduct a performance assessment.

2. Set observable and attainable goal(s).

3. Develop a schedule for evaluation.

4. Compare student performance to a goal for performance.

Self-reinforcement (external)

1. Determine desirable reinforcers for the student.

2. Establish a schedule for reinforcement.

3. Establish rules for reinforcement.

---

behavior (Hallahan & Sapona, 1983; McDougall, 1998). Self-monitoring is a key component in the self-management process. In order for students to effectively self-manage their actions, they must first be taught the skills to monitor their own behaviors, which involves seven key steps. First, *identify* the target behavior(s) of concern, and *operationally define the behavior(s)*. The target behavior needs to be observable and measurable. For example, the target behavior may be "keeping hands to self" with an operational definition of "the absence of any part of the elbow to fingertip touching another person anywhere on his body or any of his possessions."

Second, develop a plan for how students will be *cued to record their behavior* (e.g., tone played on an audio recorder, visual prompt on a form) as well as a *schedule for monitoring*. The schedule and cue may vary based on the student's level of functioning. For example, an elementary-age student may require an auditory prompt such as a tone or bell, while a middle or high school student may be prompted by the time on a clock.

Third, meet with the student to *explain the management plan*. The student and teacher discuss examples and nonexamples of the expected behaviors. For example, the teacher may ask the student "Where should your hands be during line-up time?" If the student says "At my side," the teacher reinforces the response and says, "Yes, at your side. Let me show you what that looks like and then you show me." The teacher and student should practice this several times and expand the example to include other settings (e.g., where hands should be when walking in the hallway, when sitting at a desk). For the nonexamples, the teacher should model examples of what the behavior would not look like (e.g., touching items, touching others).

Fourth, develop a *self-monitoring sheet* that can be used as a data collection method for teacher and student alike. The data collection form should be easy to use and portable so the student can bring it to other classrooms or settings if necessary. It may be beneficial for the form to have prominent visual or written prompts (e.g., "Am I keeping my hands to myself?") with a column for yes or no responses where the student can easily place a circle or tally mark to indicate self-evaluation of behavior.

Fifth, *teach the students how to use the self-management plan* by first modeling for the student the act of self-recording while verbalizing the steps out loud. For example, at the cue the teacher may say, "OK. That was the cue. Was I keeping my hands to myself? Yes! I was keeping my hands to myself so I'll check the 'yes' column and get back to work." Then the student models the steps by verbalizing the steps for the teacher to complete. Next the student performs the entire plan while also verbalizing all steps. It is important for the teacher to provide time to teach the student and for the student to practice the accurate implementation of the strategy before data collection. The student should exhibit mastery of the plan under the teacher's supervision before implementing it independently.

Sixth, *assess for accuracy of recording*. After the student can complete the plan without teacher assistance, the intervention period begins, and the teacher assesses for accuracy of recording. For example, a teacher may systematically assess the student's use of the plan and data collection by conducting independent checks every couple of sessions. If the teacher and student data match for the session, then the student receives an additional reinforcer. Initially, teachers provide reinforcement for correct recording but fade this level of assistance throughout the intervention period. The student should know that the teacher will be monitoring him; however, the actual occurrence of these checks should be completed without the student's knowledge. If the two data sets do not match, then the teacher needs to repeat step six and reteach to mastery.

Seventh, *fade the plan.* A teacher will know when the student is ready to have her plan faded when the student meets her performance goal for an extended period of time. To fade, the teacher may first remove the cue for recording and then gradually remove other elements of the program (Maag, 2004; Patton, Jolivette, & Ramsey, 2006; Wilkinson, 2008).

Self-Instruction

As part of the overall procedure of self-management, students can be taught the process of self-instruction. Teachers can teach students the steps for self-instruction in a variety of ways. The following is a three-step sequence example adapted from K. R. Harris (1982).

First, *identify the problem.* For example, a student working on task completion and accuracy may ask himself, "What am I supposed to be working on?" The student may need to be taught to use a mnemonic such as the steps to solve mathematical problems (e.g., ***Please Excuse My Dear Aunt Sally***).

Second, *attend to the situation.* In this example, the student may say, "I have to concentrate on my work" to cue himself to focus on the task at hand. He may then verify that the steps were completed in the correct order (e.g., exponents before multiplication).

Third, *plan during the phase.* The student may remind himself to "work on one thing at a time." In this case, the student looked at the entire math problem, then looked for the operations involved, then decided the order in which to complete the problem.

Self-Assessment/Evaluation

Self-assessment/evaluation is a process through which each student is taught the method of evaluating her own progress. Self-assessment/evaluation works in collaboration with other elements of self-management as it involves comparing data from the self-monitoring portion to a goal for performance (Rhode et al., 1983; Rosenbaum & Drabman, 1979). For self-assessment/evaluation to be most effective, it is essential to include a few basic steps. The following discussion highlights the essential steps for self-assessment/evaluation.

First, *conduct a performance assessment.* The teacher observes the student to determine her current level of performance. Using standardized or individualized data, the teacher then identifies the performance level the student should grow toward. This process provides information that helps lead to the second task, *to set observable and attainable goal(s).* The goal for performance is typically agreed upon by the student and

teacher and is related to the baseline performance data collected. If, for example, a student is talking out an average of 10 times per class period, the student and teacher may agree to an initial performance goal of 5 or fewer talk outs during a class period. While talking out 5 times during a class period may still be disruptive to the learning of the student and her classmates, it is recommended that initial goals be set at a point that is both realistic and attainable. Setting the goal too high may cause frustration for students, as they may feel the goal is unreachable and therefore may discontinue use of the intervention. It will be necessary to shape the goal over time to a more acceptable and less disruptive level (e.g., moving to 0 to 1 displays of talking out during a class period).

Third, *develop a schedule for evaluation.* After the student reaches the agreed-upon performance goal, the teacher should determine a schedule for evaluation. The teacher determines how often the data will be compared to the goal. It may be necessary to evaluate more frequently at the start of an intervention (i.e., after each class) and to fade the schedule for evaluation over time (i.e., one to two times per day).

Fourth, *compare student performance to a goal for performance.* The final step involves the comparison of actual student performance to the goal. Additionally, the teacher will want to offer reinforcement for correctly evaluating performance. According to Wilkinson (2008), it may be common for the teacher and student to disagree initially, but the teacher ratings are always the standard assessment of performance, and an agreement is only achieved if the teacher data indicate the criterion were met.

Self-Reinforcement

Although students can be taught to self-reinforce in two ways, externally and internally (Maag, 2004), we focus on the process of external reinforcement because it is more overt and within the teacher's control to shape the steps associated with it. Determining and implementing conditions associated with internal self-reinforcement, by contrast, is given wholly to the student herself, making the role of the teacher less central (Bandura, 1976). Following are the steps for external reinforcement.

First, *determine desirable reinforcers for the student.* The teacher should engage the student in a discussion to determine which items the student finds motivating. Over time, what motivates a student may change, so conversations on reinforcers may need to occur frequently.

Second, *establish a schedule for reinforcement.* The teacher then establishes a schedule for reinforcement to inform the student of when the desired reward will be received. For example, the student may initially reinforce himself for reaching his performance goal each time. This schedule should then be thinned over time.

Third, *establish rules for reinforcement.* Additionally, the teacher establishes rules for reinforcement (i.e., must choose from reward menu, only one choice per time). For example, if the student has a choice of computer time or free reading time for meeting a performance goal, then the teacher needs to (a) make sure the student has access to the reinforcement, and (b) ensure that the student can have/use the reinforcement at the time of achievement.

Self-Management for Students with Problem Behavior

Researchers have investigated self-management in numerous ways and have demonstrated positive outcomes for those who display problem behavior. For example, self-management has been used successfully across multiple grade levels (e.g., Blick & Test, 1987; Callahan & Radenmacher, 1999; Rock, 2005) within general education settings (e.g., DiGangi, Maag, & Rutherford, 1991; Maag, Reid, & DiGangi, 1993). For example, Blick and Test used self-management to increase the on-task classroom behaviors of 12 students with high-incidence disabilities in grades 9 to 12 in general education classrooms. The students responded to an audible cue played from an audio tape at 5-minute intervals by recording a "+" or "−" on a recording sheet if they were on task at the signal and recorded the total number of "+"s, receiving reinforcement if their criterion was met. Results suggest on-task behavior significantly increased with the use of self-management.

Self-management has been successful with students with disabilities (e.g., Coyle & Cole, 2004; DiGangi et al., 1991; Todd, Horner, & Sugai, 1999), including students with EBD (e.g., Mooney et al., 2005), learning disabilities (e.g., Todd et al., 1999), attention deficit disorder (e.g., Hoff & DuPaul, 1998), and autism (e.g., Wilkinson, 2008). For example, Prater, Hogan, and Miller (1992) used self-monitoring to improve the classroom behavior of a 14-year-old male diagnosed with a specific learning disability who displayed inappropriate classroom behaviors including interrupting others, getting out of seat during instruction, and refusing to complete assignments. Using a time-sampling procedure to record his behavior, the student decreased his inappropriate behaviors across mainstream classroom settings (resource room, mathematics, and English classrooms) over the period of the study.

Self-management also has demonstrated positive results for a variety of behavioral outcomes (e.g., on-task behavior, work completion, hand raising). For example, Todd et al. (1999) documented the use of a self-management package including self-monitoring, self-evaluation, and self-recruited reinforcement on the on-task behavior and work completion of a 9-year-old fourth grader diagnosed with ADHD and conduct disorder. Data were collected on the use of appropriate language, verbal responses to adult requests, and refraining from harassment and intimidation of peers during a reading period and project time. Results show that the self-monitoring package was successful in significantly increasing the on-task classroom behavior while simultaneously decreasing problem behaviors in both settings.

A new application of self-management is the incorporation of technology as a means for students to self-manage. For example, Gulchak (2008) evaluated the impact of self-monitoring using a mobile handheld computer on the on-task behavior of an 8-year-old male with EBD. Results indicated that on-task behavior improved and that the student was able to use the handheld computer with 100% fidelity.

Future Directions

Although self-management is supported as an effective, evidence-based practice, it is not without limitations. Future research should investigate (a) to what extent teachers and adults can implement self-management within natural contexts without external supports (e.g., researchers), (b) the role of technology in self-management procedures, (c) which student populations are most responsive to self-management strategies and what adaptations may need to be made to meet students' unique needs, and (d) what process should be followed to determine student reinforcement for performance goal attainment. These future directions will expand the self-management literature to address more fully the social and academic needs of students with problem behavior.

Conclusion

Overall, when students display problem behavior, whether at school, in the home, or in the community, teachers and adults need to implement strategies to prevent the occurrence of such behavior in the future. Teachers and adults may use pre-correction, choice making, or self-management to do that. Each of these strategies has shown promising outcomes in reducing and preventing future problem behaviors across disabilities, ages, behaviors, and settings. The literature base could be strengthened for these three strategies related to their application across learners of culturally and linguistically diverse populations as well as the systematic measurement of fidelity of the strategies used. However, teachers and adults should consider use of these three strategies for their students and children, because all three are easy to use, cost-effective, and can be used to address a plethora of behaviors.

CHAPTER 4

Students with Disabilities and Academic Engagement: *Classroom-Based Interventions*

Kevin S. Sutherland and **Stephen A. Wright** | *Virginia Commonwealth University*

Research has demonstrated a consistent and strong positive association between academic engagement and achievement (e.g., Greenwood, Horton, & Utley, 2002; Klem & Connell, 2004). Although the exact linkage between these two constructs can be elusive, several factors within the classroom environment appear to influence this relationship. For example, individual student characteristics such as inattention, hyperactivity, noncompliance, and aggression are likely to have a detrimental effect on engagement (Greenwood et al., 2002). At the same time, even for students who exhibit problem behavior, differential effects on engagement can be associated with classroom contextual factors (J. A. Baker, Clark, Maier, & Viger, 2008). Because many classroom contextual factors are malleable (e.g., instructional grouping, instructional pacing, teacher behavior), researchers have targeted these areas. Identifying an evidence base for increasing student academic engagement may be particularly salient for students with and at risk for disabilities, given both their documented risk for academic problems (M. Wagner, Newman, Cameto, Levine, & Garza, 2006) and data that suggest that both elementary (e.g., Kemp & Carter, 2006) and secondary (E. W. Carter, Sisco, Brown, Brickham, & Al-Khabbaz, 2008) students with disabilities have low rates of engagement. The importance of increasing the academic engagement of all students is further highlighted by research suggesting a reciprocal relationship between academic achievement and engagement; that is, increased academic achievement is also associated with increased academic engagement (Urdan & Schoenfelder, 2006).

Academic Engagement Defined

Yell, Meadows, Drasgow, and Shriner (2009) differentiate between allocated instructional time (e.g., amount of time the teacher sets aside for instruction) and academic engaged time (e.g., the amount of time a student is actively involved in instruction). Furthermore, academic engagement can be defined on a continuum from passive to active engagement. J. A. Baker et al. (2008) offered a broad definition of engagement that indicates "active involvement in classroom tasks and activities that facilitate learning, while inhibiting behaviors that detract from learning" (p. 1876). Within academic engagement, active student responding has been defined as observable and measurable student responses to specific academic stimuli (Gunter & Sutherland, 2005) and is the most direct measure of student responding during academic instruction (Heward, 1994).

Classroom Contexts and Academic Engagement

Classroom contexts are dynamic, complex systems where moment-to-moment interactions between teachers and students (not to mention students and their peers) exert influence on academic engagement. Individual student characteristics certainly play a role in student learning, but modifiable teacher behaviors and instructional factors also play a role. For example, proactive classroom management, whereby teachers actively promote prosocial behaviors associated with academic engagement, is associated with increased academic engagement (Kern & Clemens, 2007). J. A. Baker et al. (2008) found that instructional arrangements (e.g., direct instruction, small groups, individual seat work, interactive teaching) had a differential effect on students' engagement, with small-group and interactive teaching resulting in more engagement than direct instruction and individual seat work for students with behavior problems. Finally, research has shown the positive effects of a variety of instructional strategies on academic engagement, including but not limited to shortening task duration (Kern, Childs, Dunlap, Clarke, & Falk, 1994), frequent reinforcement (R. G. Smith & Iwata, 1997), and matching task demands to meet students' skill levels (L. M. Roberts, Marshall, Nelson, & Albers, 2001).

Given the dynamic nature of classroom environments, it is helpful to conceptualize the classroom environment as a system comprising multiple interrelated subsystems. From a theoretical perspective, this conceptualization involves behavioral principles (B. F. Skinner, 1953) embedded in social transactions (Sameroff, 1983), all the while recognizing the role of the ecology (Bronfenbrenner, 1979) on students' academic engagement. To illustrate, behavioral principles serve as the foundation for key instructional practices that serve as antecedents and consequences for academic engagement. For example, data indicate the role that antecedent instructional behavioral stimuli (e.g., providing frequent opportunities to respond during instruction) as well as behavioral reinforcement (e.g., feedback and contingent praise) serve as strategies for increasing academic engagement (e.g., Sutherland, Alder, & Gunter, 2003; Todd, Horner, & Sugai, 1999). The application of transactional theory to the classroom environment suggests that teacher–student interactions are reciprocal in nature (Sutherland & Oswald, 2005); thus, improvements in students' academic engagement likely will result in an improved classroom learning environment through both improvements in classroom behavior and learning opportunities as well as increased effective classroom-based instructional practices. Finally, from an ecological perspective, multiple influences affect students' academic engagement in the classroom, including peer and teacher influences.

In light of these multiple, interactive influences on students' academic engagement, the purpose of this chapter is to critically review the literature across a selective, yet interrelated, layer of classroom influences. Specifically, we will review the effects of (a) opportunities to respond to academic requests (OTR; antecedent procedure); (b) the Good Behavior Game (GBG; contextual procedure); and (c) praise (consequent procedure) on the academic engagement of students with or at risk for disabilities. Search criteria for experimental or quasi-experimental studies across the three procedures included the following: (a) the independent variable was either OTR, GBG, or teacher praise; (b) the dependent variable was student engagement, either self-reported or observational (including active and/or correct academic responding); and (c) research participants were students with or at risk for disabilities, including students identified as having problem behavior. Following a brief description of each procedure, including the underlying theoretical framework, we provide an implementation fidelity checklist. We then review the literature for each procedure with a focus on strengths and limitations of the research base. Finally, we discuss the implications for both practice and future research.

Opportunities to Respond

Research has shown OTR to improve the academic and social behavior of students with high-incidence disabilities, including students with emotional and behavioral disorders (EBD). Specifically, research has shown that increasing opportunities for students to academically respond is associated with increased task engagement and correct responding. In addition, as teachers increase OTR, students' disruptive behaviors decrease (Conroy, Sutherland, Snyder, & Marsh, 2008; Sutherland et al., 2003; Sutherland & Wehby, 2001). Given its ease of implementation, OTR can be an effective and inexpensive means to helping students receive better and more desirable outcomes in the academic setting. Adequate rates of OTR are necessary, as Gunter, Hummel, and Venn (1998) note. It is also important for students to have a high rate of correct responding (80% to 90%). Although OTR is important for student learning, especially for students with or at risk for disabilities, descriptive research suggests that classroom teachers rarely provide adequate OTR and require additional supports to do so (Sutherland & Wehby, 2001).

Description and Fidelity Checklist

OTR is an instructional strategy initiated and used by teachers that serves as a prompt for student academic responding. It can be defined as a questioning strategy that is used as a stimulus that begins or ends a learning trial (Carnine, 1976; Sutherland et al., 2003). A learning trial consists of a three-term, stimulus–response–consequent contingency sequence (C. H. Skinner, Fletcher, & Hennington, 1996). An OTR is used as an antecedent stimulus in the beginning of a learning trial, followed by a verbal, written, or physical student response. An example of a learning trial is when a teacher presents a question to a student (i.e., stimulus), the student answers the question (i.e., response), and the teacher delivers feedback or praise (i.e., consequence). Increasing the quantity and improving the quality of learning trials have been associated with higher learning rates (Carnine, 1976), and researchers have shown that increasing the number of learning trials can also increase learning levels during the acquisition, fluency building, and maintenance stages of learning (C. H. Skinner, Smith, & McLean, 1994).

The fidelity checklist for OTR is simple and concise. Completing the steps on this checklist before instruction allows the teacher to review the academic content to be taught and to design the OTR to use during instruction. In addition, teachers must determine the format of OTR to provide. For example, for younger students, a teacher may want to use choral responding to increase the rate of OTR and student responding, while a teacher of older students might want to use response cards (any sign, such as yes/no cards or dry erase boards, which individual students can use and can be held up simultaneously by all students in response to a teacher prompt). Three other common types of OTR are guided notes (handouts that guide a student through the lecture with standard cues), electronic response systems (remote systems that allow all students to respond simultaneously with outcomes projected publicly), and individual prompting (one student is prompted to respond). All students, including those with disabilities who may have a difficult time responding to complex questions, should have the opportunity to respond correctly to academic questions; by varying the wait-time and difficulty level, teachers may increase the likelihood of students' achieving this goal. As for increasing OTR during instruction, a teacher may decrease the intertrial interval between OTR (i.e., the amount of time between OTR); it remains desirable, however, to have a list of possible OTR available for reference. See Figure 4.1 for a fidelity checklist of procedures for OTR.

Research on OTR

Sutherland and Wehby (2001) reviewed the literature on the relationship between OTR and classroom (academic and behavioral) outcomes of students with EBD. The studies reviewed suggested that lower rates of disruptive behavior and increased rates of task engagement and academic achievement were associated with the occurrence of increased rates of OTR. Since the time this review was published, few studies have been conducted that examined the effects of OTR in the classroom settings. Following is a review of 11 studies that met the criteria for inclusion in our review; six of these studies (Carnine, 1976; C. H. Skinner, Belfiore, Mace, Williams-Wilson, & Johns, 1997; C. H. Skinner, Ford, & Yunker, 1991; C. H. Skinner & Shapiro, 1989; C. H. Skinner et al., 1994; West & Sloane, 1986) were reviewed in Sutherland and Wehby (2001), while four were conducted since that review (Sutherland, Wehby, & Yoder, 2002; Sutherland et al., 2003;

Figure 4.1   Opportunities to Respond (OTR) fidelity checklist.

Behavior	Yes	No	NA
Before Instruction			
Identify students' academic levels.			
Review academic content.			
Identify OTR format.			
Create OTR.			
OTR represent range of difficulty levels.			
During Instruction			
Present OTR at brisk pace (3–5 per min).			
Students respond correctly at rate of 80% or higher.			
Distribute OTR across students.			
Present corrective feedback and/or praise.			

Tincani & Crozier, 2008; Haydon, Mancil, & Van Loan, 2009). A final study, Darch and Gersten (1985), was not included in the Sutherland and Wehby (2001) review but did meet inclusion criteria for this review.

Study Designs

Sutherland et al. (2002) used a correlational design to measure the magnitude of the relationship between OTR and correct responding, while the remaining studies used single-subject designs. Darch and Gersten (1985), Haydon et al. (2009), Sutherland et al. (2003), and Carnine (1976) used withdrawal designs to analyze the increased rate of OTR on students' classroom outcomes. Tincani and Crozier (2008) and West and Sloane (1986) used single-subject multi-element designs, while C. H. Skinner and colleagues (1989, 1991, 1994, 1997) used alternating treatment designs.

Effect of OTR on Outcome Measures

All studies reviewed indicated positive effects of OTR on outcome measures. Carnine (1976) increased OTR by increasing the teacher's presentation rate with two first-grade students identified by the teacher as having high rates of off-task behavior. Results suggest that increased OTR were associated with increased percentages of correct responses and participation and decreased percentages of off-task behavior for the target students. In a similar study, West and Sloane (1986) examined the effects of increased OTR with five students (two boys and three girls) between the ages of 7 and 9 years. Presentation rate (fast = 20 seconds between presentations; slow = 60 seconds between presentations) was used as the independent variable in addition to a reinforcement procedure (token economy system that varied the delivery rate of point delivery for correct responding). The percentage of intervals with disruptive behaviors, academic accuracy, and correct response rate were dependent variables. Results indicated no difference among dependent variables between high and low delivery rate for reinforcement. However, a higher OTR presentation rate resulted in fewer occurrences of disruptive behaviors and increased correct response rate, although academic accuracy was slightly better during the slow OTR presentation rate.

Three additional studies also investigated the effects of increased presentation rate, resulting in increased OTR. C. H. Skinner et al. (1994) examined the effect of both a 5- and 1-second intertrial interval (ITI) procedure on the number of words mastered under each condition of three students (two boys and one girl) with EBD between the ages of 9 and 11. Results indicated that both 5-second and 1-second ITI increased presentation rate

for OTR resulted in more mastered words than the no-treatment condition. During both 5- and 1-second ITI, students were given three OTR per target reading word, compared to one OTR per target reading word during the no-treatment condition. Although the results show no difference between the 5- and 1-second ITI interventions, results do suggest that the number of responses (three) required during the intervention conditions, compared to the one response required during the no-treatment condition, may have impacted the students' mastery of the reading words. Further, the 5-second presentation rate took an average of 103 seconds longer per session than the 1-second presentation rate, so the 1-second rate may represent a more efficient use of instructional time.

Tincani and Crozier (2008) examined the effect of a wait-time procedure (brief v. extended) on response opportunities, academic responding, percentage of correct responding, and disruptive behavior of two students (ages 6 and 7 years) with challenging behaviors. The setting for this study was an empty classroom in a private clinic for students with behavior problems. Results suggest that brief wait-time had a positive effect on all of the dependent variables. When wait-time was brief, researchers noted an increase in OTR and increased responding for both students. Both students also tended to increase correct responding during the condition with increased response opportunities; while less definitive, decreases in disruptive behavior were noted during the brief wait-time condition as well. Finally, Darch and Gersten (1985) examined the effects of increased presentation rate (increased OTR) and praise on both the percentage of correct responding and percentage of on-task behavior of four students (3 boys; 7.8 to 8.6 years) with learning disabilities (LD) during reading instruction in a special education classroom. Results indicate that students' mean levels of correct responding and on-task behavior increased during the increased presentation rate phases. In sum, the research on increased presentation rate suggests that increased OTR results in desirable learning and behavioral outcomes.

C. H. Skinner and Shapiro (1989) examined the effect of increased OTR using taped words (two OTR), drill interventions (two OTR), and continuous and intermittent assessment (one OTR) on words read correctly and incorrectly per minute using an alternating-treatments design. During the taped words intervention, participants read along with a tape recording of vocabulary words, whereas in the drill condition, they read the list of vocabulary words out loud before completing an assessment (two OTRs). During the continuous and intermittent assessment, participants simply read from the list of vocabulary words (one OTR). Results indicated that the two OTR interventions resulted in 78.4 words read correctly and 3.9 words read incorrectly per minute, while having one OTR resulted in 54.4 words read correctly and 5.6 words read incorrectly per minute for five students between the ages of 14 and 18 years, suggesting that a relationship may exist between the increase in OTR and performance on the reading task.

The two remaining C. H. Skinner et al. studies (1991, 1997) examined the effect of verbal cover, copy, and compare (VCCC) and writing cover, copy, and compare (WCCC) on math responding of two students with EBD, ages 9 and 11 years old. To illustrate, during the WCCC condition, the participants looked at a math problem and wrote the answer, covered the problem and answer, wrote the problem and answer, and uncovered the problem and answer to evaluate what was written. During the VCCC condition, the procedures were the same, except that the participant stated the problem and answer verbally rather than in writing, resulting in increased OTR for participants in this condition. Across students, both the mean percentage of problems correct (74% for the VCCC intervention and 68% for the WCCC intervention and no treatment combined) and digits correct per minute (28 for the VCCC intervention and 20 for the WCCC intervention and no treatment combined) favored the condition with increased OTR. C. H. Skinner et al. (1997) further examined the effect of increased OTR using the VCCC and WCCC interventions on the number of multiplication problems completed and digits correct per minute of two students with EBD. The VCCC intervention again resulted in an increase in learning trials for both students (86 and 83 for VCCC, compared to 26 and 33 for WCCC for both students, respectively), and the data suggest that the accuracy (number of problems correct) and fluency (digits correct per minute) of one of the students increased during the VCCC intervention. Results from these two studies suggest that the increased efficiency of the VCCC condition (verbalizing responses rather than writing responses) resulted in more learning trials and, over time, more OTR, which may be associated with improved academic outcomes.

Sutherland et al. (2002) examined the relationship between teacher praise and opportunities for students with disabilities to respond to academic requests. The sample consisted of 20 teachers and 216 students (183 boys and 33 girls) identified with disabilities (112 EBD, 48 with LD, 20 with developmental disabilities, and 36 identified with other disabilities). Results indicated a significant positive correlation between OTR and students' correct responses ($r = 0.94$, $p < 0.01$). Sutherland et al. (2003) also increased OTR as the independent variable to analyze the effects on students' correct responses, disruptive behaviors, and on-task behaviors. Participants were nine students (eight boys and one girl) with EBD who ranged in age from 8 to 12 years old. Results showed mean increases in correct

responding and on-task behavior, as well as decreases in students' disruptive behavior.

Finally, Haydon et al. (2009) examined the effect of increased rates of choral responding OTR on the on-task behavior, correct responding, and disruptive behavior of a fifth-grade girl identified as at-risk for EBD. The setting was a fifth-grade general education science classroom with 19 students and a male teacher. Increased rates of OTR were associated with decreased disruptive behavior and increased task engagement. Increases in correct responding were also noted during the treatment phase.

Procedures

In general OTR was increased in the reviewed studies by an increase in presentation rate during academic instruction. Two studies (Carnine, 1976; West & Sloane, 1986) simply instructed the teacher to increase presentation rate, while Darch and Gersten (1985) instructed the teacher to provide an OTR immediately following a student response. Similarly, C. H. Skinner et al. (1994) decreased the intertrial interval between OTR, and Tincani and Crozier (2008) decreased wait time between response opportunities and student responses. Two studies (C. H. Skinner et al., 1991, 1997) used a VCCC strategy to increase OTR, simply requiring students' verbal responses rather than written responses. An observation feedback intervention was used in both Sutherland et al. (2003) and Haydon et al. (2009), whereby the teacher received feedback on his use of OTR following each observation session. In each case the teacher also set a goal for his use of OTR.

Implementation Fidelity

Nine of the eleven studies reviewed provided some form of treatment fidelity data. The lack of an intervention in Sutherland et al. (2002) precludes the need for fidelity data, while Darch and Gersten (1985) provided no data to indicate that rates of OTR actually increased during their intervention. Haydon et al. (2009) and C. H. Skinner et al. (1989, 1994) used various forms of checklists to measure treatment fidelity. For example, Haydon et al. (2009) used a checklist on 25% of the sessions to record the steps of the choral responding sequence, noting 100% fidelity. Similarly, C. H. Skinner et al. (1989) noted 100% fidelity on 17% of the sessions, and C. H. Skinner et al. (1994) noted 100% fidelity for 11 intervention-phase sessions. Treatment fidelity was measured by direct observation in five studies (Haydon et al., 2009; C. H. Skinner et al., 1989; Sutherland et al., 2003; Tincani & Crozier, 2008; West & Sloan, 1986), which strengthens the findings from these studies by providing evidence of increased rates of OTR.

Strengths and Limitations of Research on OTR

Findings across the 11 studies reviewed here are consistent: Increases in OTR are associated with increased academic achievement and task engagement and decreased disruptive behavior. The measurement of treatment fidelity (9 of 10 intervention studies reported treatment fidelity data) is a strength of this literature, increasing our ability to link increases in dependent variables to actual increases in OTR. At the same time two significant limitations in the research must be noted. First, only three of the eleven reviewed studies (Haydon et al., 2009; Sutherland et al., 2003; Tincani & Crozier, 2008) provided information on the race/ethnicity of student participants; additionally, these three and Sutherland et al. (2002) also provided race/ethnicity information for teacher participants. Second, the lack of a reintroduction of the intervention in Haydon et al. (2009) limits the interpretation of experimental effects in this study. Nonetheless, research on the antecedent procedure of OTR suggests that it can be a useful tool for teachers attempting to provide instruction for students with and at risk for disabilities. We will next review the literature on a contextual intervention on academic engagement, the Good Behavior Game.

Good Behavior Game

The Good Behavior Game (GBG), which has its theoretical roots in behavioral psychology, has been described as a behavioral vaccine (Embry, 2002). Embry defines a behavioral vaccine as "a simple procedure that can dramatically change an adverse outcome" (p. 274). Hallmark characteristics of effective behavioral vaccines related to our discussion include their ability to be combined with other treatments in a synergistic manner as well as their low costs and generalizability (Embry, 2002). In 1969 Barrish, Saunders, and Wolf published the first study on the GBG, and in the ensuing years both empirical studies (e.g., Lannie & McCurdy, 2007, Salend, Reynolds, & Coyle, 1989) and reviews of the literature (e.g., Embry, 2002; Tingstrom, Sterling-Turner, & Wilczynski, 2002) have documented the positive effects of the GBG on a variety of developmental outcomes, including proximal decreases in disruptive behavior and increases in prosocial behavior as well as more distal outcomes such as problem behavior and drug or alcohol use in young adulthood (Poduska et al., 2008; Tingstrom et al., 2002).

Description and Fidelity Checklist

The GBG is a group-contingency classroom management procedure that may occur during any group activity and is designed to reduce problem behavior. Before implementing the GBG, the teacher first (a) identifies and operationally defines up to three negative behaviors to be targeted for change (e.g., talking out, out-of-seat behavior, aggression); (b) assigns students to one of three to four teams (three to four students per team), taking care to create heterogeneous groups based on behavior (externalizing and internalizing); (c) collects baseline data on team behavior to ensure that teams are similar on base rates of behavior; and (d) reorganizes groups if necessary based on baseline data showing marked differences in behavior between groups. During the pre-implementation phase, the students do not know that the teacher is collecting data on these behaviors.

Before implementation of the game, the teacher describes the game and provides examples and nonexamples of the behaviors. Each team may appoint a team leader and assign their team a group name. The teacher then informs the students that groups that receive fewer than a certain number of check marks (e.g., five during a 15-minute session) may receive a predetermined reward at the end of the activity. Throughout the activity period, the teacher monitors the students for occurrences of the targeted behaviors. If a student displays any one of the behaviors, she earns a check mark for her team, thus holding the group responsible for the behavior of each of its members. If all groups exceed the determined number of check marks, then the group with the fewest number wins the reward. If all teams tie or have fewer than the criterion number of checks, all students on those teams receive the reward. The team leaders are then responsible for dispensing the rewards (if tangible) to their team members and marking their team's reward on a progress chart. Once the students are familiar with the game, the teacher may begin the game unannounced at any time, thus teaching students to consistently self-monitor their behavior. See Figure 4.2 for a fidelity checklist of procedures for the GBG.

Research on the GBG

After the initial study on the GBG (Barrish et al., 1969), a series of studies documented the positive effects of the GBG on a variety of youth outcomes. Perhaps the most well-known evaluation of the GBG is a series of studies conducted by Kellam and colleagues (e.g., Kellam, Ling, Merisca, Brown, & Ialongo, 1998; Poduska et al., 2008) in a randomized control trial with a longitudinal design in 19 elementary schools in Baltimore, Maryland. A review of this literature is well beyond the scope of this chapter, and only a small subset of these studies ($N = 4$) met the criteria for inclusion in our review of measuring a dependent variable of student engagement. However, it is important to mention that the effects of the GBG on both proximal and distal measures of disruptive behavior

Figure 4.2   Good Behavior Game (GBG) fidelity checklist.

Behavior	Yes	No	NA
Before Implementation (1–2 Weeks)			
Identify and define undesirable behaviors.			
Create teams.			
Collect baseline data.			
Reorganize teams based on baseline data (if necessary).			
Implementation			
Announce game before beginning.			
Announce group members before beginning.			
Read the classroom rules.			
Explain the classroom rules.			
Explain the requirements to win.			
Explain the rule violation process.			
Set the game timer.			
Announce the start of the game.			
Handle disruptive behaviors appropriately.			
Review scores.			
Review rules.			
Record proper information.			
Provide reinforcement.			

and aggression, particularly for high-risk students, have been overwhelmingly positive. Following is a review of the four studies (Darch & Thorpe, 1977; Darveaux, 1984; Fishbein & Wasik, 1981; Lannie & McCurdy, 2007) that met the criteria for inclusion in our review.

Study Designs

Two of the studies (Darveaux, 1984; Lannie & McCurdy, 2007) used an ABAB single-subject design, while one (Darch & Thorpe, 1977) used an ABACA single-subject design. The reversal design used in these studies allows for an evaluation of the effects of the independent variable on dependent variables as the participants serve as their own controls. Fishbein and Wasik (1981) used an ABCB single-subject design, which limits the interpretation of results due to a lack of experimental control.

Effect of the GBG on Outcome Measures

All studies reviewed indicated positive effects of the GBG on outcome measures. Similar to the majority of studies on the GBG, three of the four studies reviewed included a measure of disruptive behavior (Darveaux, 1984; Fishbein & Wasik, 1981; Lannie & McCurdy, 2007), and data indicated that students' disruptive

behavior covaried with the introduction and implementation of the GBG across studies. Two studies (Darch & Thorpe, 1977; Lannie & McCurdy, 2007) included a measure of student on-task behavior, and results also indicated that on-task behavior covaried with the introduction and implementation of the GBG. For example, Lannie and McCurdy reported that on-task behavior increased from 53.3% and 47% in the two baseline phases to 68% and 75.6% in the two treatment phases when the 22 first-grade students in their study played the GBG. Similarly, Darch and Thorpe reported that on-task behavior increased from 26%, 51%, and 34% during baseline conditions to 86% (for GBG with group consequences) and 75% (for GBG with individual consequences) for the 10 highest-risk students in a disruptive fourth-grade classroom. Interestingly, the students' level of on-task behavior during the reintroduction of the GBG without group contingency (i.e., students worked for individual rather than group consequences) was not as high as the group contingency condition, suggesting the importance of the peer-group reinforcement in this study.

Results for outcomes other than on-task behavior have also been positive. For example, Darveaux (1984) found that assignment completion rates increased from 40% to 75% for two second-grade boys identified as high risk when their classroom participated in the GBG.

In addition, Fishbein and Wasik (1981) found increases in task-relevant behaviors, such as answering or asking lesson-related questions, writing, and raising a hand, and decreases in off-task behaviors of 25 fourth-grade students who had been identified as disruptive when the GBG was introduced. Interestingly, in the third phase of this study, winning teams received verbal reinforcement rather than a tangible (e.g., fun classroom activity) reinforcer, and rates of both task-relevant and off-task behavior decreased to approximate levels demonstrated during the baseline phase, indicating the importance of tangible reinforcement in this study.

Procedures

Embry (2002) noted that a strength of the GBG is its relatively easy implementation procedures. Of the four studies reviewed here, only two reported the level of support provided to implement the procedures of the GBG. Darveaux (1984) noted that a school psychologist provided a total of 1 hour of training to the teacher, and Lannie and McCurdy (2007) noted that the researcher provided training to the teacher in GBG procedures, although the amount of time and training was not provided.

Several adaptations were made to the GBG in reviewed studies that warrant mention. Three of the studies (Darveaux, 1984; Fishbein & Wasik, 1981; Lannie & McCurdy, 2007) used reinforcement rather than punishment procedures as the students in these studies earned points for desirable behaviors. This adaptation is notable, particularly as it relates to students with and at risk for disabilities, given the long history of beneficial effects of positive reinforcement on students' academic and behavioral outcomes. Darveaux also used an innovative procedure whereby students could use earned points to "take away" negative check marks that teams had earned; this strategy might be particularly useful when teams have exceeded a set criteria for negative behaviors, allowing them to continue working toward a reward rather than "giving up" for the session. Finally, an adaptation in Darch and Thorpe (1977) involved the principal's acknowledging winning teams by coming into the classroom once a day and providing verbal reinforcement.

Implementation Fidelity

Unfortunately, only one study (Lannie & McCurdy, 2007) provided data on implementation fidelity. These researchers used a checklist that was rated for 29% of the observed GBG sessions. Results indicated that across sessions, 88% of the procedures were implemented.

Strengths and Limitations of the Research on the GBG

Interpreting the research on the effects of the GBG on student engagement is made difficult by the small number of studies reviewed. Again, however, it is important to note that the research base for the GBG is much larger than that reviewed here; the vast majority of research studies on the GBG did not meet criteria for inclusion in this review. That said, several limitations in the reviewed studies should be taken into account when considering outcomes. First, none of the four studies in this review included information on the race or ethnicity of their participants, limiting the generalizability of results. Second, the lack of a return to baseline in the Fishbein and Wasik (1981) study did not allow for a demonstration of experimental control. Finally, of the four studies reviewed, only one (Lannie & McCurdy, 2007) provided treatment fidelity data. This omission limits the interpretation of findings from the research reviewed on the GBG, particularly given the number of procedural steps necessary to implement the intervention with fidelity. Results of the reviewed research, even in light of these limitations, do suggest that a contextual intervention such as the GBG can have positive effects on the engagement of students with and at risk for disabilities. We next review the literature on teacher praise—a consequent procedure—and its effect on students' academic engagement.

Praise

Teacher praise is widely recognized as an effective consequent strategy for promoting desirable student classroom behavior (Gable, Hester, Rock, & Hughes, 2009). Teachers use praise to communicate positive evaluations of a student's performance or effort to the student (Henderlong & Lepper, 2002), and praise can be used to promote both academic responding and behavioral skills. Effective praise can increase intrinsic motivation, promote appropriate behavior, and decrease disruptive behavior (Henderlong & Lepper, 2002; Stormont, Smith, & Lewis, 2007). Although providing effective praise can be a simple consequent strategy for a teacher to use, it may be difficult to find opportunities for praise within the ongoing dynamic classroom environment. This assertion is supported by descriptive research that suggests that praise statements, particularly for students with or at risk for disabilities, are delivered infrequently (Van Acker, Grant, & Henry, 1996; Wehby, Symons, Canale, & Go, 1998). Ironically, students with academic or behavioral deficits are precisely the ones who need the most positive attention (Haager & Klinger, 2005).

Description and Fidelity Checklist

Praise is a social reinforcer and is one of the most effective and convenient positive reinforcers teachers can use to manage student behavior. It is inexpensive, because it costs nothing but the teachers' observation and time. Paine, Radicchi, Rosellini, Deutchman, and Darch (1983) report that effective praise has several important components:

- Good praise adheres to the "if–then" rule, which states that if the student is behaving in the desired manner, then (and only then) the teacher praises the student.
- Good praise frequently includes students' names.
- Good praise is descriptive.
- Good praise conveys that the teacher really means what is said (i.e., it is convincing and sincere).
- Good praise is varied.
- Good praise does not disrupt the flow of individual or class activities.

In addition, researchers (Dweck, 2007; Sutherland & Singh, 2004) recommend that praise be effort related. That is, praise should be focused on the process of responding, whether academic or behavioral. Process praise focuses on students' effort and strategies that are modifiable when faced with difficult tasks, resulting in maintained high expectations and more positive affect (Kamins & Dweck, 1999). This focus differs from person praise (e.g., "You're so smart!"), which is related to characteristics of the student that are not modifiable. See Figure 4.3 for a fidelity checklist for teacher praise.

Research on Teacher Praise

A large literature base has examined the effect of praise on a variety of student outcomes. However, only five studies met criteria for inclusion in this review (Connell & Carta, 1993; Darch & Gersten, 1985; Sutherland, Wehby, & Copeland, 2000; Sutherland et al., 2002; Todd et al., 1999).

Study Designs

Sutherland et al. (2002) used a correlational design to measure the magnitude of the relationship between praise and correct responding, while the remaining studies used single-subject designs. One study used a multiple baseline design across participants to determine whether the implementation of the self-assessment intervention influenced rates of student active engagement, competing behavior, and teacher prompting to the target students during in-class transition (Connell & Carta, 1993). Another study (Todd et al., 1999) began with a functional assessment and then employed withdrawal and multiple baseline design elements. Two studies (Darch & Gersten, 1985; Sutherland et al., 2000) used withdrawal of treatment designs.

Effect of Praise on Outcome Measures

We described the setting and measurement of two studies (Darch & Gersten, 1985; Sutherland et al., 2002) earlier. Sutherland et al. found a positive association between teacher praise and correct academic responding ($r = 0.49$, $p < 0.05$) in 20 classrooms for students with EBD, while Darch and Gersten noted increases in both

Figure 4.3   Praise fidelity checklist.

Behavior	Yes	No	NA
Before Instruction			
Identify desirable social behavior.			
Identify desirable academic behavior.			
Generate list of possible praise statements.			
During Instruction			
Provide praise for desirable social behavior.			
Provide praise for desirable academic behavior.			
Praise is contingent on desirable behavior ("if–then rule").			
Praise statement includes student name.			
Praise is descriptive (e.g., behavior specific).			
Praise is sincere.			
Use a variety of praise statements.			
Praise is related to effort.			

correct responding and on-task behavior when praise was increased for four students with LD, particularly when these increases were paired with increases in OTR.

Connell and Carta (1993) investigated an intervention package that combined a self-assessment procedure with teacher praise for appropriate behavior during transition time in three early childhood special education classrooms. Participants included one student from each of the three classrooms and the corresponding teachers who were all certified in early childhood special education. Results suggest that the intervention resulted in mean increases in students' engagement across classrooms; however, praise was included as part of an intervention package including students' self-assessment of behavior, and as such the effects of praise on engagement are difficult to ascertain. Results of this study do suggest, however, that teaching students to self-assess performance of in-class transition skills, accompanied by moderate levels of teacher praise, can have a positive effect on student active engagement and independent responding.

Todd et al. (1999) examined the effects of a self-management procedure in the context of positive behavior support, including increased teacher praise. Participants were nine third- and fourth-grade students (one target student with LD and eight randomly selected students) in a mixed third- and fourth-grade classroom with 29 students and one teacher. Results suggest that implementation of self-monitoring, self-recruitment of teacher attention, and increases in teacher praise were associated with decreases in problem behaviors, increases in on-task behavior, and increases in task completion. In a similar study, Sutherland et al. (2000) examined the effect of increases in a teacher's behavior-specific praise on the on-task behavior of nine fifth-grade students with EBD in a self-contained classroom. Using an observation/feedback procedure, the teacher set a goal of six behavior-specific praise statements per 15-minute observation period and received feedback on his use of praise statements. Increases in the teacher's behavior-specific praise were associated with increased on-task behavior.

Procedures

Procedures for increasing rates of praise varied across the five studies reviewed, although it should be noted that the Sutherland et al. (2002) study was descriptive in nature and thus measured naturally occurring rates of teacher praise. Darch and Gersten (1985) simply instructed the teacher to increase rates of praise during treatment phases; no other procedures were noted. Similarly, Connell and Carta (1993) instructed the teachers in their study to praise desirable student behavior at least when students were transitioning between activities during the treatment phases. Additionally, the teachers

completed a self-assessment scale following transitions that allowed them to note occurrences of students' target behavior. Finally, the researcher in Sutherland et al. (2000) provided the teacher with feedback immediately following observations on the teacher's rate of behavior-specific praise related to the teacher's goal of six praise statements per observation period.

Implementation Fidelity

Given the descriptive nature of Sutherland et al. (2002), fidelity data were not noted, although rates of teacher praise and correct responding were provided. Darch and Gersten (1985) did not provide rates of teacher praise; thus, interpreting the effect of their increased praise condition on student engagement is limited. Connell and Carta (1993) used a checklist to measure treatment fidelity across phases of their study. These authors noted that fidelity of implementation of the praise component were 93%, 56%, and 84% across three classrooms. Todd et al. (1999) used direct observations of teacher behavior to document increases in teacher praise; results indicated increased means during treatment phases with some data overlap. Sutherland et al. (2000) reported direct observation data on the teacher's use of behavior-specific praise statements; results indicated that the teacher's rate of praise statements was 1.3 and 1.7 per minute during baseline phases and 6.7 and 7.8 per minute during intervention phases.

Strengths and Limitations of the Research on Praise

The small number of studies makes it difficult to generalize the findings of the research reviewed here; however, results suggest a positive association between teacher praise and various measures of students' academic engagement. The treatment fidelity data in two of the studies strengthen these findings. However, one study (Darch & Gersten, 1985) did not provide data on rates of teacher praise, making it difficult to link any increases in praise to improvements on the measured variables. Finally, only one of the five reviewed studies (Sutherland et al., 2000) provided race/ethnicity for student participants, while an additional study (Sutherland et al., 2002) provided race/ethnicity information for teacher participants, limiting the generalizability of findings from this research.

Summary

The purpose of this chapter was to review the effects of three classroom-based interventions on academic engagement among students with disabilities. OTR to academic requests (antecedent strategy), the GBG (contextual strategy), and teacher praise (consequent strategy) were evaluated, and this review resulted in a total of 18 studies that met criteria for inclusion. Following is a discussion of the collective strengths and limitations of the research reviewed, as well as recommendations for research and practice.

Strengths of the Research Base

Overall the studies reviewed in this chapter suggest positive effects of the independent variables on a variety of student engagement measures. Because 17 of the 18 studies reviewed used single-subject methodology, the criteria for determining whether a study meets acceptable methodological rigor recommended by Horner et al. (2005) are helpful in identifying both strengths and limitations of the reviewed studies. In general, both dependent and independent variables were provided with operational and replicable precision. The variety of student engagement measures, including correct academic responding (including reading, math, and science responding), off-task behavior, and task engagement, showed desirable change across studies, a finding that suggests that the interventions can have a positive effect on both passive and active student engagement. Demonstrations of experimental effects were evident across studies and at a minimum were replicated across participants. In addition, given the association between student engagement and academic achievement, the dependent variables in the research reviewed are socially valid, and the independent variables, particularly OTR and teacher praise, are practical and cost-effective to implement.

A relative strength of the OTR and praise literature reviewed was the reporting of treatment fidelity data. Of 13 intervention studies that examined the effect of OTR or praise, 12 provided some form of treatment fidelity data. Only Darch and Gersten (1985) failed to provide fidelity data, and this limits the interpretation of findings from this study, because it is not clear that rates of OTR and praise actually increased. Finally, although all of the research studies examining the effects of the three interventions reviewed do not necessarily meet the criteria for methodological rigor suggested by Horner et al. (2005), confidence in the effects of the three interventions reviewed is enhanced by the number of different research teams and geographical locations represented by the studies. To illustrate, of the 11 OTR studies reviewed, 7 were conducted by different research teams, while all 4 of the GBG studies and 4 of the 5 praise studies were conducted by different research teams.

Limitations of the Research Base

Although the results of the research reviewed in this chapter are promising, several significant limitations in this literature were evident. First, Horner et al. (2005) note the importance of describing research participants with sufficient detail. Of the reviewed 18 studies, only 4 provided information on the race/ethnicity of student participants, with one more providing information on the race/ethnicity of teacher participants. This limitation significantly limits the generalizability of the reviewed research and raises questions about the potential effects of the interventions on students from culturally and linguistically diverse backgrounds. Second, methodological limitations were noted in several studies. Specifically, the lack of a return to baseline in the Fishbein and Wasik (1981) study did not allow for a demonstration of experimental control, and the lack of a reintroduction of the intervention in Haydon et al. (2009) limits the interpretation of experimental effect in this study. Finally, of the four GBG studies reviewed, only one (Lannie & McCurdy, 2007) provided treatment fidelity data. This omission limits the interpretation of findings from the research reviewed on the GBG, particularly given the number of procedural steps necessary to implement the intervention with fidelity.

Recommendations for Future Research

Limitations of the reviewed research should inform future studies examining the effects of classroom-based interventions on the active student engagement of students with and at risk for disabilities. For example, studies should provide data on the race/ethnicity of student and teacher participants in order to help determine the potential effects of interventions for all students, including those from culturally and linguistically diverse groups. Additionally, collecting data on treatment fidelity is crucial as the field attempts to determine if particular interventions are associated with desirable student outcomes. Specifically, it is important that educators do not discount interventions with potential positive effects on student outcomes due to weak treatment effects when fidelity of implementation was poor or unexamined.

While encouraging practitioners to implement interventions with fidelity has been of interest to school-based researchers for some time, the science of measuring implementation of interventions remains behind that of the development and identification of these practices (McLeod, Southam-Gerow, & Weisz, 2009). Thus, it is critical that researchers not only measure treatment fidelity but also be thoughtful in the development of fidelity measures so as to capture those characteristics of fidelity that are most related to treatment effectiveness. From an educational perspective, *adherence* to a treatment protocol (e.g., base rates of target behavior) and *quality* (e.g., purposeful use of target behavior) might have differential effects on students' task engagement. Although many of the studies reviewed in this chapter used observed rates (i.e., *adherence*) of OTR and praise as measures of treatment fidelity, the *quality* with which these strategies were used was not measured. Mediational models of analysis can provide important information to researchers about the relationship between treatment fidelity and treatment outcomes, allowing for more targeted intervention packages that have the potential for greater treatment gains.

The selection of interventions to review in this chapter was purposeful. Each represents a different layer in a complex, interactive classroom system, and examining these interventions in concert therefore might be useful. To illustrate, Sutherland et al. (2002) found a sequential association between teacher praise and OTR, such that OTR were likely to occur with 5 seconds of a teacher praise statement at a rate higher than suggested by chance occurrence. Given that these two strategies are part of a learning trial (and given the promising results of each in isolation per this review), examining the effects of increased rates of praise and OTR might yield particularly powerful effects on student outcomes. In addition, examining the effects of increased rates of praise and OTR within the context of the GBG might also be a worthwhile research focus. For example, three of the GBG studies reviewed in this chapter (Darveaux, 1984; Fishbein & Wasik, 1981; Lannie & McCurdy, 2007) utilized reinforcement rather than punishment procedures as a procedural modification, and this adaptation might hold promise for students with and at risk for disabilities.

Recommendations for Practice

Although the limitations of the studies reviewed here provide some hesitation in the strength of recommendations, a few general suggestions for practitioners can be made. The research does suggest that increasing OTR is associated with improved student engagement, and increasing learning trials therefore should be a goal for teachers. A variety of means to increase rates of OTR are available to teachers, including decreasing intertrial interval, response cards, and choral responding. Selecting the method for increasing OTR should be based on a variety of factors, including but not limited to the age and developmental level of the students, the material to be learned, and the teacher's professional judgment. Additionally, teachers should attempt to identify and praise students' desirable behavior, both academic and social, as research strongly suggests the positive effects of praise. Delivering high-quality praise (e.g., behavior specificity, sincerity, contingent on target behavior) and appropriate, frequent OTR should be consistent goals of all practitioners. Finally, the GBG does appear to hold promise for students with and at risk for disabilities. Although adhering to the treatment protocol of the GBG is critically important, it may also be important for students with and at risk for disabilities to receive instruction on desirable behaviors and to have opportunities to be reinforced for performing desirable behaviors. Findings from three of the four studies on the GBG reviewed in this chapter, in which teachers provided points for desirable behavior rather than punishment procedures for undesirable behavior, support this assertion (Darveaux, 1984; Fishbein & Wasik, 1981; Lannie & McCurdy, 2007).

CHAPTER 5

Strategies to Improve Compliance

Carol Ann Davis and **Annie McLaughlin** | *University of Washington*

Following instructions is one of the basic readiness skills children need as they move into public school settings (Ladd, Kochenderfer, & Coleman, 1997). Without this skill, a child is less likely to perform well in school and more likely to have poor social relationships (Shores & Wehby, 1999). Long before children reach age 5, parents and day-care workers struggle with preschool children who do not follow instructions or are considered noncompliant (Webster-Stratton, 2006). In fact, Gilliam and Shahar (2006) reported preschool expulsion rates as 27 per 1,000 students. This alarming rate reflects not only those children with known disabilities but is indicative of the behavioral difficulties of the general population of young children (Patterson & Reid, 1973; G. R. Walker, 1993). Recent reports have listed noncompliance, or not following directions, as one of the primary causes for children being asked to leave their day-care settings. Children and youth who are noncompliant are at greater risk for exclusion from the day-care or general education classrooms and have fewer opportunities to engage in a variety of activities in the community (e.g., Gilliam & Shahar, 2006).

Noncompliance has been defined as a failure to initiate an adult request or direction in a timely manner, or as a failure to complete the task requested of the individual (Schoen, 1983). The study of compliance has a long history in the field of education and parenting (Englemann & Colvin, 1983; Forehand & McMahon, 1981). In fact, compliance to typical routine instructions within the educational environment is a critical skill for students to succeed in school. Issues related to compliance therefore affect the amount of instructional time a teacher can provide and, thus, directly influence students' success (Belfiore, Basile, & Lee, 2008).

While the primary purpose of this chapter is to discuss research-based strategies for improving compliance, it is important to acknowledge this literature's influence on other areas of instruction and behavior and provide a rationale for why we, as educators, should still be interested in a literature that focuses on compliance and compliance training. Much of what we know about improving compliance comes from the early work of Forehand, MacMahon, Patterson, and other colleagues examining family interactions (Forehand & McMahon, 1981; Forehand, Wells, & Sturgis, 1978; Patterson, 1982). These researchers, along with several others, studied interactions in the home and school and differentiated the types of requests delivered to children and students and their corresponding compliance to those requests (S. M. Johnson, Wahl, Martin, & Johansson, 1973). Findings showed that higher rates of compliance were associated with higher rates of "initiating commands," which required the student to begin an activity (e.g., "Please sit down") as opposed to "stop commands," which required the student to stop doing something (e.g., "Stop touching the glass"). H. M. Walker, Ramsey, and Gresham (2004) suggest it is important to deliver instructions that are specific (i.e., explicitly telling the student what to do), direct (e.g., "Please put the paper down" rather than questioning, e.g., "Could you put the paper down?"), and simple (e.g., not wordy, one request at time). This body of research on the delivery of requests, taken together, provides guidelines regarding ways to improve students' overall compliance by simply changing how adults deliver requests. The literature also provides several demonstrations of the successful use of compliance training with requests "to do" as well as "to stop doing" something (see Houlihan & Jones, 1990; Neef, Shafer, Egel, Cataldo, & Parrish, 1983).

Much of the early work on compliance assisted the field of special education in determining ways to increase appropriate responding and improve compliance. That is, we know how to change the environment, context, and type of request to increase the likelihood that students will engage or stay engaged in an activity (i.e., comply). We also recognize the importance of how teachers and other adults respond (or do not respond) to student noncompliance. That is, researchers have indicated that inconsistent responding to a child's noncompliance is likely to contribute to continued problems with noncompliance (e.g., Patterson, 1982; Dishion & Patterson, 2006). In addition, we know that increasing reinforcement (i.e., attention) when a learner follows a direction is likely to result in continued or improved compliance (Madsen, Becker, & Thomas, 1968; Sutherland, Wehby, & Copeland, 2000).

What we know about working with students with challenging behavior has evolved over time. The field has shifted its emphasis to focus on preventing and teaching skills rather than relying on only changing the consequence to influence the behavior. This shift in focus is evident in the expansive work on effective instruction and functional behavioral assessment. The literature, as well as chapters in this book, offers many strategies that if implemented can increase engagement and therefore increase compliance (see Chapter 4 in this volume).

More recently, appropriate strategies for increasing compliance have focused on determining the function of noncompliance and identifying a replacement behavior for noncompliance. Some perceive compliance training negatively (I. M. Evans & Meyer, 1990; McDonnell, 1993; Meyer & Evans, 1989), as it seems to focus only on conformity and does not address the underlying issue or mislearning that has occurred. Said differently, some professionals believe that the use of effective instruction and functional behavioral assessments to inform prevention efforts or identify a replacement behavior for noncompliance has alleviated the need for strategies that focus on the somewhat mechanistic procedures of compliance (i.e., simply "do as I say" approach). For example, we can change the environment or the conditions under which we deliver the requests to alleviate

noncompliance rather than direct intervention only at student compliance.

Nonetheless, we believe some situations and some learners may benefit from direct strategies to improve compliance. Take, for example, the adolescent who refuses to sit down and buckle the seat belt when asked by the airplane attendant or the fourth grader who still refuses to engage in the academic task, even when the teacher has increased the power of the consequence or opportunities to respond in the activity. In these instances, using effective instruction such as opportunities to respond or teaching a replacement behavior will not result in an acceptable alternative. Yet, the lack of compliance to a request or rule is likely to have dire consequences for those individuals. These instances provide us with examples to consider the need for strategies that increase a student's engagement (i.e., improving compliance) that other research-based strategies (e.g., increasing opportunities to respond, addressing the function of behavior) do not provide.

As acknowledged in the previous paragraph, our field's shift to applications of preventive and function-based approaches provides us with many strategies that increase the likelihood a learner will engage in the learning activities or respond appropriately to a request. However, some learners are particularly resistant to the typical interventions that increase engagement. In some cases, it may be necessary to first implement strategies that teach the skill of "compliance" or "following directions" so the learner may be ready or more willing to access those instructional strategies that increase or maintain engagement. The two strategies discussed within this chapter—compliance training and high probability requests—focus on improving compliance. In the sections that follow, we will present definitions, provide some theoretical background for the strategies, and list in a "how-to" format the steps of the strategies.

Compliance Training
Definition and Theoretical Background

Compliance training is simply the use of reinforcement to establish a particular behavior under stimulus control of an instruction or a request. For example, a teacher identifies those requests to which the learner does not respond appropriately, delivers one request, and then provides reinforcement when the appropriate response occurs. If the student does not respond within 10 seconds (typically) or engages in an incorrect behavior, a correction procedure is used by redelivering the request and providing prompts or assistance to complete the request.

The teacher provides reinforcement for the student's responding appropriately and does not provide reinforcement when the student does not respond appropriately. Differential reinforcement (i.e., reinforcing appropriate responses and not reinforcing inappropriate responses) is used to teach the student that appropriate response to a task demands occasional reinforcement. Several studies have indicated that providing reinforcement for following a subset of similar requests (also known as a response class) increases "instruction-following" behavior for other requests (Neef et al., 1983; Russo, Cataldo, & Cushing, 1981).

More recently, the more traditional procedures for compliance training have been modified to incorporate what Ducharme, Sanjuan, and Drain (2007) refer to as "errorless compliance training." This procedure structures the instructional trials (i.e., the delivery of a request, student compliance behavior, and the delivery of reinforcement) in phases that are categorized by the type of request. The types of requests are defined by the likelihood the student will respond. That is, level-1 requests are those that the student will respond to 75% to 100% of the time, level-2 requests are those that the student will respond to 51% to 75% of the time, level-3 requests are those that the student will respond to 26% to 50% of the time, and level-4 requests are those that the student will respond to 0% to 25% of the time. During the first phase, the interventionist or teacher delivers level-1 requests that the student will respond to 76% to 100% of the time. The interventionist starts at this level to ensure that the student will experience success by responding appropriately and thus begin to pair the reinforcement with the instruction and subsequent appropriate responding. Once the student demonstrates stable responding to level-1 requests, the interventionist begins to deliver only level-2 requests. Once the student responds to level-2 requests consistently, the teacher moves to level-3 and then level-4 requests, typically delivering only one level of request at a time (Ducharme, Harris, Milligan, & Pontes, 2003). In the section that follows, we offer a "how-to" guide for conducting compliance training in the classroom.

A "How-To" Guide

Identify the Instructions or Task Demands

For most teachers, identifying instructions that an individual does not consistently complete or does not complete in a timely manner is easy. These are typically the instructions (e.g., "Get out your book," "Come to circle time," "Clean up your activity") that we are most aware of because they cause us great concern or take many opportunities for the individual to accomplish them. For some learners, it is often a group of instructions (i.e., stimulus class) that are not followed consistently. A group of instructions (i.e., stimuli) can be defined by the elements they share. These common instructions may make up a stimulus class. In this case, the group of instructions or the stimulus class is defined by their effects on the behavior (i.e., noncompliance). The group of instructions that produce noncompliant responses is individual to each learner. For some learners, the group of instructions that result in noncompliance might include "Come here," "Put the _____ away," "Hand me the _____." For other students the instructions may be related to academic tasks and include "Begin working now," "What is the capital of Texas?" or "It is your time to read out loud."

Identify Reinforcers

Much has been studied and written about the use and role of reinforcement in the stimulus–response paradigm, particularly the role it plays in stimulus (or instructional) control. A stimulus is defined as a condition or event that occurs before a response or behavior that elicits its occurrence. A reinforcer is defined by the effect it has on the increased occurrence of a particular behavior (J. O. Cooper, Heron, & Heward, 2007). That is, a stimulus provided contingent on the production of a behavior that maintains or increases that behavior is termed a *reinforcer*. Consider, for example, a situation when a student responds to an instruction or request (i.e., stimulus) and a teacher provides praise contingent on that response. If the student's responses to the teacher's requests increase, then teacher-provided praise is considered reinforcement, and the student's response is likely to occur again when the teacher gives that request or instruction in the future. Much has been studied and written about the identification of reinforcers (J. E. Carr, Nicolson, & Higbee, 2000). Although reinforcers are individually determined and specific to each learner, we do have reliable and valid ways to ensure we identify stimuli that serve as reinforcers (Morgan, 2006; Piazza, Fisher, Hagopian, Bowman, & Toole, 1996) through direct observation and choice assessment.

When preparing to directly teach "instruction following," it is necessary to identify and validate reinforcers for the learner. This can be done by observing which items or activities the learner engages with during a "free-choice" condition in which items that are likely to function as reinforcers are accessible. Reinforcers can also be identified by presenting likely preferred items to the learner in a forced choice condition. That is, the interventionist provides a choice of potential reinforcers (typically two to three items or activities selected from a larger pool) and then asks the learner to choose among them. The interventionist records the learner's selection and then presents another choice of two to three potential reinforcers (items and activities from the larger pool may be represented). Choice of items or activities is presented repeatedly, and a hierarchy of preferred items are then identified based on the frequency with which the learner chose a particular item.

Decide on a Correction Procedure

As with all interventions or teaching trials, it is important to remember that a behavior is not under the control of the stimulus until it has been paired with reinforcement. On those occasions early in the teaching cycle, it is important to identify what the procedure will be when the desired behavior (e.g., instruction following) does not follow after the stimulus (e.g., instructions). The consequence for noncompliance or correction procedure can include physical guidance, time-out, or ignoring. Physical guidance is the process of physically guiding the learner through the desired behavior. That is, if the instruction is to "Give me the paper" and the learner does not respond, the interventionist would physically prompt the student to give the paper (or provide physical assistance to the learner to hand the paper to the interventionist). If a teacher chooses to use time-out as the consequence for noncompliance, she would move the student to an area of the room in which all reinforcement is removed and unavailable for the learner to access. Finally, a teacher might decide to ignore the noncompliance by not providing any feedback or verbal redirection. The literature on functional assessment indicates that we should choose an intervention that will not provide the learner with reinforcement for the noncompliance. For example, if the noncompliance is a function of escape, the teacher should avoid choosing time-out or ignoring, because these two consequences would lead to reinforcing the function of the noncompliant behavior.

Provide Opportunities to Follow Instructions and Receive Reinforcement

Once the components have been identified, the interventionist provides opportunities for the student to respond, and when the learner provides the target response, the learner receives reinforcement. For example, the teacher says, "Please put down your pencil," and delivers the reinforcer to the student immediately when the student puts down her pencil. The teacher repeats the set of steps (instruction, behavior, reinforcement) over and over to provide numerous opportunities for the learner to experience both the instruction and the reinforcement. It is through multiple trials of the three-part contingency of the (a) teacher delivering the stimulus, (b) student

Table 5.1 Steps to Implementing Compliance Training

Steps	Examples
1. Deliver the instruction.	"Johnny, sit down."
2. Student responds.	Johnny sits in his chair.
3a. Teacher delivers reinforcement for instruction following.	"Nice sitting, Johnny," while the teacher gives Johnny a high-five.
3b. Teacher delivers corrective feedback for incorrect responding.	If Johnny does not sit down, the teacher may physically guide him to his seat.

responding appropriately, and (c) student receiving the reinforcement that compliance is taught. See Table 5.1 for an illustration of steps to implementing compliance training.

Consider, for example, a teacher who wants a student to sit down so she will stop wandering the classroom. The teacher gives the student the direction, "Sit down." If the student responds by sitting down, the teacher delivers the reinforcer by stating, "Great following directions, thank you for finding your seat." Of course, at any time the student does not respond by sitting down, the teacher delivers the correction procedure (e.g., physically guides the student to sit down) as previously described.

Errorless Compliance Training

Errorless compliance training is based on the same principles as errorless learning. That is, errorless learning structures the teaching opportunities in a way that increases the likelihood the learner will succeed and provide the correct response. Errorless compliance training is a specific form of compliance training that involves exposing the learner to increasingly and successively more challenging instructions at a pace that provides many opportunities for the student to experience success and gain reinforcement.

When implementing errorless compliance training, one of the first tasks is to identify a set of requests and categorize them into four categories related to the student's ability to perform them: easy requests (i.e., those the student has a history of completing), easy moderate requests, moderate requests, and hard requests. Clearly, some of these requests will be those for which the learner responds, and other requests will be those for which the student does not respond. In order to ensure success, the instruction begins with delivering easy requests and continues to deliver easy requests until the student is successful 80% of the time. Once the easy requests are mastered, the instruction then moves to the next level of requests, easy moderate, and so on until all requests

Table 5.2 Steps to Implementing Errorless Compliance Training

Steps	Examples
1. Identify requests (i.e., instructions), and categorize the requests into four groups (easy, easy moderate, moderate, and hard).	Make a list of requests the student always follows, usually follows, sometimes follows, hardly ever follows.
2. Deliver instruction for easy requests.	Deliver a request in which the student will always follow, "What is your favorite after-school activity?"
3. Deliver reinforcement for instruction following (ignore inappropriate responding).	Deliver some form of reinforcement, "That sounds like a great thing to do."
4. Provide many opportunities for the student to succeed at responding appropriately to the request.	Deliver requests in which the student always follows until you have 80%–100% compliance across 10 opportunities.
After teaching easy requests (to 80% responding for all requests), provide instruction on the next level of requests.	Deliver requests in which the student usually follows and so on until you are delivering instructions that the student typically does not follow.

have been taught. While appropriate responding is provided reinforcement (typically contingent praise), inappropriate or no responding is ignored. That is, errorless compliance training is based on the use of differential reinforcement; reinforcement is provided when the learner follows the direction, and reinforcement (or any other correction procedure) is not provided when the learner does not follow the instruction. See Table 5.2 for illustrative steps to implementing errorless compliance training.

Research Base

The literature on compliance training has a long history and influenced much of how we now prepare teachers to provide instruction in the classroom. However, this research is primarily focused on young children and involves parent training programs (R. McMahon & Forehand, 2003; Webster-Stratton, 2006). For the purpose of this chapter, we will provide a brief summary of the literature on compliance training and errorless compliance training together (see R. McMahon & Forehand, 2003, for a comprehensive review of the parent training literature).

Populations

Given the importance compliance, or responding to requests, plays in the early interaction of parents and

children, it is not surprising that the majority of this research has been conducted with young children, primarily 3 to 8 years of age (Bernhardt & Forehand, 1975; Ducharme et al., 2010; Forehand & Scarboro, 1975; M. Roberts, McMahon, Forehand, & Humphreys, 1978; Scarboro & Forehand, 1975). These participants have included learners who are typically developing (Ducharme, Popynick, Pontes, & Steele, 1996; Ford, Olmi, Edwards, & Tingstrom, 2001), with parents who use physical punishment (Ducharme, Atkinson, & Poulton, 2001), and learners with developmental disabilities (Ducharme & Di Adamo, 2005; Ducharme & Popynick, 1993; Russo, Cataldo, & Cushing, 1981).

Settings and Interventionists

The early research occurred in clinical settings, which allowed the researchers to isolate particular attributes of the instructional package to be evaluated (see summary of literature in R. McMahon & Forehand, 2003), and subsequently in the home setting (Ducharme, DiPadova, & Ashworth, 2010; Ducharme & Drain, 2004; Ducharme & Popynick, 1993). This research conducted with families laid the ground work for what we know about increasing compliance and effective instruction and has led to applications in preschool and school settings (Ducharme et al., 2010; Ducharme & Harris, 2005; Ford et al., 2001; Neef, Shafer, Egel, Cataldo, & Parrish, 1983). A range of individuals have implemented the intervention in research studies, beginning with parents who were prompted by the researchers (Ducharme & Popynick, 1993; Forehand & Scarboro, 1975; M. Roberts et al., 1978), and have included clinical therapists (Russo et al., 1981), researchers (Ducharme & DiAdamo, 2005), and teachers (Ducharme et al., 2010; Ford et al., 2001).

Delivery of Intervention

Compliance training is a package of several components related to the delivery of instructions, the prompted responses, and consequences provided upon the learner's response. We know that limiting the number of instructions (Forehand & Scarboro, 1975), using instructions that are clear and concise (M. Roberts et al., 1978), and providing instructions that require a learner to "do" something rather than "don't" do something (Neef et al., 1983) lead to increased compliance. In addition, the research literature indicates it is important for those implementing this intervention to use a consequence based on the learner response. If a learner follows the instruction, interventionists can increase compliance in the future by reinforcing the behavior through attention (Kotler & McMahon, 2003) or specific praise (Bernhardt & Forehand, 1975). On the other hand, interventionists can increase the likelihood of future compliance by implementing time-out (Hobbs, Forehand, & Murray, 1978; M. Roberts et al., 1978; Yeager & McLaughlin, 1995), ignoring (Davies, McMahon, Flessati, & Tiedemann, 1984), or physical guidance (Neef et al., 1983; Parrish, Cataldo, Kolko, Neef, & Egel, 1986) when the learner does not follow the instruction. Interestingly, McMahon and his colleagues found that including a verbal rationale along with the time-out procedure increased learner compliance and parental satisfaction with the intervention. Finally, the literature indicates that intervening on compliance can lead to changes in other behavior (Parrish et al., 1986).

General Strengths of the Research

As mentioned previously, compliance training has a long history demonstrating how to increase compliance. From the research findings of evaluating the implementation of compliance training, we have learned what types of requests or instructions are likely to lead to compliant responses (i.e., following directions). The research that forms the literature base is rich and varied. Studies have been conducted in a variety of settings such as clinics, homes, and schools, and effectiveness of compliance training has been documented in multiple replications. Much of the literature regarding compliance training has established the basis for what we know about effective instruction and the prevention of problem behavior.

General Limitations of the Research

Compliance training, while clearly effective, sometimes suffers from a lack of social validity, particularly from indirect consumers. That is, it is not often considered by caregivers and other educators as "functional" or meaningful learning when a student is repeatedly asked to perform simple tasks or instructions (e.g., "Come here," "Hand me the pencil"). This perspective may be due to the historical nature of the research (A. McDonnell, 1993). Much of the compliance training literature is older and was conducted at a time when education did not see the value of embedded instruction. That is, students were taught to read during reading class and to do calculations during math class. Thus, instruction often looked like "drill and practice." Many studies have taken place in clinical settings and under conditions in which mass trials of the same (or a limited group of) instructions have been taught instead of in actual classrooms. This is not to say the strategy itself is not effective or does not have social validity; in fact, parents and interventionists report meaningful changes in outcomes for learners and agree the intervention is easy to use (Ducharme et al., 2007). However, the way in which the strategy has been reported to have been implemented in the past possibly contributes to the sometimes negative perceptions of the intervention.

Recommendations for Future Research

Following instructions continues to be a critical skill in the classroom and is clearly linked to the future success of students, both academically and socially. Most of the research in this area to date has been in clinical or segregated settings. With the contemporary emphasis on inclusion, compliance training should also explore ways in which the intervention can be delivered within the context of less restrictive environments. Such research might consist of examining the ways in which the intervention can be embedded within the school day or the dosage of the intervention necessary to be effective.

High-Probability Requests
Definition and Theoretical Background

The high-probability requests (HPRs) teaching strategy is designed to increase a learner's compliance with instructions to which she does not usually comply. By providing a series of requests with which the learner is likely to respond favorably (HPRs) before providing the request with which the learner is not likely to respond (low-probability request), results have shown increases in compliance. Since the mid-1990s, a plethora of research has been conducted examining the use of HPR sequences on compliant responses to a variety of task demands across a variety of learners (Davis, Brady, Hamilton, McEvoy, & Williams, 1994; Killu, Sainato, Davis, Ospelt, & Paul, 1998; Zarcone, Iwata, Hughes, & Vollmer, 1993). Most often, HPR sequences have been implemented when the target outcome is to increase instances of following instructions or completing tasks and the function of the noncompliant behavior is escape (e.g., to avoid tasks that are difficult or uninteresting, to get away from social situations). HPRs have also been associated with or noted as being similar to "pre-task requesting" (Singer, Singer, & Horner, 1987) and "interspersed requesting" (Horner, Day, Sprague, O'Brien, & Heathfield, 1991).

HPR sequences is an intervention package consisting of an interventionist delivering three to five quick requests to which the student has a history of responding (HPR) immediately before delivering a request to which the student does not typically respond (low-probability request). The student is provided with reinforcement after he has responded appropriately to each request.

Table 5.3 High-Probability Request Sequence Examples

Request (high- and low-p)	Student Response	Teacher Response
"Clap your hands." (high-p)	Student claps hands.	Teacher praises student's response.
"Give me five." (high-p)	Student claps teacher's hand.	Teacher praises student's response.
"Touch your nose." (high-p)	Student touches nose.	Teacher praises student's response.
"Clean up toys." (low-p)	Student cleans up toys.	Teacher praises student's response.

Request (high- and low-p)	Student Response	Teacher Response
"Put your name on the paper." (high-p)	Student writes name on paper.	Teacher praises student's response.
"How many problems are on the paper?" (high-p)	Student says, "Ten."	Teacher praises student's response.
"Point to the fifth problem." (high-p)	Student touches problem number 5.	Teacher praises student's response.
"Start work now." (low-p)	Student begins work.	Teacher praises student's response.

A high-probability (high-p) request is a request to which the individual typically complies with 80% to 100% of the opportunities. A low-probability (low-p) request has been defined as a request in which the person typically complies with 50% or less of the presented opportunities. The HPR sequence, then, is made up of the interventionist delivering (a) a series of three to five high-p requests, (b) a low-p request, and (c) reinforcement for the compliance to each high- and low-p request. The requests, both high-p and low-p, are individually determined. An example of the implementation of this intervention is located in Table 5.3.

A considerable amount has been written about the possible theoretical explanations for the success of HPR. Although considerable discussion of and challenges to these explanations exist (see Houlihan & Brandon, 1996; Mace, 1996; Nevin, 1996), we focus on the two most frequently cited explanations in the research: behavioral momentum and response generalization.

Behavioral Momentum

Behavioral momentum is an analogy frequently used to describe the behavior principles at work in the HPR sequence (Mace et al., 1988). In Newton's law of physics, momentum is the product of an object's mass and velocity. For example, a car traveling at 60 mph (velocity) has more momentum than the same car traveling at 20 mph. Therefore, it would be more difficult to stop the car traveling at 60 mph. Nevin, Mandell, and Atak (1983) applied Newtonian physics and the associated concept of momentum to describe behavior such that the behavior response strength is analogous to mass and response rate is analogous to velocity. The product of the response strength (behavioral mass) and the response

rate (behavioral velocity) is a behavior's momentum. A behavior's momentum can increase when the response rate or response strength is increased. When a behavior's momentum is increased, the behavior is less likely to change and more likely to persist across time. A behavior with a high momentum, then, is likely to persist over time even when conditions change. For example, the behavior's (i.e., compliant responding) velocity is increased by increasing the response rate (i.e., presenting three to five high-p requests in close proximity). The mass, or response strength, is increased by delivering continuous reinforcement for the compliant responses to the high-p requests. This succession of request/compliance/reinforcement creates a momentum for compliant responding even when the more difficult task, the low-p request, is presented.

Response Generalization

HPR sequences have also been explained using the principles of response generalization (Horner et al., 1991). In their article using interspersed requests, Horner and colleagues suggest the sequence of high-p requests serves as varied stimuli from the same stimulus class of "instructions." That is, a learner begins to follow one "instruction" and then generalizes this response to other instructions. These instructions are followed by the learner's correct responses, all representing the same response class of "instruction following," and reinforcement. The authors suggest that the reinforced responses to the varied instructions increase the probability of the learner responding to the low-p request (i.e., a request from the same stimulus class of "instructions") because response generalization has occurred.

Regardless of the explanation for the phenomena, sequencing several high-p requests before initiating a low-p request can help students learn to successfully respond to low-p requests. In the section that follows, we offer a "how-to" guide on how to conduct HPRs.

A "How-To" Guide

Identify Low-P Requests

Teachers can typically easily identify low-p requests. Students refuse to follow these requests, delay starting them, or fail to complete them in a timely manner. Before beginning the HPR sequence, it is important to make sure the teacher directs the student to the complete task clearly and explicitly. For example, the language the teacher uses should be task-oriented (e.g., "Begin writing") and not in the form of a question (e.g., "Are you ready to begin writing?") and should use minimal words (e.g., "Begin writing" instead of "If you are ready to begin writing now you can go ahead and get started"). The teacher should also ensure that the student understands the expectation and is capable of responding appropriately. Only tasks that students can perform but are not performing well or are refusing to perform should be included in the HPR sequence. To identify low-p requests, the teacher can consult with those who frequently work with the student and create a list of possible low-p requests. Once these requests have been identified, teachers can validate the low-p requests by observing that they are not complied with at least 50% of the time.

Identify High-P Requests

High-p requests should be tasks or requests to which the student has a history of responding and readily completes. In addition, these requests should be instructions that can be completed in a relatively short amount of time (i.e., seconds versus minutes). Easy directives to which the student can respond to quickly, such as "Give me five," "Touch your nose," "Tell me your name," "Point to the light," are the focus of high-p requests. To identify possible high-p requests, interview those who typically work with the student and/or observe the student within her usual routine. It is important to make sure that you identify a pool of high-p requests from which to draw the three or four to make an HPR sequence and to later develop new sequences. Davis and Reichle (1996) found that HPR sequences that used the same three high-p requests were less successful than those sequences that were chosen from a variety of high-p requests. After identifying these high-p requests, it is necessary to validate that the learner will actually respond to the requests at least 80% of the time. If the sequences are built from requests the learner does not readily complete, the intervention will be ineffective.

Validate High-P and Low-P Requests

To validate low-p requests, simply provide the student with opportunities to complete a task, and record the student's response (see Figure 5.1). Those requests to which the student responds 50% of the time or less are considered low-p requests. To validate the requests as high-p, create a list from the interview and observation. Over the course of a few days and within a typical routine, ask the student to perform the high-p request. Spread the tasks out over the course of the school day. Over approximately five trials, record whether the student complied with the request. Requests that result with 80% success or better can be considered high-p requests.

To determine high-p requests for written assignments, develop one high-p worksheet and one typical worksheet. Both worksheets should contain the same number of letters or numbers. For example, if you are assessing addition, the low-p worksheet has five two-digit-by-two-digit problems (20 digits, total). The high-p worksheet needs to have 20 digits as well: 10 one-digit-by-one-digit problems. This equality ensures that the assessment focuses on the type of task and not the amount of work. Place one type of each worksheet on the desk, and ask the student to pick one of them. Over the course of a few days, repeat this procedure approximately five times. Record the student's choice each time. Again, the type of worksheet the student chooses 80% or more of the time can be considered to contain high-p content. If the student does not select one of the choices 80% of the time, you should re-evaluate the choices of high-p requests. Find different potential high-p requests and repeat the process again.

Select the HPR Sequences

Because we know that delivering the same or a select number of high-p sequences decreases the effectiveness of the intervention (Davis & Reichle, 1996), it is helpful for the interventionist to select and determine a pool of sequences before implementing the intervention. For example, the pool could include 10 different high-p requests so that whenever the interventionist uses an HPR sequence, plenty of options are available instead of repetitions of the same requests.

Implement the HPR Sequence

The considerations for implementing HPR sequences for verbal requests differ from those for written requests. When implementing the HPR sequence with verbal instructions, the sequence is initiated by asking the learner to complete the first high-p request. On completion of the high-p request by the learner, the interventionist delivers

Figure 5.1   Verify high-probability and low-probability requests.

Request	1	2	3	4	5	Percentage	High- or Low-p?

a reinforcer. The reinforcer can be in the form of verbal praise or a tangible (Mace et al., 1988; Mace, Mauro, Boyajian, & Eckert, 1997). The second and third high-p requests should be delivered within 5 to 15 seconds from the delivery of the reinforcement for the previous request. Some evidence indicates that the longer the intertrial interval, the less effective the intervention seems to be (McLaughlin & Davis, 2010). After the delivery of the reinforcer for the third high-p request, the interventionist should deliver the low-p request quickly (typically within 5 seconds) (Mace et. al., 1988). The interventionist then provides reinforcement for completion of the low-p request, as well. Figure 5.2 provides an implementation checklist for the HPR sequence intervention.

When implementing the high-p request sequence for written tasks, arrange the written tasks with three to five high-p tasks (e.g., single-digit addition problems) immediately before the low-p task (e.g., double-digit addition problems). Provide reinforcement for completion of the low-p task. For some written tasks, reinforcement is not provided following the high-p requests until the learner has finished the low-p request. This differs from the verbal HPR sequences.

Evaluate the Effectiveness of the Intervention

In evaluating the success of HPR, the interventionist should consider collecting data on both high-p and low-p compliance (Figure 5.2 also serves as a data collection sheet). Monitoring the rate of compliance to high-p requests allows the interventionist to determine the fidelity of the intervention. That is, if the learner is not complying with the high-p requests, then the high-p request is not functioning as a stimulus for reinforcement, and the intervention will not work. The compliance to high-p requests does not need to be monitored for each sequence, but compliance should remain at about 80%. It is also important to monitor compliance with low-p requests. For verbal low-p requests, record compliance to the request, and for written low-p requests,

Figure 5.2 High-probability requests implementation checklist and data collection form.

Type of request	Student Response		Reinforcement w/in 5 s	
High-p: (write request)	C	IC	Y	N
High-p	C	IC	Y	N
High-p	C	IC	Y	N
Low-p	C	IC	Y	N

Type of request	Student Response		Reinforcement w/in 5 s	
High-p: (write request)	C	IC	Y	N
High-p	C	IC	Y	N
High-p	C	IC	Y	N
Low-p	C	IC	Y	N

Type of request	Student Response		Reinforcement w/in 5 s	
High-p: (write request)	C	IC	Y	N
High-p	C	IC	Y	N
High-p	C	IC	Y	N
Low-p	C	IC	Y	N

Type of request	Student Response		Reinforcement w/in 5 s	
High-p: (write request)	C	IC	Y	N
High-p	C	IC	Y	N
High-p	C	IC	Y	N
Low-p	C	IC	Y	N

Type of request	Student Response		Reinforcement w/in 5 s	
High-p: (write request)	C	IC	Y	N
High-p	C	IC	Y	N
High-p	C	IC	Y	N
Low-p	C	IC	Y	N

Request	Total delivered	Total correct	Percentage ([Total Correct/Total #] x 100)
High-p requests			
Low-p requests			

record the number of letters or numbers that the student completes. Evaluate whether the student is completing more of the low-p requests over time.

Fade the Intervention

Eventually, you can begin to fade the intervention by reducing the number of high-p requests delivered before the low-p request (Ducharme & Worling, 1994).

Although some evidence indicates that fading is not necessary (Davis, Brady, Williams, & Hamilton, 1992), other research leads us to recommend the interventionist systematically reduce the number of high-p requests slowly (Ducharme & Worling, 1994). If compliance to low-p behaviors decreases, then it may not be appropriate to decrease the high-p requests at that time. Implement the HPR sequences again, and plan to fade its use in the future.

Research Base

Research has provided a great deal of understanding regarding the effects of HPR. To date, over 40 peer-reviewed articles from a variety of researchers examine not only the efficacy of HPR, but also what variables or components of the strategy contribute to its effectiveness. The following is a summary of the literature on HPR.

Populations

HPR has been validated among individuals with a range of disabilities, as well as individuals without disabilities (Ardoin, Martens, & Wolfe, 1999; Austin & Agar, 2005; Rortverdt & Miltenberger, 1994; Bullock & Normand, 2006). Specifically, HPR has shown to be successful with people with behavior disorders (Belfiore, Lee, Scheeler, & Klein, 2002; Davis, Brady, Williams, & Hamilton, 1992), developmental disabilities (Killu et al., 1998; Mace et al., 1988; Zarcone et al., 1993), learning disabilities (Wehby & Hollahan, 2000), autism (Romano & Roll, 2000; Ray, Skinner, & Watson, 1999), and traumatic brain injury (D. L. Lee & Laspe, 2003). In addition, HPR has been used successfully across a variety of ages, including toddlers (Bullock & Normand, 2006), preschoolers (Rortverdt & Miltenberger, 1994), elementary-aged students (Ray et al., 1999; Davis et al., 1994), high school-aged students (Belfiore, Lee, Vargas, & Skinner, 1997), and adults (Fisher, Adelinis, Thompson, Worsdell, & Zarcone, 1998; Romano & Roll, 2000).

Outcomes

Most of the research on HPR has focused on increasing compliance to general requests. However, researchers have also targeted other behaviors, such as increasing social interactions (Davis et al., 1994; McComas et al., 2000), increasing functional communication skills (Sanchez-Fort, Brady, & Davis, 1995), improving academic skills (Belfiore et al., 1997), increasing compliance to a medication routine (Harchik & Putzier, 1990), decreasing task duration and response latency to instruction following (Mace et al., 1988; Belfiore et al., 1997; Wehby & Hollahan, 2000), decreasing transition latency (Ardoin et al., 1999), and decreasing challenging behaviors (Horner et al., 1991; Zarcone, Iwata, Mazaleski, & Smith, 1994). The different behaviors shown to be affected by using HPRs are wide in variety and indicate versatility in its application.

Variety of Settings and Interventionists

HPR studies have been conducted in both clinical and applied settings. These settings include schools (Davis & Reichle, 1996; Houlihan, Jacobson, & Brandon, 1994; Wehby & Hollahan, 2000), preschools and day-care centers (D. L. Lee, Belfiore, & Ferko, 2006; Santos & Lignugaris-Kraft, 1999), family homes (Bullock & Normand, 2006; Ducharme & Worling, 1994), hospitals (McComas, Wacker, & Cooper, 1998), and group homes (Romano & Roll, 2000). In schools, HPRs have been used in various locations on school grounds, such as general education classrooms (Ardoin et al., 1999), self-contained/segregated special education classrooms (Belfiore et al., 2008), hallways (Banda & Kubina, 2006), and inclusive classrooms (Davis et al., 1994).

The majority of the studies have used one interventionist to implement the HPR sequence with one individual (Banda & Kubina, 2006; Belfiore et al., 2008). However, Ardoin et al. (1999) delivered the HPR sequence to a class with three students targeted for intervention. Use of HPR increased compliance and decreased response latency for two of the three targeted students. In addition, Singer et al. (1987) implemented the intervention to a class of students when returning from recess with 100% success for two of the target students and 97% success for two other target students.

Interventions have been implemented by researchers or trained research assistants (Belfiore et al., 1997; Bullock & Normand, 2006; Zarcone et al., 1994) and by teachers or teacher assistants (Banda & Kubina, 2006; Belfiore et al., 2008; Davis et al., 1994). Additionally, peers have been trained to deliver the HPR sequence within the context of classroom activity (Davis & Reichle, 1996). A social validity survey and direct follow-up observations in Davis, Reichle, and Southard (2001) indicate that the intervention is practical for teachers to use on a daily basis in their classrooms. Overall, HPR sequences have been used in a variety of settings, spanning a large range of ability levels, and implemented by different people as interventionists.

Delivery of High-P and Low-P Requests

Much of the research regarding HPR has defined high-p requests as those requests to which the participant complies with 80% or more of instances of the requests being delivered (Ardoin et al., 1999; Belfiore et al., 2008; Davis & Reichle, 1996; Zarcone et al., 1994). However, Romano and Roll (2000) examined the use of high-p sequences (>80% compliance) and medium-p request sequences (50% to 70% compliance) to increase compliance of individuals with developmental disabilities. Romano and Roll showed that no systematic differences existed between the medium- and high-probability sequences on increasing the compliance with low-p requests. The results of this study indicate that both high- and medium-probability requests may be successful antecedents to low-p requests.

When examining research regarding the implementation of HPR sequences, we know that it is important to vary the individual high-p requests. Davis and Reichle (1996) used high-p requests to increase initiated social interactions of young children with behavioral disorders and found that using variant high-p request sequences was more effective than using invariant sequences. Research has also indicated that it is important to attend to the time between the delivery of the reinforcers and the high-p and low-p requests (intertrial intervals). For example, Mace et al. (1988) examined differences in 5 seconds and 15 seconds between the delivery of the reinforcer for the last high-p request and the delivery of the low-p request (interprompt time). They found that the 15-second inter-prompt time failed to elevate the rates of compliance above baseline; instead, shorter inter-prompt times increased the rate of reinforcement, and compliance with low-p requests persisted over time. These findings were replicated by Houlihan et al. (1994) and Kennedy, Itkonen, and Lindquist (1995). Moreover, McLaughlin and Davis (2010) found that HPR sequences were more effective when the intertrial intervals between the reinforcer of the high-p requests and the next high-p request are in close temporal proximity (e.g., 5 seconds).

Reinforcer Quality

In addition to varying the high-p requests in sequences and shorter intertrial intervals, Mace et al. (1997) found that increasing the quality of the reinforcer increased the compliance to low-p requests. For example, Mace et al. (1997) used social praise alone and then food as reinforcers for compliance to the low-p requests. They found that using food (a higher-quality reinforcer) produced higher rates of compliance. Additionally, Mace et al. (1997) found that responding to multiple low-p requests persisted better when a higher-quality reinforcer such as food was used.

Consequences for Not Responding to Low-P Requests

When using HPR, we typically expect the learner to comply with the low-p request when followed by a sequence of high-p requests. However, as with most interventions, the use of an HPR sequence does not always produce the effects or compliant responding to the low-p request that is targeted. Zarcone and her colleagues (1993, 1994) examined the use of escape extinction on noncompliant responding to the low-p requests. For example, if a student engages in noncompliance to escape having

to do the task, using escape extinction would look like not allowing the student to escape the task. That is, if a teacher asks a student to put away his materials and the student does not comply, the teacher's physically prompting the student to put away the materials would be an example of escape extinction. Zarcone's research indicated that using escape extinction for noncompliance to the low-p request produced more effective results than when the noncompliant responding was ignored. However, several studies also indicate positive effects when noncompliant responding to the low-p request was ignored (Davis, Brady, Williams, & Hamilton, 1992; Davis et al., 1994).

General Strengths of the Research

The research on HPR has shown positive outcomes for individuals with a range of disabilities as well as individuals without disabilities. The research has also shown an influence on a variety of outcomes, with most being conducted in applied settings with practitioners implementing the intervention. The applied nature of the research base allows teachers in schools to envision a variety of opportunities in which the HPR sequence might be utilized.

General Limitations of the Research Reviewed

Although HPR clearly has been documented as a successful invention, as with compliance training, some professionals consider its perceived contrived nature as a limitation (I. M. Evans & Meyer, 1990). For example, most of the research using the HPR sequence with people with intellectual disabilities often uses one-step directions (high-p requests) that peers without disabilities may not comply with due to social disapproval. That is, many interventionists cannot imagine an adolescent complying with being asked to "Give me five." However, the breadth of this literature provides opportunity to identify socially and contextually valid high-p requests (either verbally or nonverbally) that are effective with a variety of individuals and in a variety of situations.

Recommendations for Future Research

As with any intervention, once the strategy has been validated as successful, it is up to researchers and practitioners to work together to provide further information about its utility in applied settings. In addition, when we examine intervention packages such as HPR, it is also helpful to have a better understanding about the influence of fidelity of implementation on the effectiveness on the intervention. Moreover, as HPR continues to be studied across a wide variety of learners and in a variety of settings, it will be important for us to consider the impact of the context on the implementation of the intervention. For example, examining how the age of the participant influences which high-p requests are used, or how the preferences of the interventionists (e.g., teacher, parent) impact whether or not escape extinction is plausible would be important contextual variables that would further our understanding.

Conclusion

Compliance, or the lack thereof, influences the interactions between learners and adults in school and other settings in ways that can adversely affect a student's outcomes and future opportunities for learning. In this chapter, we reviewed the procedures and supporting literature for two effective and straightforward strategies that are supported by research as improving compliance—compliance training and HPRs. Each of these strategies not only has provided teachers and families with specific interventions that can increase compliance, but also has contributed to our understanding of (a) how to increase effective instruction in schools, (b) how to increase positive interactions in families, and (c) how these strategies work in combination with other research-based strategies to provide an optimal learning environment for both students and teachers. Although both practices are supported by strong research bases and are relatively simple to implement, it is important to remember these strategies should be used in the classroom alongside the other advances in our field (i.e., functional assessment and positive behavior support).

CHAPTER 6

Strategies to Address Internalizing Behavior Problems

Lee Kern | *Lehigh University*

Alexandra Hilt-Panahon | *Minnesota State University, Mankato*

Anuja Divatia Mukherjee | *University of Texas Health Science Center at Houston*

Overview of Internalizing Problems

The mention of youth emotional and behavioral problems usually brings to mind externalizing or acting out behaviors, such as aggression and disruption (e.g., see Chapters 2 and 7, this volume). Because these types of behaviors are evident to others in the environment and usually disrupt learning and order in classroom and school settings, they beseech the most attention. Equally problematic, however, are behaviors that are not readily observable, yet cause individual interruptions in learning, social relationships, and everyday functioning. Problems of this nature, classified as *internalizing behaviors,* are directed inwardly and represent overly controlled patterns of behavior (Gresham & Kern, 2004).

Internalizing problems pose unique challenges for identification and assessment, particularly for school-based practitioners, for a number of reasons. First, the covert and nonintrusive types of behaviors that characterize internalizing problems are often overlooked by teachers and other school-based practitioners. This is because they are seldom disturbing or disruptive to

others (Algozzine, 1977). Second, unlike externalizing behaviors, internalizing behaviors do not challenge a teacher's authority or ability to manage the classroom and provide instruction. Third, the definition of emotional disturbance, as specified in the Individuals with Disabilities Education Act (IDEA), does little to facilitate identification of students needing intervention. Specifically, the IDEA denotes three limiting criteria for identification, including the presence of a disorder: (a) of sufficient severity or "to a marked degree," (b) exhibited for a "long period of time," and (c) that "adversely affects educational performance." These criteria are extremely subjective and provide particularly little guidance in identifying internalizing disabilities, especially given their covert nature (e.g., Kauffman, 2001). Finally, the academic performance of many students with internalizing problems is not adversely affected to an extent that most schools or districts require for special education identification. This does not diminish the need for intervention, but rather eliminates the possibility that it will be mandated through the educational system. Exclusion for this reason is particularly unfortunate because, although the large majority of students with emotional health needs do not receive services, for those who are able to access intervention, schools are the primary provider (B. J. Burns et al., 1995). Specifically, schools provide 70% to 80% of the services that school-age students receive for their emotional problems.

A comprehensive definition of internalizing disorders requires familiarity with two systems of classification, education and psychiatry. The IDEA definition of "emotional disturbance" encompasses both externalizing and internalizing problems, but a close inspection reveals that the majority of criteria pertain to internalizing problems. Specifically, "emotional disturbance" is defined as:

(i) . . . a condition exhibiting one or more of the following characteristics over a long period of time and to a marked deter which adversely affects school performance: (a) an inability to learn which cannot be explained by intellectual, sensory, or health factors; (b) an inability to build or maintain satisfactory relationships with peers and teachers; (c) inappropriate types of behaviors or feelings under normal circumstances; (d) a general mood of unhappiness or depression; (e) a tendency to develop physical symptoms or fears associated with personal or school problems.

(ii) The term includes children who are schizophrenic. The term does not include children who are socially maladjusted, unless it is determined that they also are emotionally disturbed.

As the federal definition reflects, students with internalizing problems typically experience difficulties with learning, relationships with others, feelings, moods, and/or physical symptoms/fears. To reiterate, the definition is quite ambiguous and lacks clarity, providing little direction for school-based practitioners when determining eligibility.

The *Diagnostic and Statistical Manual of Mental Disorders IV,* published by the American Psychiatric Association (1994), specifies a number of types of internalizing disorders and describes characteristics of those disorders. Disorders falling under the category of internalizing problems, and their definitions, are provided in Table 6.1. This system of classification, the most commonly used for identifying psychopathology in the United States, provides more specificity than the IDEA definition. Still, this system has limitations, particularly with respect to use in schools (Gresham & Gansle, 1992). One issue is that diagnosis, even by skilled clinicians, has been unreliable (e.g., Sattler & Hoge, 2006). In addition, the descriptions focus on associated feelings or behaviors, rather than related environmental events (e.g., Watson & Robinson, 1998). The absence of focus on environmental triggers and responses to internalizing

behavioral problems or symptoms is an important omission because it does facilitate the development of strategies to address associated environmental events, a critical component of a comprehensive behavior plan. In spite of the limitations, it is important to understand both the educational and psychiatric classifications, given that students with internalizing disorders may meet diagnostic criteria for a DSM IV diagnosis but not IDEA classification and vice versa.

It is essential for educators to understand effective interventions for reducing internalizing behaviors for numerous reasons. First, without effective intervention, internalizing problems are associated with a range of negative outcomes, including low self-esteem, social withdrawal, sadness, physical health problems, lack of concentration, poor academic performance in school, disrupted day-to-day functioning, and, in severe cases, even suicide. These problems last far past the school years, interfere with productive adult functioning, and cause a tremendous burden to the individual herself as well as society. Effective intervention is imperative for healthy development and long-term quality of life. In addition, the large numbers of students who experience internalizing problems during the school-age years underscore the need for services. For instance, research indicates that as many as 8% of adolescents in the United States experience depression (Collins, Westra, Dozois, & Burns, 2004; Costello, Erkanli, & Angold, 2006). Estimates of the prevalence of mental health issues suggest that more than 30% of students will experience a significant problem during their school career (Hammen & Rudolph, 1996). Also, as noted, it is unlikely that students will receive intervention if it is not provided in schools. Finally, growing evidence indicates that intervention is most effective if delivered when symptoms first emerge, before problems become severe (Kern et al., 2007). Hence, providing intervention at the early stages of internalizing disorders will prevent the development of associated problems and will require less intensive efforts.

Because internalizing problems have garnered less attention than externalizing problems, a relative paucity of research supports intervention effectiveness. Further, although some interventions, such as medication, have been tested with adults, far fewer evaluations have been conducted with school-age students. In the following sections, we review the interventions that are most commonly used, have the most empirical support, and appear to be either efficacious or promising: cognitive behavior therapy, anxiety management/relaxation training, and pharmacological intervention. Due to the large and diverse number of internalizing problems, we focus primarily on the most common two, depression and anxiety.

Table 6.1   DSM IV Internalizing Disorders and Characteristics

Disorder	Description
Adjustment disorder	Emotional or behavioral symptoms in response to an identifiable stressor or stressors. There are six subtypes of adjustment disorders, depending on whether symptoms include depressed mood, anxiety, mixed anxiety and depressed mood, disturbance of conduct, mixed disturbance of mood and conduct, or are unspecified.
Anorexia nervosa	An eating disorder characterized by an obsessive fear of gaining weight and resulting in extremely low body weight and body image distortion. Body weight is often controlled through voluntary starvation, excessive exercise, or diet pills and diuretic drugs.
Bulimia nervosa	An eating disorder characterized by recurrent binge eating, followed by compensatory behaviors (e.g., self-induced vomiting, purging, fasting, use of laxatives, over exercising) to avoid weight gain.
Dysthymic disorder	A chronic mood disorder with low-grade depression, less severe than major depressive disorder. In children, the disorder may be characterized by irritability, rather than sadness.
Generalized anxiety disorder	Excessive, uncontrollable, and generally irrational worry that is disproportionate to the actual source of worry.
Major depressive disorder	Low mood, low self-esteem, and loss of interest or pleasure in nearly all activities. In children, the disorder may be characterized by irritability, rather than sadness.
Obsessive-compulsive disorder	Recurrent intrusive thoughts, which may include feeling compelled to perform irrational, time-consuming behaviors.
Posttraumatic stress disorder	Severe ongoing emotional reaction to an extreme and traumatic stressor, such as someone's death, a threat to own or another's life, serious physical injury, or unwanted sexual act.
Reactive attachment disorder of infancy or early childhood	Disturbed and developmentally inappropriate ways of relating socially in most contexts, ranging from failure to initiate or respond to displaying excessive familiarity with strangers. The disorder begins before age 5.
Selective mutism	Failure to speak in person given situations, or to specific people, when capable of speech.
Separation anxiety disorder	Excessive anxiety regarding separation from home or from people to whom the person has a strong attachment.
Social anxiety disorder	Excessive distress and impaired functioning in social situations, particularly pertaining to a fear of being embarrassed or humiliated by one's actions or being judged by others.
Somatization disorder	Chronic and persistent complaint of varied physical symptoms with no identifiable physical origin.

Source: Information from American Psychiatric Association. (2000). *Diagnostic and statistical manual of mental disorders* (4th ed.). Washington, DC: Author.

Effective Practices

Cognitive Behavioral Therapy

Definition and Theory for Effectiveness

The term *cognitive behavior therapy* (CBT) describes techniques that incorporate both cognitive and behavioral methods of intervention. Cognitive approaches are rooted in the work of Aaron Beck, who developed a treatment for depression based on cognitive theory. Specifically, he hypothesized that people experienced depression because of deficits in information processing that cause a negative self-view, as well as a negative outlook of the world and the future (Kazdin & Marciano, 1998). This negative world view then leads to maladaptive thought processes, such as a short-term focus, excessively high performance standards, and lack of self-reinforcement. In fact, research has shown that students with depression can exhibit a wide range of cognitive distortions including low self-esteem and selective attention to negative events (Kendall, Stark, & Adam, 1990; McCauley, Burke, Mitchell, & Moss, 1988). Given these distorted and negative views, the goal of cognitive therapy is to confront, challenge, and modify maladaptive thought processes.

Unlike cognitive interventions that attempt to change the thoughts of an individual with depression, behavioral interventions focus on changing specific behaviors that will then lead to decreased symptoms. According to behavioral theory, depression leads to decreases in engagement in pleasurable activities due to a restricted range of response-contingent reinforcement, fewer social reinforcers, and inadequate social skills. Behavioral interventions for depression therefore are designed to teach skills and provide opportunities to increase positive social experiences and pleasurable activities (i.e., reinforcers). When combined, these two types of interventions target both the thoughts and actions of individuals with depression.

Implementation

Although many variations of cognitive-behavioral therapy exist, all CBT treatments have several common features (Harrington, Whittaker, & Shoebridge, 1998). The overarching commonality is that both cognitive and behavior techniques are combined to affect change in thoughts and behavior. In addition, several other common features exist in all CBT programs. First, the focus of CBT is the child/adolescent. Although intervention also may involve parents or family members peripherally, the focus of change is on the individual. Another common feature is that the therapist is an active participant in therapy, collaborating closely with the child to solve problems and identify solutions. The therapist acts as a teacher, providing instruction to the child on how to monitor his thoughts and behavior. The child also is taught to keep a record of thoughts and behavior for later reflection (Harrington et al., 1998).

One advantage of CBT is that it can be implemented in relatively brief periods of time. Intervention typically lasts 5 to 12 weeks, and requires 8 to 15 sessions, ranging in length from 30 to 90 minutes per session. In addition, CBT is most frequently conducted in group sessions, making it cost-effective.

In a recent review of school-based interventions for students at risk for depression, Hilt-Panahon, Kern, Divatia, and Gresham (2007) identified the most common techniques and combinations of techniques used in CBT interventions. Among 15 studies identified, cognitive restructuring was used in the majority of studies ($n = 8$). Cognitive restructuring involves teaching students to challenge distorted and negative cognitions about themselves and their environment and to replace those cognitions with more realistic ones. This technique is based on the assumption that students are depressed due to a maladaptive style of information processing (i.e., interpreting events as negative). If cognitions are more realistic (and potentially more positive), then the individual should experience less depression.

Problem solving, also considered a CBT approach, was the second most frequently implemented technique,

occurring in six studies. Problem solving involves teaching students to evaluate stress-provoking situations by gathering relevant information, thinking about alternative responses, and choosing the best response. For example, students may be taught how to identify social conflict and then develop appropriate ways to handle those situations (Cardemil, Reivich, & Seligman, 2002). Pleasant activity scheduling is an intervention that entails systematic planning of students' daily activities to incorporate pleasant and desirable events, and it was implemented in five studies. For instance, students generated a list of preferred activities, which were incorporated into their daily routines to increase positive experiences. Weisz, Thurber, Sweeney, Proffitt, and LeGagnoux (1997) incorporated this technique into CBT by focusing therapy sessions on the student's learning to both identify and engage in activities that the student found to be mood enhancing.

Self-management, in many forms, is also a major component of CBT. For students to begin to think and act differently, they must be able to identify and address their own thoughts, feelings, and actions. Several specific techniques fall into this category including self-change (making self-evaluations and changing behavior as a result), self-instruction, self-modeling, and attribution retraining (teaching students to make more realistic and adaptive attributions). In addition, activities to link thoughts, feelings, and behavior (teaching students how all three are linked and influence each other) can assist students in managing their own behavior. For example, Jaycox, Reivich, Gillham, and Seligman (1994) taught children to understand the link between their own thoughts and feelings and how one influenced the other. Participants in the therapy learned how to develop a list of potential explanations for the negative events in their lives and then to identify the most plausible explanation based on what they know about the situation.

As highlighted by Hilt-Panahon et al. (2007), it is important to emphasize that these interventions have been used in schools with great success in the context of research protocols; however, little is known about the feasibility of implementation of CBT in schools with school staff as intervention agents. In fact, of the studies reviewed, only one used school personnel to implement the intervention, and that was with the collaboration and supervision of the researcher. In addition, extensive training and supervision were provided in a number of studies reviewed, regardless of who was implementing the intervention. CBT is designed to be implemented by or in conjunction with someone who has been trained in its use.

As described in the previous sections, CBT is not a specific intervention but rather a combination of therapeutic techniques. These interventions should be implemented in conjunction with a professional trained in the use of CBT. Figure 6.1 provides guidelines for the implementation of CBT by school personnel. Given that many possible components can be implemented in combination, it is difficult to provide a specific protocol for implementation. Instead, in the following sections, we provide an example of an intervention protocol, as described as part of an efficacy study conducted by Reynolds and Coats (1986).

The intervention package was designed to be delivered over a short period of time. Intervention was intense, with students participating in small groups for 10 sessions, each 50 minutes in duration, across a 5-week period. Students received reinforcement contingent on their participation and attendance. Intervention was conducted at the high school the students attended. The program consisted of three phases that emphasized the training of self-control and self-change skills. Specific techniques used in the intervention package included self-monitoring, self-evaluation, and self-reinforcement. In addition to the specific skills taught, the participants

Figure 6.1 Steps for implementation of cognitive-behavior therapy.

1. Operationally define problem behavior.
2. Collect data to determine frequency and severity of problem behavior.
3. Is the problem behavior frequent and severe enough to impact the student's socioemotional well-being?
   a. Yes—go to step 4.
   b. No—intervention not indicated.
4. Consult with experienced professionals to determine the benefits of referral for cognitive–behavioral interventions.
5. Consult the school district's policy for such referrals.
6. If cognitive behavior therapy (CBT) is implemented, determine the roles of different school personnel for the following tasks:
   a. Implementation of intervention (must be conducted by or under the supervision of someone with extensive training in cognitive–behavioral techniques).
   b. Behavior-progress monitoring.
   c. Home–school communication.
7. Establish data collection procedures, such as:
   a. Develop a checklist for monitoring intervention fidelity.
   b. Conduct behavioral observation techniques for behavior-progress monitoring.
   c. Establish home–school communication through home–school note system.
8. Implement CBT:
   a. Identify most appropriate intervention components for individual student or students.
   b. Identify time, place, and content of sessions.
   c. Implement with fidelity.
   d. Review discussion in text of detailed research protocol.
9. Continue to collect data.
10. Review data periodically, answering the following questions:
    a. Are CBT procedures being implemented as indicated?
    b. Has the problem behavior reduced to desired level?
    c. Are parents/guardians informed regularly by the school about the students' behavioral progress?
    d. Is the school informed regularly by the parents about any changes at home?
11. Make data-based decisions such as:
    a. Continue the current intervention if data indicate high fidelity of implementation and progress in student behavior.
    b. Reconsider school-based CBT if behavioral data indicate a lack of desired level of progress.
    c. Refer for private/community services if depression is still clinical after treatment.

also were provided training in basic techniques for developing a self-change plan that they could use when applying the self-control skills.

The general format of each session consisted of a presentation and a discussion of self-control principles followed by the assignment of homework exercises and a review of the preceding session's assignment. Session 1 began with an introduction to the program that included a description of CBT as well as the theory behind the intervention's effectiveness. The remainder of the first session focused on how to self-monitor and the importance of accurate self-observation. All participants were asked to complete daily log forms, monitoring their positive activities and moods that day. Each subsequent session began with a short summary of the rationale and format of the last assignment.

In Session 2, an exercise was used to highlight the relation between the two aspects of mood and activity related to depressive behavior. Students graphed the number of both positive activities and mood ratings daily. This exercise was designed to show the connection between the activities that the students engaged in and the way that they felt (mood). Research has shown that depressed individuals tend to focus on the immediate rather than long term-effects of their behavior (Reynolds & Coats, 1986). This faulty self-monitoring resembles Lewinsohn's (1974) concept that depressed behavior functions to elicit immediate rather than more important delayed forms of reinforcement. Session 3 therefore focused on activities designed to aid students in attending more closely to the delayed positive consequences of behavior, facilitated by an immediate versus delayed effects exercise.

Beginning in Session 4 the focus of therapy changed to individual self-evaluation. Given the distorted self-views that depressed individuals hold, the importance of evaluating oneself accurately was stressed. According to cognitive theory (A. T. Beck, Rush, Shaw, & Emery, 1979), depressed persons often hold faulty beliefs about their responsibility for events. Thus, students were taught to look closely at assumptions people make in assigning credit, blame, or responsibility for events. In Session 5, students were presented with strategies for developing a self-change plan. These methods included (a) defining the problem, (b) collecting baseline data, (c) discovering antecedents and consequences, (d) setting goals, (e) contracting, and (f) obtaining reinforcement (Lewinsohn, Munoz, Youngren, & Zeiss, 1978). Students were asked to identify a specific problem to work on and begin collecting baseline data while paying attention to antecedent and consequent events. Session 6 focused on setting realistic and obtainable goals as part of a self-change plan. Students were encouraged to identify goals that were positive, attainable, overt, and within their own

control. The students were asked to continue to collect baseline data regarding their target problems and then identify appropriate goals. Session 7 began the self-reinforcement phase of the program. The therapist presented general principles of reinforcement and related these to the problems of depression. The therapist highlighted how errors in an individual's thinking can often lead to too much self-punishment and too little self-reward. In addition to the identification of negative interpretations, students also created a "reward menu." As students met goals identified in earlier sessions, they administered rewards to themselves from the menu as points were earned. Session 8 included a brief presentation relating both covert self-reward and self-punishment to depression, followed by an activity on covert self-reward. Students were asked to monitor themselves and to use covert self-reinforcement (e.g., state "I'm doing well" to oneself) in addition to other rewards, according to their plans. The remaining two sessions were arranged to obtain information indicating how subjects complied with treatment instructions, to work on remedial efforts, and to provide a review of the program. Students were encouraged to continue using cognitive-behavioral procedures in the future and were given extra copies of log sheets and related forms.

Research Base

A strong research base exists to support the use of CBT for individuals with depression, including school-age students. Several literature reviews have summarized the evidence to support CBT for use with adult (Gillham, Shatte, & Freres, 2000) and child (Curry, 2001) populations. Specifically, research has shown that individuals who participate in CBT show symptom reduction and are less likely to relapse than individuals treated with other interventions, particularly psychopharmacology (M. D. Evans et al., 1992; Paykel et al., 1999). Researchers hypothesize that the reduced rate of relapse with CBT occurs because CBT teaches individuals the skills necessary to cope with stressful situations. After therapy is complete, individuals continue to use the skills learned. This differs from medications, which, when removed, leave individuals with no means to deal with stress, and depressive symptoms are likely to return (Gillham et al., 2000). In addition, CBT has been shown to lead to more rapid reduction of symptoms than other interventions (Brent et al., 1997).

Although a great deal of evidence supports the efficacy of CBT interventions, the majority of studies have focused on its use in clinical settings. For example, a review by Curry (2001) examined the effectiveness of psychosocial interventions for childhood and adolescent depression. Curry reviewed a total of 15 studies, and the findings indicated that CBT was both efficacious and superior to control (no intervention) and other types of intervention (e.g., family therapy, relaxation training). These findings were encouraging; however, the majority of studies ($n = 10$) were conducted in clinical settings. Considering that the vast majority of students receive mental health intervention at school, it is imperative to examine effectiveness when implemented in school settings (e.g., Kahn, Kehle, Jenson, & Clark, 1990).

The aforementioned review by Hilt-Panahon et al. (2007) examined interventions for school-age students at risk for depression. Those authors identified 15 studies that met inclusion criteria, and they evaluated a variety of variables related to intervention implementation and effectiveness. CBT emerged as the intervention with the strongest evidence base for effectively reducing depressive symptoms. Eleven studies implemented CBT in the school setting, with effect sizes ranging from 0.16 to 2.22. The effect sizes across the majority of studies were moderate to large, with low effect sizes found in only two studies. In one study (Hains & Szyjakowski, 1990), an effect size of 0.18 for depressive symptoms was hypothesized by the authors to be a result of low levels of initial symptoms in both experimental and control groups. The low effect size for the other study (Cardemil et al., 2002) was attributable to a subgroup of participants. That is, the same intervention program was provided to two ethnically diverse groups of students at two different schools. While results were positive for the Latino students (ES = 1.01), little positive effects were noted for the African American participants (ES = 0.16). The authors provided several possible explanations for these results, including regression to the mean, differential expression of symptoms across ethnic groups, and ethnic variation in the response to different intervention components.

CBT has been used in both public and private school settings, as well as at the middle and high school levels (Hilt-Panahon et al., 2007). To date, no studies have evaluated the effectiveness of school-based implementation of CBT with an elementary school population. School-based CBT interventions have primarily been implemented in a group format, although about a third of reviewed studies have implemented a combination of group as well as individual sessions. Group size has been as small as 2 students to as many as 12.

Anxiety Management/Relaxation Training

Definition and Theory for Effectiveness

Anxiety management/relaxation training (AM/RT) interventions are derived from the body of literature supporting that stressors, both major life events as well as minor hassles, can contribute to depression (Reynolds & Stark, 1987). An individual's response to those stressors has a major impact on mood and levels of anxiety. By teaching a person more appropriate ways to respond to stressful life events, the negative effects can be reduced. Although the intervention does not specifically align with any of the major theories of depression (Reynolds & Coats, 1986), several empirical studies have shown AM/RT to be an effective means of reducing depressive symptoms (e.g., Biglan & Dow, 1981). As a result, AM/RT has been used in the treatment of depressive symptoms and anxiety.

Implementation

Descriptions of AM/RT vary in the literature but have several similar components. First, an explanation of the intervention is provided. Next, the relationship between anxiety, stress, and depressive symptoms is discussed. It is important for students to understand how their stress and anxiety are related to feelings of depression and how managing their reactions to stress can lessen depressive symptoms. Finally, students are taught through therapy that these are techniques that they can use at any time and that are under their control (Reynolds & Stark, 1987).

A second common feature is some form of progressive relaxation training (PRT). PRT consists of training individuals to systematically tense and release each of 16 muscle groups within the body. This technique was developed and modified based on the seminal work by Jacobsen (1938). Individuals are taught to tense and relax the various muscle groups, which then leads to a release of tension and increased relaxation. These procedures have been used in connection with the treatment of numerous disorders including anxiety and depression.

Muscle groups are tensed, the position held for a short period, and then relaxed in progressive order, causing the body to feel relaxed. To begin PRT, the student makes a tight fist with the dominant hand, holds the position, and then releases the muscles. Then, with the dominant bicep, the student pushes his elbow down against a chair. The student repeats these actions for the nondominant hand and bicep. To tense the forehead, the student lifts the eyebrows as high as possible and for the central section of the face, the student squints and wrinkles his nose. For the lower face and jaw, the student bites hard and pulls back the corners of the mouth. To tense the neck, the student pulls the chin toward (but not touching) the chest. Then, to tense the chest, shoulders, and upper back, the student pulls the shoulder blades together and makes his stomach hard to tense the abdomen. To tense the legs, the student then tightens the top and bottom muscles of the dominant upper leg and to tense the calf, the student pulls the toes of the dominant calf toward his head. Finally, the student points and curls the toes of the dominant foot inward to tense them. This tensing sequence is then repeated for the nondominant leg, calf, and foot. Descriptions in the literature of the implementation of PRT have indicated that as an individual becomes more skilled at the technique of PRT, the number of muscle groups used can be decreased without an apparent loss of effects (e.g., Hains, 1992; Kahn et al., 1990). PRT can be conducted alone (e.g., by oneself) or in a group setting, a flexibility that makes it an ideal intervention for classroom implementation. For those interested in implementing relaxation techniques in the classroom, see Figure 6.2 for an implementation checklist.

Research Base

Hilt-Panahon et al. (2007) identified three studies that evaluated relaxation training in isolation implemented in the school setting. Effect sizes were large, ranging from 1.14 to 2.45. In a study by Reynolds and Coats (1986), the effectiveness of both CBT and relaxation training interventions was evaluated for reducing

depression in 30 high school-age adolescents with moderate depression. Participants in both intervention groups met in small groups for ten 50-minute sessions. Sessions were held over a 5-week period at the students' school. CBT consisted of training participants in self-control and self-change skills. Relaxation training sessions were implemented following a general introduction to the program, which included a presentation of a rationale for the treatment that highlighted the relation between stress-related problems and depression. It was explained that the goal of relaxation training was to understand the relation between stress, muscle tension, and depression and to learn specific skills to facilitate self-relaxation. Students were asked to practice the techniques they would learn during the sessions as homework assignments. Then, in subsequent sessions, students were taught to implement PRT as described previously. Sessions 2 to 5 focused on teaching students the specific procedures outlined by Jacobsen (1938), which consisted almost exclusively of practicing standard progressive muscle-relaxation exercises and of reviewing homework assignment log sheets. The next four sessions (6 to 9) were devoted primarily to helping students generalize the techniques learned in previous sessions. In the final session, the procedures were

Figure 6.2   Steps for implementation of relaxation training techniques.

1. Provide an explanation of the intervention to the student including rationale for effectiveness.
2. Explain the relationship between anxiety, stress, and depressive symptoms.
   a. Stress and anxiety are related to feelings of depression.
   b. Managing stress can reduce feelings of depression.
3. Teach students Progress Relaxation Training (PRT).
   a. Make a tight fist with the dominant hand, hold for a short period, and then release.
   b. Push elbow down against a chair for the dominant bicep.
   c. Repeat steps a and b for the nondominant hand and bicep.
   d. Tense the forehead by lifting the eyebrows as high as possible.
   e. Squint and wrinkle the nose to tense the central section of the face.
   f. Bite hard and pull back the corners of the mouth to tense the lower face and jaw.
   g. Pull the chin down toward (but not touching) the chest to tense the neck.
   h. Tense the chest, shoulders, and upper back by pulling the shoulder blades together.
   i. Tense the abdomen by making the stomach hard (pull in the stomach muscles).
   j. To tense the legs, tense the top and bottom muscles of the dominant upper leg.
   k. To tense the calf, pull the toes toward the head.
   l. Finally, point the toes of the feet and curl them inward.
4. Practice PRT until students are fluent.
5. Help students to generalize skills outside of the therapy situation.
   a. Practice in other settings and situations.
   b. Students may reduce the number of muscle groups tensed at one time based on their own needs.
6. Encourage students to use skills whenever they feel stress or anxiety.

reviewed and the students were encouraged to continue using the skills in tension-producing situations.

Results of the Reynolds and Coats (1986) study indicated that both CBT and relaxation training were superior to a wait-list control condition for reducing depression in adolescents. Participants, who had moderate depression pre-intervention, showed no depression at post-test as well as at 5 weeks' follow-up. In addition, the researchers found no difference in effects across the two interventions. In other words, relaxation training was as effective as CBT in reducing depression in the students who participated in the intervention. This result is important to note, given the simplicity of relaxation training and the relatively little training that is needed for implementation, especially as compared to CBT.

In a second study, Kahn et al. (1990) compared the effects of CBT, relaxation training, and self-modeling on the depressive symptoms of 68 middle school students. Relaxation training was similar to interventions described in other studies. Sessions began with an introduction to and rationale for the intervention. The link between anxiety, stress, and depression was highlighted, along with how the techniques could reduce feelings of anxiety and stress, leading to a reduction of depressive symptoms. This session was followed by several sessions in which progressive relaxation techniques were modeled and practiced. After this, generalization procedures were taught as well as alternative methods of relaxation, including the use of fewer muscle groups, imagery, and counting. Results indicated that all three interventions were superior to wait-list control in the reduction of depressive symptoms.

The third study, by Hains (1992), evaluated the effects of anxiety management training with a traditional cognitive restructuring technique. Participants in the anxiety management intervention were taught to recognize cues that signaled the onset of anxiety and then to react to those cues using relaxation techniques including visualization and progressive relaxation training. As treatment progressed, control was gradually shifted to the students rather than the therapist. Results indicated that treatment succeeded in reducing levels of anxiety, anger, and depression, and the results were maintained at 11 weeks' follow-up.

AM/RT has been implemented as an intervention in both public and private school settings and at both the middle and high school levels. Moreover, intervention has been delivered in a group format, with group sizes ranging from 2 to 12 students, with the duration of intervention of 9 to 12 sessions over 5 to 8 weeks, and with sessions ranging from 30 to 50 minutes in length. A promising feature of this intervention is that it appears to be quite simple to implement and could be conducted with relatively little training.

Pharmacologic Intervention

Definition and Theory for Effectiveness

In addition to CBT and AM/RT, psychotropic medication or psychopharmacological intervention is an important and widely used intervention for internalizing disorders, such as depression and anxiety. Psychotropic medications are prescribed by a primary care physician, pediatrician, or a psychiatrist and are typically taken orally. Although originally developed for and used with adults, psychotropic medications are now commonly used to address internalizing disorders in students. With new research regularly emerging to document the efficacy of medications for internalizing disorders in students, their use has increased substantially in the last decade (Abrams, Flood, & Phelps, 2006). It should be stressed that medications are recommended to supplement, *not substitute for*, behavioral or cognitive–behavioral interventions (Abrams et al., 2006; Merrell, 2001).

The use of medications for internalizing behavior disorders, such as anxiety or depression, is based on the theories that postulate anomalous functioning of the different neural channels and chemicals in the brain of individuals with symptoms of psychological disorders (Reiter, Kutcher, & Gardner, 1992). Specifically, pharmacological agents in psychotropic medicines affect the malfunctioning neurotransmitter systems in the brain, and consequently reduce the symptoms of the psychological disorder that an individual experiences.

Implementation

The first step with respect to the use of pharmacologic interventions for internalizing behavior difficulties is determining need. Before a recommendation of medication (or concurrent with, in very extreme cases), behavioral or cognitive behavioral interventions should be implemented. Medications are generally restricted to students whose symptoms of internalizing disorders reach very high levels of severity and cannot be reduced through nonpharmacological interventions. Although school personnel cannot prescribe specific medications, as members of the multidisciplinary team, school personnel can play an important role in helping parents decide whether pharmacological interventions should be considered for a child or adolescent. Merrell (2001) provided a comprehensive guideline to help the multidisciplinary team with this decision. Some of the important considerations for a medication referral include severity or symptoms, chronicity of symptoms, interference of symptoms with students' socioemotional and academic functioning, threat of harm to self or others, symptoms of psychotic behavior (i.e., hallucinations, abnormal thought process, delusions), persistent failure of other sound and evidence-based psychological or behavioral interventions, and strong family history of mental disorders (Merrell, 2001). If one or a combination of these symptoms is present for a child or adolescent, a referral for pharmacological intervention may be appropriate. If a teacher or school psychologist has little experience in this area, it is advisable to consult more experienced colleagues as well as to consult the school's policy before making such a recommendation.

Medications should *not* be viewed as an exclusive or superior treatment for internalizing disorders. Medications should not replace, but rather supplement, other evidence-based behavioral interventions. Studies comparing behavioral and pharmacological treatments for students with anxiety and depression have consistently found that treatments combining cognitive behavioral therapy and medications yielded greater efficacy as compared to exclusively pharmacological interventions (Bernstein et al., 2000; Forness, Freeman, & Paparella, 2006; Pediatric OCD Treatment Study Team, 2004; Treatment for Adolescents with Depression Study Team, 2004). These results signify the importance of continuing behavioral, cognitive–behavioral, or other school-based intervention with students, regardless of the medical treatment they obtain.

After a student is placed on medication, monitoring is needed by school personnel. Because medications are often taken multiple times during the day and many students receive their medications at school, one form of monitoring involves ensuring that students take the medications as prescribed. Typically, the school nurse provides the medications and monitors ingestion.

In addition to ensuring that medications are taken, it is important for the teachers, school psychologists, and other relevant school personnel who interact with a student to understand the type of medications the student is prescribed, the symptoms for which they are taken, the expected effects on students' behavior, and the potential side effects. In case of deviations in the student's typical behavior, the medication-monitoring data can be particularly important. For example, a student who begins taking a new medication or experiences a dosage change may engage in atypical types of behavior (e.g., initial fatigue). When school personnel know that the student has begun a new medication, they can evaluate whether the medication change is influencing her behavior. Conversely, a student may revert back to maladaptive behavior if medications are not taken as prescribed. A teacher who notices such changes in the student's behavior can refer to the medication-monitoring data to determine whether the student took the medications as prescribed.

It also is important for school-based practitioners to evaluate specific behaviors to determine medication effectiveness. Although medical doctors (general practitioners, pediatricians, and psychiatrists) prescribe medications, given their infrequent contact with the student, they cannot regularly monitor behavior changes in response to the medication. More typically, they rely on parent reports and student self-report to determine medication effectiveness, which can be very subjective. School personnel, on the other hand, have the advantage of being in close contact with the student for several hours every day. Given this frequent and close contact, they can play a vital role in monitoring a student's behavior during the pharmacological intervention.

When monitoring medication effects, it is important to again note that even when medication is considered necessary, best practice suggests continuation of behavioral, cognitive–behavioral, or other effective psychological interventions in addition to the pharmacological interventions (Forness et al., 2006). Thus, it is critical that school personnel ensure students are receiving a comprehensive package of interventions, including evidence-based psychosocial approaches. In addition, it is important for school-based practitioners to assist in monitoring the effectiveness of medications.

Ideally, psychosocial interventions (i.e., cognitive behavioral therapy) should begin before the implementation of medications. If effective, medications may not be warranted. If, however, nonpharmacologic interventions are not sufficient, data can provide an interesting and important analysis of the combined effects of the two interventions versus the effects of a behavioral intervention in isolation. If the progress-monitoring data show that medications provide very little or no effectiveness beyond the behavioral interventions, the implementation of medications may be reconsidered.

To determine whether medications are having the intended effects, it is best to collect periodic data on a target behavior or set of behaviors. In the case of internalizing problems, the behaviors will be those associated with the disorder, such as withdrawal, somatic complaints, or anxiety-related behaviors. Data collection to assess and monitor the level of internalizing behavior challenges can be conducted in numerous ways. For example, a teacher may collect frequency data on the number of somatic complaints made by a student. For internalizing problems that are more difficult to observe, behavioral indicators can be identified. For instance, social anxiety might be operationally defined as lack of interpersonal interaction and/or refusal to respond to social initiations by peers or adults. These behaviors can be measured using duration data to indicate the amount of time the behaviors occurred throughout a school day. This type of ongoing data collection not only provides information on whether or not medications are effective in reducing problem behaviors, but also on their level of efficacy. If such progress-monitoring data reveal a lack of change in behaviors, the medications (i.e., the type of medication and the dosage) as well as other interventions can be reevaluated.

In addition to monitoring medication effectiveness, school personnel can facilitate communication between individuals involved in the intervention and coordination of intervention. Students frequently receive multiple services at doctor's offices, the school, the home, and outpatient settings. This is particularly true for students who are prescribed medications. Thus, it is important that all intervention agents and stakeholders communicate with each other and coordinate their interventions in order to best serve the student. School personnel can play an important role in coordination of services. Home–school communication is important for medication monitoring as well as for behavior intervention monitoring. Home–school communication can be conducted by the regular exchange of notes between the parents and teachers. It also is important to communicate with the student's doctor to maintain updated information about the prescribed medications. In addition, physicians and/or psychiatrists should be provided all data, particularly objective data that are collected to evaluate medication effects (both beneficial effects and side effects). Family members also should be involved in data collection regarding medication effects. Checklists, on which each respondent can mark whether or not medications were administered as prescribed and whether or not various expected positive effects and potential negative effects of the medications were observed, may be best suited for this purpose. This is a feasible system that is likely to be more objective than other formats (e.g., notes) and will allow the individual prescribing the medications to fully evaluate if the desired outcome is achieved and whether the dosage is optimal. A regular schedule of communication should be arranged. Generally, home–school communication should be daily, especially when new medications are evaluated, while communication with physicians or psychiatrists may be less frequent (e.g., bi-weekly, monthly, just before scheduled visits). To establish communication with the doctor prescribing the medication, it is important for the school personnel to obtain consent from the parents. Subsequently, communication arrangements can be made that are mutually agreeable and optimally beneficial for all parties. See Figure 6.3 for an implementation checklist.

Research Base

Most psychotropic medications are categorized into classes based on the biochemical brain system they impact, the disorder or symptoms they target, or both (Abrams et al., 2006). The three main classes of medication for pediatric internalizing disorders are tricyclic antidepressants (TCAs), selective serotonin reuptake inhibitors (SSRIs), and benzodiazepines. Other medications, such as monoamine oxidase inhibitors (MAOIs) and Buspirone, commonly used with adults, are understudied with students. The few studies assessing the efficacy of MAOIs and Buspirone had weak research designs and resulted in contradictory findings. Therefore, we will discuss only the three main classes of medications, tricyclic antidepressants (TCAs), selective serotonin reuptake inhibitors (SSRIs), and benzodiazepines, which have been systematically evaluated in a number of double-blind research studies specifically with school-age students.

Tricyclic antidepressants (TCA) were one of the first medications used to treat symptoms of depression and anxiety disorders in children (Wolraich, 2003). TCAs are termed tricyclic because of their three-ring antihistaminic structure. TCAs increase the supply of norepinephrine and serotonin in the brain, which allows the flow of nerve impulses to return to normal levels, thereby reducing the symptoms of depression and anxiety. Some of the commonly used TCAs include amitriptyline (Elavil), clomipramine (Anafranil), desipramine (Norpramine), imipramine (Tofranil), and nortriptyline (Pamelor).

Literature to support for the efficacy of the TCAs for internalizing disorders is somewhat inconclusive. Although some double-blind studies have found the TCAs to be more effective than placebos for pediatric depression (Braconnier, Le Coent, & Cohen, 2003; Sallee, Hilal, Dougherty, Beach, & Nesbitt, 1998; Sallee, Vrindavanam, Deas-Nesmith, Carson, & Sethuraman, 1997) and anxiety (Gittelman-Klein & Klein, 1971), others have found that they are no more effective than placebos (Barney, Klovin, & Bhate, 1981; Geller, Reising, Leonard, Riddle, & Walsh, 1999; Klein, Koplewicz, & Kanner, 1992). Common side effects of the TCAs include dry mouth, drowsiness, tremors, visual difficulties, sleep disorders, and impacted cognition (Abrams et al., 2006; Velosa & Riddle, 2000). In addition, overdoses of TCAs can increase the risk of seizures. The overdose of desipramine, in particular, has been reported to have lethal effects in some cases (Riddle, Geller, & Ryan, 1993; Varley & McClellan, 1997; Velosa, & Riddle, 2000).

In the 1990s, TCAs were very popular medications for depression and anxiety. Their popularity as the primary pharmacological treatment for pediatric internalizing disorders has decreased significantly. The reduced use is a result of contradictory research evidence on their efficacy in treating pediatric internalizing disorders, their potentially serious side effects, and the availability of alternative medications (e.g., SSRIs) with stronger efficacy and milder side effects (Merrell, 2001).

Selective serotonin reuptake inhibitors (SSRI) work by blocking the reabsorption, or reuptake, of a

Figure 6.3   Steps for school professionals working with students receiving pharmacological interventions.

1. Operationally define problem behavior.
2. Collect data to determine frequency and severity of problem behavior.
3. Determine whether the problem behavior is frequent and severe enough to impact the student's socioemotional well-being.
   a. If Yes—go to step 4.
   b. If No—attempt relatively nonintrusive classroom-based interventions.
4. Determine whether behavioral interventions alone might address the problem behavior.
   a. If Yes—implement intervention (e.g., CBT, relaxation techniques).
   b. If No—consider concurrent pharmacological intervention referral.
5. Consult experienced professionals to determine the benefits of referral for pharmacological interventions.
6. Consult the school district's policy for such referrals.
7. If pharmacological intervention is implemented, determine the roles of different school personnel for the following tasks:
   a. Medication monitoring.
   b. Behavior progress monitoring.
   c. Home–school communication.
8. Establish data collection procedures, such as the following:
   a. Develop a checklist for medication monitoring.
   b. Conduct behavioral observation techniques for behavior progress monitoring.
   c. Establish home–school communication through a home–school note system.
9. Continue to collect data.
10. Review data periodically, answering the following questions:
    a. Are medications being administered as prescribed?
    b. Has the problem behavior reduced to the desired level?
    c. Are parents/guardians informed regularly by the school about the student's behavioral progress?
    d. Is the school informed regularly by the parents about any changes in the prescribed dosage or types of medications?
11. Make data-based decisions such as the following:
    a. Continue the current intervention if data indicate high fidelity of implementation and progress in student behavior.
    b. Enhance medication monitoring methods if data indicate that medications are not taken as prescribed.
    c. Reconsider the type and dosage of medication if behavioral data indicate a lack of desired level of progress.

neurotransmitter in the brain called *serotonin,* consequently increasing its overall level in the brain. Low levels of serotonin have been found to be associated with symptoms of mood and behavioral disorders. Hence, increased levels of serotonin, as a result of SSRIs, help reduce symptoms related to mood disorders. Some of the common SSRIs are fluoxetine (Prozac), sertraline (Zoloft), paroxetine (Praxil), fluvoxamine (Luvox), and citalopram (Celexa).

SSRIs, as a group, have the strongest research support as medications for internalizing disorders in children (Abrams et al., 2006; Whittington et al., 2004; Velosa & Riddle, 2000; Wolraich, 2003). Fluoxetine is the most widely researched SSRI for the treatment of depression and anxiety in children. A number of recent double-blind randomized control studies have demonstrated significantly higher efficacy of fluoxetine for reducing symptoms of depression and anxiety when compared with a placebo (Birmaher et al., 2003; Emslie et al., 2002; Treatment for Adolescents with Depression Study Team, 2004). Additionally, other SSRIs, such as sertraline (J. S. March et al., 1998; Rynn, Siqueland, & Rickels, 2001), paroxetine (Braconnier et al., 2003; Keller et al., 2001), and fluvoxamine (The Research Unit on Pediatric Psychopharmacology Anxiety Study Group, 2001, 2002) also have demonstrated efficacy in treatment of anxiety and depression in children in double-blind studies.

The previously cited research base evaluating the efficacy of the SSRIs included nine double-blind randomized control trial studies conducted since 2000. The studies collectively included 1,593 children and adolescents aged 5 to 20 years. Females were slightly overrepresented (61%) as compared to males in the collective sample. Only six studies reported the details of ethnic and linguistic diversity of the sample. The samples of these studies included the highest proportion of Caucasians (above 80%), followed by African Americans, Hispanics, Asian Americans, biracial, and other racial groups consisting of about 15% or less in each respective sample. All studies were implemented in the clinic or home, wherein the medications were delivered to the participants' parents on their weekly or biweekly clinic visits. While five studies mentioned medication-monitoring services provided by a case manager or a nurse on the clinic visits, none of the studies provided sufficient detail to determine integrity procedures. This emphasizes the point that, given the lack of close and constant contact, clinic-based practitioners may not be in the best position to thoroughly monitor medication intake.

In the cited research, the symptom reduction was measured by a number of standardized informant and self-rating scales. All studies found the SSRIs to be effective in reducing the symptoms of depression and anxiety, with one study demonstrating positive medication effects lasting up to 6 months in a follow-up assessment (The Research Unit on Pediatric Psychopharmacology Anxiety Study Group, 2002). Overall, the research indicated strong support for SSRIs to address internalizing difficulties in children and adolescents. More research in the area of involvement of school personnel; better communication between clinics, homes, and the schools; and home- and school-based implementation fidelity assessment may overcome the current limitations in the existing literature base.

SSRIs have relatively mild side effects, which include nausea, dry mouth, diarrhea, headaches, and insomnia. The overdose of SSRI does not have fatal effects. Given the strong empirical evidence and relatively milder side effects, SSRIs have replaced TCAs as the most commonly prescribed medication for anxiety and depression in children. In fact, in one survey, 91% of family care physicians and 58% of pediatricians reported having prescribed an SSRI for depression at least once (Rushton, Clark, & Freed, 2000).

Benzodiazepines are typically used to address symptoms of anxiety in children. They are effective because of their sedative, anticonvulsant, and muscle relaxant effects, which help reduce the symptoms of anxiety. Commonly prescribed benzodiazepines include alprazolam (Xanax) and clonazepam (Klonopin). Although benzodiazepines have been extensively researched with adults, research on their efficacy with children is sparse and contradictory. A few early double-blind studies have demonstrated that alprazolam (Simeon & Ferguson, 1987) and clonazepam (Biederman, 1987; Kutcher & Mackenzie, 1988) were significantly more efficacious than placebos. A number of later studies, however, failed to demonstrate statistically significant differences between benzodiazepines and placebos (Bernstein, Garfinkel, & Borchardt, 1990; Graae, Milner, Rizzotto, & Klein, 1994). The literature to date, and particularly more recent research, is equivocal regarding the use of benzodiazepines with school-age children.

Summary

The research base suggests that CBT and SSRIs benefit from the strongest research support for decreasing depression and anxiety in school-age children and adolescents. To support this conclusion, we applied criteria developed by Chambless and Hollon (1998) to identify empirically supported efficacious interventions. Their criteria include (a) a randomized control trial with results superior to no treatment or equivalent or superior to another treatment of known efficacy; (b) the use of a treatment manual, a specified population, valid and reliable outcome measures; and (c) the use of appropriate statistical analyses. Further, the criteria must have been met in studies conducted in at least two different research settings. Applying these criteria, both CBT and SSRIs are considered efficacious, evidence-based interventions.

In addition, the research regarding AM/RT interventions, to date, shows that this approach is promising for addressing internalizing behaviors. Although this type of intervention does not yet meet the definition of an evidence-based practice, as defined by Chambless and Hollon (1998), the only criterion that was not met was the use of a treatment manual, an implementation variable that was absent in two of the three studies. Thus, we consider it a promising practice.

The research regarding tricyclic antidepressants yielded mixed findings, and that class of medications is less frequently used at the present time, in favor of SSRIs with more consistent and overall positive research support. The research on benzodiazepines also is inconclusive with respect to efficacy for treating internalizing problems.

For those effective and promising interventions (CBT, SSRIs, AM/RT), in spite of research support, a number of limitations remain in the literature base. First, few research studies have considered contextual variables related to implementation and outcomes. Specifically, in all but one research study, CBT and

AM/RT procedures were implemented by trained clinicians. Consequently, it is unclear whether these interventions could be implemented as effectively by typical school personnel. Further, involvement by school personnel is essentially absent in the SSRI research.

A related concern pertains to feasibility of implementation in school settings. The CBT and AM/RT interventions required an average of approximately 10 hours of implementation, which seems a minimal amount of time given the high risk of negative sequelae absent intervention. Still, it is important to determine whether school personnel will find time for such interventions—time related to implementation as well as time devoted to training professionals.

In light of these limitations, future research should determine the type and amount of training and supervision required for school personnel to implement CBT and AM/RT with integrity. In addition, research is needed to document how schools can make critical behavioral and mental health interventions a part of ongoing school practices. Finally, future research might identify barriers to implementation and delineate strategies to overcome such barriers.

Another limitation is the paucity of evidence-based research with elementary-age students experiencing depression and anxiety. Although medication trials have included this age group, CBT and AM/RT research has been conducted only with middle and high school-age adolescents. Given that disorders may be most easily and effectively treated when symptoms initially emerge, it is critical for future research to examine whether these and other interventions are efficacious with younger children as well.

The absence of research to support intervention efficacy across racial and ethnic groups is another limitation. This is particularly concerning in light of the differential effectiveness of CBT across racial groups found by Cardemil et al. (2002). Given that the intervention had little effect on the depression of African American participants, while large effects were found for Latino children, additional research is needed to determine whether CBT and other interventions are effective with racial, ethnic, and other subgroups. Similar research across diverse groups is needed for medications. Although some of the research on SSRIs included somewhat diverse racial/ethnic samples, outcomes were not parceled out by subgroup. Thus, in addition to including diverse students as study participants, outcome data also must be differentially analyzed.

In general, a great deal of additional research is needed in the area of internalizing problems, and research in this area, unfortunately, appears to have slowed over time. To illustrate, only 2 of the 15 studies evaluating CBT or AM/RT were conducted after 2001. This is particularly discouraging given the need to further evaluate issues related to the applicability and feasibility of these interventions with existing school-based resources.

In light of the current research base, we recommend that practitioners begin arranging for implementation of CBT and AM/RT in schools. Evidence for effectiveness is sufficient at the present time. Further, given that youth are unlikely to receive intervention unless provided by their schools, these evidence-based strategies become particularly urgent. Although training is required for CBM implementation, no specialized certification or skill base for practitioners was evident in the research literature. AM/RT appears to be a somewhat easier intervention to implement, requiring less training, and therefore could be rapidly implemented. Finally, the combined use of medication and psychosocial interventions can be improved greatly via data collection and communication. Simple checklists, as described in this chapter, provide a means to thoroughly and more objectively evaluate the additive effectiveness of medications across settings, which can be regularly communicated to those who are prescribing.

Given only preliminary evidence for effectiveness of CBT and AM/RT, particularly in school settings and when implemented by natural intervention agents, along with limited evaluation/communication regarding medications, we recommend collection of procedural and outcome data to guide decisions. Further, responsiveness should be examined individually to determine effectiveness on students of different age, racial, and gender groups. In the case of medication, desirable effects must be carefully considered and balanced in terms of unwanted side effects. Practical applications should be carefully documented and publicly disseminated. Such documentation will greatly inform science and practice, particularly around issues of feasibility.

CHAPTER 7

Strategies for Decreasing Aggressive, Coercive Behavior: *A Call for Preventive Efforts*

Kathleen Lynne Lane | *Vanderbilt University*

Hill Walker | *University of Oregon*

Mary Crnobori, Regina Oliver, Allison Bruhn, and **Wendy P. Oakes** | *Vanderbilt University*

Students with emotional and behavioral disorders (EBD) represent between 2% and 20% of school-age youth, with conservative estimates approximating 6% (Kauffman & Landrum, 2009). This category includes students with externalizing (e.g., aggression, coercion) and internalizing (e.g., anxiety, depression) behaviors. Clearly, these students experience a host of short- and long-term negative outcomes within and beyond the school setting, as evidenced by grade-level retentions, school dropout rates, impaired social relationships, high rates of mental health services, unemployment, and even criminality (Stouthamer-Loeber & Loeber, 2002; M. Wagner, Kutash, Duchnowski, Epstein, & Sumi, 2005). Yet, only 1% of students are likely to qualify for special education services under the category of emotional disturbance (ED; Individuals with Disabilities Education Improvement Act [IDEA], 2004). Thus, many of these students will spend their educational careers in K–12 general education settings with teachers who report feeling ill-prepared to meet the multiple needs of these students (Lane, Menzies, Bruhn, & Crnobori, 2011).

Students with externalizing behavior patterns are most recognized for their antisocial behavior tendencies, which include a propensity to misinterpret social cues, engage in high rates of negative social interactions despite average levels of positive social interactions, and invoke aggressive tactics as a means of resolving conflicts and getting their own needs met (Cullinan & Sabornie, 2004). Given these social skills acquisition and performance deficits, it is not surprising that these students' behaviors escalate quickly, resorting to an aggressive mode of interacting with peers and adults (Colvin, 2004). Without intervention these aggressive behaviors tend to become intractable over time (Kellam, Ling, Merisca, Brown, & Ialongo, 1998).

In addition, students with externalizing behaviors do not fare well academically. They exhibit low levels of academic engagement (DeBaryshe, Patterson, & Capaldi, 1993), which are associated with low levels of compliance with teacher directives, low rates of homework completion, and poor academic performance (Greenwood, Hart, Walker, & Risley, 1994). These students have broad-based academic deficits in core academic areas (e.g., reading, writing, mathematics) that tend to remain stable or even decline over time (Landrum, Tankersley, & Kauffman, 2003; J. R. Nelson, Benner, Lane, & Smith, 2004). G. R. Mayer (1995) suggested that academic failure may serve as a setting event for antisocial behavior tendencies. Namely, these students may act out to escape demands that are beyond their skill set (Penno, Frank, & Wacker, 2000).

Regardless of the nature of the link between multiple deficits, what is clear is that the collective behavioral, social, and academic characteristics pose significant challenges to educators, parents, and the students themselves, as well as to society as a whole (Kauffman & Brigham, 2009; Lane, 2007; H. M. Walker, Ramsey, & Gresham, 2004). Consequently, early detection and socially valid, evidence-based supports are critical to improve outcomes on multiple levels. For example, not only is it important to prevent student-to-student violence, it is also important to prevent student-to-teacher violence (American Psychological Association [APA] Classroom Violence Directed Against Teachers Task Force, 2011). It may surprise some to learn that approximately 6% of elementary teachers and 8% of secondary teachers have been threatened with injury by students, and 4% of elementary teachers and 2% of secondary teachers have been physically attacked by students (Dinkes, Kemp, & Baum, 2009). In fact, school-based violence and lack of safety in some schools and communities are keystone factors in some teachers' decisions to exit—or even not enter—the field of education (Dinkes, Kemp, Baum, & Snyder, 2008).

A teacher's ability to prevent and respond to aggressive behaviors as manifested in the form of verbal or physical aggression, or even property destruction, is paramount to providing a safe, productive learning environment. Yet, this is a challenging task given that aggression is a powerful means to achieve a desired outcome. From a behavioral perspective, aggression is a reliable, efficient tool in the sense that it typically allows the student who exhibits aggression to access (positive reinforcement) or avoid (negative reinforcement) attention, tasks, or sensory experiences (Cooper, Heron, & Heward, 2007). In short, aggressive behavior works for students to "get their way." Rather than engage in other, more constructive, prosocial strategies that may or may not lead to their desired source of reinforcement, many students resort to aggression, thereby challenging the behavior management skills of even highly trained teachers.

The Importance of Early Intervention

Given that aggressive behavior is so efficient for some students, it is wise to intervene early at two critical junctures: (a) on initial school entry when students are most amenable to intervention efforts (Kazdin, 1987) and (b) early in the acting-out cycle by responding effectively to lower levels of undesirable behaviors (e.g., disruption, noncompliance) before *behavior earthquakes* occur (Colvin, 2004). The first intervention goal is to intervene before students become highly efficient in their use of aggression by providing a comprehensive approach to teaching and reinforcing prosocial, productive behavior. First Step to Success (FSS; H. M. Walker, et al., 1997) is one such program designed to meet this charge. In brief, FSS provides school-based and home-based instruction on key social skills necessary for academic success by involving key social change agents in the child's life: parents, teachers, and peers. Ideally, all students who need this level of support could be detected on initial school entry using methodical screening tools such as the Systematic Screening for Behavior Disorders (SSBD; H. M. Walker & Severson, 1992) or the Student Risk Screening Scale (SRSS; Drummond, 1994) and subsequently supported with FSS.

Educators also need other effective practices for students who are not identified early. For example, it is important to have evidence-based practices to support older students whose aggressive tendencies may develop later in life (e.g., late-onset conduct disorders; Moffitt, 1993) or for those who have continued to be nonresponsive to primary and secondary prevention efforts (Lane, Kalberg, Parks, & Carter, 2008). As a result, the second intervention goal is to intervene early in the acting-out cycle to prevent low levels of disruptive behavior from escalating. In this instance, the ultimate goal is to prevent the damaging consequences of violence and facilitate a productive, safe instructional environment (Colvin, 2004). A clear understanding of the progression of aggressive behavior is necessary so that (a) interventions can be targeted early in the escalating behavior chain to prevent aggression; (b) the student can be taught problem-solving strategies and academic skills if necessary; and (c) aggressive behavior is not inadvertently reinforced. A functional assessment-based intervention (FABI) is one approach that can be used to meet this charge. In brief, FABIs focus on identifying the reasons why the target behavior is occurring and then teaching students functionally equivalent behaviors that are more reliable and efficient in meeting their objectives. Such interventions involve modifying antecedent conditions, adjusting rates of reinforcement, and extinguishing reinforcers that previously maintained the undesirable behavior (Umbreit, Ferro, Liaupsin, & Lane, 2007).

In sum, it is important for teachers to have evidence-based practices to prevent and respond to aggression during the early school years to prevent antisocial behaviors from becoming stable (e.g., FSS). At-risk students need to learn new ways to get their needs met so that they will not resort to less desirable (yet efficient) coercive behaviors (e.g., FABI).

Purpose

In this chapter we review two highly effective practices to prevent and respond to aggressive behavior patterns: First Step to Success (FSS) and functional assessment-based interventions (FABIs). To rigorously evaluate each of these practices, we conducted a systematic review of the literature to identify the full scope of treatment outcome studies. Specifically, we identified articles by using a systematic search process that included electronic searches using specific key words, hand searches in relevant journals, and personal queries with authors who had contributed to these bodies of literature. A total of 9 articles pertaining to FSS and 31 related to FABI met inclusion criteria and were evaluated.

In the sections that follow, we provide (a) a definition of the practice, including the theoretical underpinnings; (b) a description of the practice; and (c) a review of the treatment-outcome literature base. We conclude by discussing (a) the strengths and limitations of each literature base, (b) recommendations for future research, and (c) recommendations for practice.

First Step to Success

First Step to Success Definition and Description

FSS is a manualized program designed to interrupt the progression of antisocial behavior for at-risk students on school entry (H. M. Walker, Stiller, Severson, Feil, & Golly, 1998). FSS has three components: (a) proactive universal screening, (b) school intervention, and (c) parent training (see Table 7.1 for procedures). This early intervention program involves parents, teachers, and peers as key social agents in the student's developmental process. A school professional coordinates and delivers the program by acting in the role of behavioral coach to the teacher and parents (i.e., FSS consultant).

The first component requires screening of all kindergarten students to identify those who may require intervention on initial school entry. Early identification is crucial to determine which students demonstrate the initial indicators of antisocial behavior and later delinquency. Then, treatment may be implemented when it has the greatest likelihood of success, before adolescent involvement in deviant peer groups and delinquency (Patterson, Reid, & Dishion, 1992). Screening procedures range from teacher nominations to more complex three-stage gating procedures (H. M. Walker & Severson, 1992). These stages include (a) teacher nominations and rank ordering of nominated students on external and internal behavior dimensions, (b) assessment of student behavior using teacher behavior ratings, and (c) direct observations in the school setting.

In the initial stage of screening, students are nominated by their teachers, based on externalizing and internalizing behavioral characteristics. Five students per class are nominated as at risk for externalizing and five for internalizing behavior problems and then rank ordered from most-like to least-like the characteristics provided. The three highest-ranked students enter the next screening stage, where teachers rate each student on specific critical behaviors and frequency of adaptive and maladaptive behavior. Students exceeding predetermined normative cut scores are then observed directly in the classroom and on the playground to determine the quality and duration of their academic engagement and social interactions with peers. Students exceeding normative criteria at this final stage are typically identified as having severe behavioral adjustment problems and referred for early intervention. This screening process is conducted after students have been in school for at least

Table 7.1   First Step to Success Procedures

FSS Component	Implementer	Time Line	Duration	Goal
Systematic Screening	Consultant with input from teachers.	After 6 weeks of attending school year.	1–2 days to collect data.	Identify students who are at risk for aggression.
Contingencies for Learning Academic and Social Skills (CLASS)	Consultant with fading to classroom teacher.	Begins after student is identified. • Initially 2- to 20-min sessions with extension to ½ or full day once teacher takes over.	Typically 30 days.	Teach important social skills with short lessons, and provide feedback on behavior through the use of a behavior card and rewards.
Home Base	Consultant works with parents. Parents work with child.	Begins on day 10 of implementation. • 45-min daily consultant sessions with parents. • 15- to 20-min daily parent sessions with child.	Typically 6 weeks.	Reinforce social skills taught in CLASS component at home with parents. Improve parent–child interactions.

30 days, allowing the teacher sufficient exposure to the student to make screening decisions.

After students are identified and parents are brought into the process (e.g., parental consent), the FSS school component is implemented. The school component consists of an adapted version of the Contingencies for Learning Academic and Social Skills (CLASS) Program for Acting-Out Child developed by Hops and Walker (1988) with the key components of (a) frequent adult praise and monitoring of student performance; (b) awarding points to the student based on program guidelines and student performance; and (c) individual, group, and home rewards. Features of the classroom-based component teach important prosocial behaviors by using powerful behavioral strategies such as frequent monitoring and feedback, positive reinforcement, and group contingencies that provide positive peer social involvement (Lane, Menzies, et al., 2011).

Initially, two 20-minute sessions occur daily (one in the morning and then another in the afternoon) and are conducted by the consultant in the classroom (Epstein & Walker, 2002). The consultant sits by the student to accomplish behavioral monitoring and to provide feedback. A red and green card is used to signal the student about his behavior, to record points, and to note praise and bonus points. Sample behaviors are provided on the cards (e.g., follows directions, works quietly, gets along with others), but the teacher may add or change an additional two behaviors based on the goals for the student. The green card is placed face up when the student is performing appropriate behaviors and is immediately turned over to the red side if the student exhibits any inappropriate behavior. The changing of the card acts as a cue to the student and provides immediate visual feedback. Verbal feedback is also provided when the student responds to the red card (e.g., "You made a good choice." "You know how to work."). Points are awarded, and verbal praise provided, during predetermined intervals established for each day of the program. If the student reaches 80% of the criteria for that program day, the whole class is given a reward. The card goes home at the end of the day for a parent signature, and the student receives home privileges contingent on meeting the performance criteria for that day.

The consultant sits farther away from the student once the student demonstrates success. Students can progress to the next program day only after they have mastered the criteria; otherwise, the program day is repeated. Student performance goals progressively increase, and reinforcement is faded (e.g., every other day), making meeting the criteria more challenging while shaping behavior. Eventually, the program is extended to half day or full day, and the teacher assumes control of implementation after the sixth day of the program. The teacher uses the green/red card in the same way as during the consultant phase, with the criteria for student success becoming increasingly difficult. The program requires at least 30 days to complete, although it typically takes longer as students repeat program days that are not mastered initially (H. M. Walker, Stiller, et al., 1998). A maintenance phase is built into the program to fade out the use of the card and classroom reinforcement, typically around day 30.

Parents of targeted students are enlisted to support the school component with the home-based FSS program component shortly after the school component is initiated. Home base begins on day 10 and typically lasts 6 weeks. Parents are trained by the consultant to teach their children important school success skills such as accepting limits, cooperation, and problem solving. The home-based component contains lessons, guidelines, and games and activities that parents can use with their child for 10 to 15 minutes daily. Parents teach and reinforce skills being taught in the school-based component. The goal of involving parents in the process is to build a partnership with the school to support their child's development and improve home–school communication (Epstein & Walker, 2002). The home-based component also indirectly teaches parents valuable parenting skills and interrupts the coercive interaction patterns responsible for aggressive behavior (Patterson et al., 1992).

First Step to Success: Theoretical Underpinnings

FSS is a comprehensive early intervention program for aggressive children in grades Pre-K–3 who are at risk for developing antisocial behaviors and later delinquency (H. M. Walker, et al., 1997). It is based on a social learning model of antisocial behavior developed by Patterson and colleagues (1992). Early aggressive behavior patterns begin at home with coercive cycles of parent–child interactions. These patterns are developed over time and are a result of the bidirectional influence of caregiver–child interactions. Contextual variables such as family stress, divorce, poverty, or parental antisocial behavior establish a family system marked by inconsistent and harsh discipline, poor monitoring, and overall poor family management skills. In fact, families with antisocial children tend to rely heavily on coercion in their daily interactions, exchange high rates of aversive initiations, maintain longer durations of negative interactions, and use more negative reinforcement strategies (Patterson et al., 1992).

Coercive interaction patterns develop through a system of escape conditioning (Patterson et al., 1992) that begins with overly harsh parental discipline, to which the child responds with aversive behaviors such as crying, aggression, or tantrums. The caregiver responds by removing any demands previously issued or by engaging in conversation and negotiation with the child, which stops the aversive child behavior. The child and caregiver are both negatively reinforced by removal of these undesirable events (e.g., demands, crying). This cycle escalates with inconsistent parenting and increased use of coercion during parent–child interactions, thus creating a breakdown in parental effectiveness that inadvertently teaches the child to use aggression to achieve desired outcomes. As such, it is critical to involve parents and the home context in any comprehensive intervention program to stop this cycle in the home.

The next stage of the coercion model begins when the child enters school unprepared to handle the social and academic demands of schooling. Children who enter school with antisocial, coercive behavior patterns already established at home often use the same coercive techniques with teachers and peers (Patterson et al., 1992). As a result, the student experiences rejection by teachers and peers and associated poor academic outcomes. Having experienced teacher and peer rejection, students with antisocial tendencies tend to seek out students with similar behavior patterns that perpetuate and reinforce coercive interactions. Without early intervention, these students often do not learn important social skills such as cooperation, problem solving, negotiating, and friendship making. Over time, they tend to demonstrate increasing levels of aggressive behavior, substance use, and delinquency. Thus, the school becomes a critical context for arresting the progression of antisocial behavior and the development of prosocial behavior patterns and appropriate peer interactions.

Given the nature of the progression of antisocial behavior, intervention should be targeted as early as possible in the developmental sequence to divert students with aggressive tendencies from this trajectory (Kazdin, 1987). Comprehensive intervention for aggressive, antisocial behavior should involve the family context as well as the school context to address this cycle of behavior. The FSS program areas address issues in both these critically important contexts.

Research Base

Of the nine FSS articles reviewed, data are reported for all 342 included participants (see Appendix 7.1 at the end of this chapter for details). The majority of participants were young boys (77%), ranging in age from 5 to 10 years in first through third grades (72%), who did not have a disability (77%), but who were identified through systematic screening tools. Most students were Hispanic (54%) or Caucasian (30%). All interventions occurred in elementary schools, with one school located on an Indian reservation (Diken & Rutherford, 2005).

Purpose

The purpose of the initial studies using FSS was to evaluate the multicomponent intervention as an approach to preventing antisocial behavior in schools. Over a 4-year period, the initial evaluation (H. M. Walker, Kavanagh, et al., 1998) examined two cohorts of kindergarteners with follow up into first grade. All three components (i.e., universal screening, CLASS, home base) were implemented by an FSS consultant with fading of implementation gradually to the classroom teacher. To confirm previous findings and explore issues of feasibility, subsequent studies replicated these initial results and expanded the research goal to evaluating social validity (e.g., Golly, Stiller, & Walker, 1998).

Intervention

Nearly all studies implemented all three components of the FSS intervention. All studies used universal screening procedures and the classroom-based intervention (i.e., CLASS). In addition, home-based intervention occurred for 99% ($n = 339$) of participants, with only three participants receiving school-based intervention only (D. R. Carter & Horner, 2007; Golly, Sprague, Walker, Beard, & Gorham, 2000). One study also used a FABI consisting of check-in procedures, various antecedent adjustments, and skill-building strategies for a participant who did not respond to the FSS intervention (D. R. Carter & Horner, 2007). Screening measures used to determine risk status and treatment eligibility were limited to the Early Screening Project (ESP; H. M. Walker, Severson, & Feil, 1994; $n = 3$), Systematic Screening for Behavior Disorders (SSBD; H. M. Walker & Severson, 1992; $n = 3$), and Student Risk Screening Scale (SRSS; Drummond, 1994; $n = 2$), with one study omitting information regarding the type of screening measure used.

Design and Dependent Variables

Of the nine studies, five (56%) used a group design to evaluate the effects of FSS, while the other four (44%) used single-case methodology. A randomized cohort group design was used for three of the five group studies (Seeley et al., 2009; H. M. Walker, Kavanagh, et al., 1998; H. M. Walker et al., 2009) and the remaining two studies used a nonrandomized pretest/post-test group design (Golly et al., 1998; Overton, McKenzie, King, & Osborne, 2002). Of the studies using single-case methodology, multiple baseline was the predominant design, two across participants (Golly et al., 2000; Lien-Thorne & Kamps, 2005) and one across groups (Diken & Rutherford, 2005), with one study using a within-subjects reversal design (D. R. Carter & Horner, 2007).

The number of dependent variables measured within studies ranged from 2 to 10 ($M = 5.7$), with greater numbers of dependent measures in group studies ($M = 7.4$) compared to studies using single-case methodology

($M = 3.75$), resulting in a total of 34 separate measures across studies. The dependent measures themselves evaluated a range of behaviors from specific (e.g., talk outs, out of seat) to broad behavioral constructs (e.g., maladaptive, adaptive) with a variety of those measured through direct observation (e.g., academic engaged time) or reports from teachers or parents (e.g., Child Behavior Checklist—Teacher Report; Achenbach, 1991). The most common measure was direct observations of academic engagement, used in eight studies (88.8%).

Components Related to Valid Inference Making

Reports of the reliability of the dependent variable, treatment integrity, and social validity are all important variables necessary to make valid inferences about study outcomes (R. H. Horner, et al., 2005). Fortunately, all studies reported reliability for the dependent measures. However, treatment integrity and social validity were reported less frequently. Only two studies (Seeley et al., 2009; H. M. Walker et al., 2009) discussed data collection procedures and reported outcomes for treatment integrity for both CLASS and home-base components. Three studies (D. R. Carter & Horner, 2007; Diken & Rutherford, 2005; Overton et al., 2002) discussed treatment integrity data collection and reported outcomes for the CLASS component only, while two studies (H. M. Walker, Kavanagh, et al., 1998; Lien-Thorne & Kamps, 2005) mentioned that treatment integrity was considered but did not report outcomes. Similar patterns were found for social validity. Social validity data were reported in five studies (Diken & Rutherford, 2005; Golly et al., 1998; Overton et al., 2002; Seeley et al., 2009; H. M. Walker et al., 2009), with one study (Lien-Thorne & Kamps, 2005) mentioning it without reporting, and one study (Golly et al., 2000) offering anecdotal reports.

Outcomes

In general, significant decreases in antisocial behaviors and increases in prosocial behaviors were found across studies, although variability was found based on type of behavior and who was reporting. In terms of antisocial behavior, teachers reported significant decreases in maladaptive and aggressive behavior in two group studies (Golly et al., 1998; H. M. Walker, Kavanagh, et al., 1998), and significant decreases in externalizing behavior were reported by both parents and teachers in another group study (Overton et al., 2002). In another group study, parents, but not teachers, reported significant decreases in aggressive behavior. Moderate-to-large effects were also found for maladaptive and problem behavior and for behavior symptomatic of ADHD in group studies

reporting those outcomes (Seeley et al., 2009; H. M. Walker et al., 2009). However, researchers found no significant improvement reported by parents or teachers for withdrawn (Golly et al., 1998; H. M. Walker, Kavanagh, et al., 1998) or internalizing behavior (Overton et al., 2002).

Functional relations between FSS and decreases in specific behaviors were found in some single-case studies. Observations of talk outs, out of seat, touching others, and touching property demonstrated initial decreases in behavior across participants ($n = 4$) with slight variability (Golly et al., 2000). Inappropriate behavior decreased and maintained across participants ($n = 3$) for one study (Lien-Thorne & Kamps, 2005). Decreases in problem behavior were also found in one study (D. R. Carter & Horner, 2007) during FSS, and decreased further when a FABI was implemented for the participant ($n = 1$). Also, nonsocial play decreased for three participants with slight variability for the fourth (Diken & Rutherford, 2005). Parent and teacher reports of problematic behavior in studies that used single-case methodology were less clear. Inconsistency in parent and teacher reports was found across participants for two studies (Diken & Rutherford, 2005; Lien-Thorne & Kamps, 2005); parent reports of problem behavior indicated decreases for most participants, while teacher reports indicated variability across participants with little change.

The outcomes for prosocial behavior appeared stronger and more consistent across studies. Adaptive behavior improved significantly (Golly et al., 1998; Seeley et al., 2009; H. M. Walker, Kavanagh, et al., 1998; H. M. Walker et al., 2009), as did social skills based on both parent and teacher reports (Seeley et al., 2009; H. M. Walker, Kavanagh, et al., 1998). The most consistent finding across studies was significant improvement in academic engagement (Golly et al., 1998, 2000; Lien-Thorne & Kamps, 2005; Overton et al., 2002; Seeley et al., 2009; H. M. Walker, Kavanagh, et al., 1998; H. M. Walker et al., 2009), with some variability (Golly et al., 2000) for at least one participant. Some indication that these improvements in academic engagement may maintain over time was evident (Overton et al., 2002). Academic competence also improved significantly (Seeley et al., 2009; H. M. Walker et al., 2009). The outcomes for studies using nonexperimental designs (Golly et al., 1998; Overton et al., 2002), although generally consistent with that of experimental designs in the current review, should be interpreted with caution.

High variability in treatment integrity was found for studies that did report it, with strong correlations between treatment integrity and outcomes. The percentage of items implemented by teachers for the CLASS component ranged from 75% to 100% (Overton et al., 2002), 83.3% to 100% (Diken & Rutherford, 2005), and 20% to 100% of intervals (D. R. Carter & Horner, 2007). Two studies examined the relationship between the quality of implementation and study outcomes (Seeley et al., 2009; H. M. Walker et al., 2009). These correlations were found to be strong across parents, teachers, and coaches ($r = 0.52$; $r = 0.67$; $r = 0.93$, respectively), indicating outcomes improved when the quality of implementation was high.

In general, social validity data indicated favorable ratings of FSS, although some variability was found. One study (Golly et al., 1998) specifically examined social validity. Teachers in this study gave favorable ratings to the training content of FSS. Follow-up surveys from teachers indicated the primary reason for lack of implementation was that no students were found to require intervention, with the expense and impracticality of implementation cited next.

Functional Assessment-Based Interventions

Definition and Description

Functional assessment-based interventions (FABIs) refer to interventions that are constructed based on the reason(s) *why* a target (problem) behavior occurs (Umbreit et al., 2007). For example, if the target behavior is physical aggression, the intent of a function-based approach is to determine *why* aggressive behavior is occurring. In other words, what is happening before physical aggression occurs (antecedents) to set the stage for the occurrence? And, what occurs after physical aggression occurs to increase (or decrease) the probability of future occurrences (consequences)? The motive for the specific behavior is identified by conducting a functional behavioral assessment. In brief, a functional behavioral assessment includes the full range of descriptive (e.g., interviews, direct observations of behavior, rating scales) and experimental (e.g., functional analysis) procedures conducted to identify antecedent conditions that prompt a target behavior as well as the maintaining consequences. This information is analyzed to determine a hypothesis statement (e.g., aggression is maintained by peer attention and escape from too-difficult tasks) that can be tested within the context of an experimental (functional) analysis. All behaviors occur to either access (positive reinforcement) or avoid (negative reinforcement) social attention, activities or tasks, or sensory conditions (Umbreit et al., 2007). The intent of these tools is to determine the function of the target behavior (see Table 7.2 for procedures).

Once the function of the behavior is identified and confirmed, an intervention is designed, based on the function of the target behavior. Rather than simply designing topographical interventions that focus on suppressing a specific behavior, such as physical aggression, the intent of a FABI is to teach students a more reliable, efficient, functionally equivalent method of meeting their objective (e.g., accessing peer attention and requesting help or a break from too-difficult tasks; Cooper et al., 2007). This new behavior is referred to as a *replacement behavior*. In general, function-based interventions contain three core components: (a) antecedent adjustments to set the stage (prompt) for the replacement behavior to occur, (b) modification of reinforcement rates to increase the likelihood that the replacement behavior (and not the target behavior) will occur in the future, and (c) extinction of the target behavior.

After the intervention is designed, then it is implemented using a scientifically rigorous single-subject

Table 7.2 Functional Assessment-Based Interventions Procedures

Step	Sample Tools	Purpose
1. Collect data to determine function of behavior.	Teacher, parent, or student interviews Behavior rating scales Antecedent-behavior-consequence (ABC) observation data Scatter plot Record reviews	To collect data from multiple settings, multiple times of day, over at least 3 days, 3 hours (or 8 instances of the behavior), and multiple respondents. Data provide information about antecedents and consequences that reliably predict target behavior.
2. Analyze data to determine function of target behavior.	Function matrix (Umbreit et al., 2007)	To organize data systematically to identify the function and develop a hypothesis statement.
3. Design the intervention linked to function of the behavior.	Function-Based Intervention Decision Model (Umbreit et al., 2007)	To identify which method, or combination of methods, are needed in the intervention to address the target behavior and identified function.
4. Evaluate the extent to which the intervention produces changes in the desired behaviors.	Progress monitoring Time series graphs	To determine if the intervention is working or if adjustments need to be made.

research design such as a withdrawal (ABAB) or multiple baseline across settings to ensure that a functional relation is established between the introduction of the intervention and changes in the target and/or replacement behavior (Gast, 2010). To draw accurate conclusions regarding intervention outcomes, it is important for (a) reliability of the dependent variable (interobserver agreement), (b) treatment integrity (the accuracy with which the intervention is implemented as planned), (c) social validity (social significance of the goals, social acceptability of the treatment procedures, and social importance of the outcomes; M. M. Wolf, 1978), and (d) generalization and maintenance of student outcomes to be addressed.

One of the challenges associated with describing the step-by-step process of designing and evaluating FABIs is that tremendous variability occurs in the procedures used to (a) collect data to determine the function of the behavior, (b) analyze data collected to determine the function of the target behavior, (c) design an intervention linked to the results of the functional assessment, and (d) evaluate the extent to which a functional relation is established between the introduction of the intervention and changes in the target and/or replacement behavior.

Umbreit and colleagues (2007) attempted to address some of these concerns by developing a systematic approach to designing, implementing, and evaluating FABIs. In their model, they introduce a systematic approach to (a) determining the function of a given target behavior and (b) constructing interventions linked to results of the functional assessment. In brief, this systematic approach involves a new tool, the Function Matrix, which is used to analyze data from all functional assessment tools (e.g., interviews, direct observations, school record searches, behavior rating scales, functional analysis; Umbreit et al., 2007; see Figure 7.1). The Function Matrix is a six-celled grid used to determine if the behavior is maintained by positive and/or negative reinforcement to attention, tangibles/activities/tasks, or sensory stimuli. Data collected from each tool are placed into the

appropriate cell. For example, consider the antecedent-behavior-consequence (ABC) chain in this sequence: teacher again prompts Frank to "get back to work" (A), Frank throws the assignment at the teacher coupled with some colorful words (B), and the teacher sends Frank to on-campus suspension (C). In this instance of the target behavior (#5—the fifth time that the target behavior was observed during ABC data collection), the analysis indicates that the behavior was being maintained by escape from task. Thus, #5 could be placed in the cell that intersects with negative reinforcement and task (meaning that the result of this behavior is that the student avoided the task). After reviewing all data in the Function Matrix, a hypothesis statement describing the function(s) of the target behavior is generated. For example, if the majority of comments from the interviews (teacher, student, and parent) and the direct observation data were coded under negative reinforcement and activity, the teacher might hypothesize that when presented with work that he perceives as too difficult, Frank uses inappropriate language to escape the teacher-assigned task.

Another feature of this systematic approach is the Function-Based Intervention Decision Model (Umbreit et al., 2007; see Figure 7.2). This tool was developed to guide intervention planning using two key questions: (a) Is the replacement skill in the child's repertoire? and (b) Does the classroom environment represent effective practices? Answers to these questions direct the intervention to one of three methods:

- *Method 1: Teaching the Replacement Behavior* is reserved for students who do not have the replacement behavior in their repertoire (acquisition deficit) and when the classroom represents effective practices. This method focuses on explicitly teaching the replacement behavior. For example, a validated intervention designed to teach social skills may be implemented to teach the student specific skills that she lacks.

Figure 7.1 Function matrix for developing functional assessment-based intervention.

	Positive Reinforcement (Access Something)	Negative Reinforcement (Avoid Something)
Attention		
Tangibles/Activities		
Sensory		

Source: Reprinted with permission from Umbreit, J., Ferro, J., Liaupsin, C., & Lane, K. (2007). *Functional behavioral assessment and function-based intervention: An effective, practical approach* (p. 84). Upper Saddle River, NJ: Prentice-Hall.

Figure 7.2   Function-Based Intervention Decision Model.

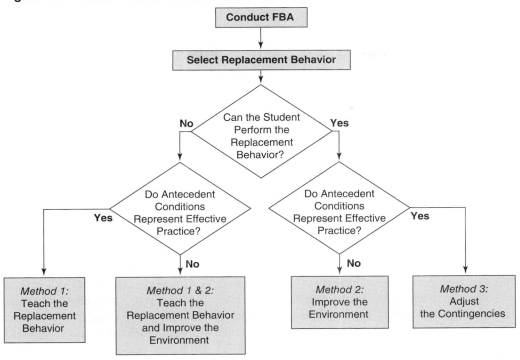

Note: FBA = functional behavior assessment.

Source: Reprinted with permission from Umbreit, J., Ferro, J., Liaupsin, C., & Lane, K. (2007). *Functional behavioral assessment and function-based intervention: An effective, practical approach* (p. 98). Upper Saddle River, NJ: Prentice-Hall.

- *Method 2: Improve the Environment* is reserved for students who have the replacement behavior in their repertoire but are in classrooms where the antecedent conditions may be less than optimal in terms of facilitating instruction (Lane, Weisenbach, Phillips, & Wehby, 2007). This intervention involves (a) adjusting (or removing) existing aversive events and (b) providing a context that supports the replacement behavior. For example, a teacher might withhold reinforcement for the disruptive behavior (i.e., talking out) by using planned ignoring and by asking the student to use communication cups to appropriately signal a need for assistance (communication cups involve students being given a red, yellow, and green cup to arrange on their desk to serve as a signal to the teacher: red = I am stuck and need help before I can move on; yellow = I am a little confused, but I can do some of this task; green = I am clear on the directions and able to do the assignment).

- *Method 3: Adjust the Contingencies* is reserved for students who have the necessary replacement behavior in their repertoire and are in classrooms where antecedent conditions represent effective practices. This intervention method focuses predominantly on adjusting reinforcement rates to decrease the rate for the target behavior and

increasing the rate for the replacement behavior. For example, an escape-motivated student who was previously sent to the office for misbehavior for failing to complete assignments will now gain access to the office contingent on work completion.

Each method includes three core components: teaching or modifying antecedents; reinforcing the occurrence of the replacement behavior; and extinction of the target behavior. Yet, each method has a predominant emphasis tailored to the student needs and environmental context. Once the intervention method is selected, the interventionist designs socially valid (feasible) plan tactics.

The Function-Based Intervention Decision Model is only one approach to conducting functional assessments; a number of other methods also can be used to design, implement, and evaluate FABIs. Ideally, any approach to functional assessment should gather multiple sources of information through the tools mentioned previously to identify converging evidence of the hypothesized function of the target behavior. And regardless of the method for identifying the function, we encourage the reader to intervene early in the acting-out cycle, before aggressive behavior ensues (Colvin, 2004). It is important to measure treatment fidelity of the *intervention* to be implemented as well as the procedural fidelity to measure the *process* of conducting the functional assessment, analyzing data, and designing the plan.

In the following section, we discuss the logic behind FABIs. We also illustrate some of the controversy surrounding applications of this practice within naturalistic contexts (e.g., classrooms).

Theoretical Underpinnings and Legal Foundations

The logic behind FABI is that this approach to intervention recognizes the communicative intent of behavior. Namely, behavior occurs for a reason: to either access (positive reinforcement) or avoid (negative reinforcement) social attention; activities, tasks, or tangibles; or sensory conditions (Umbreit et al., 2007). Once the function of the behavior is determined, the intervention can be developed based on this information. FABIs provide a respectful method of analyzing undesirable behaviors with a goal of providing an intervention designed to expand the student's repertoire by teaching her a new, more adaptive skill or how to use the replacement behavior more consistently and appropriately. Initial studies of functional assessment procedures were conducted in clinical settings with individuals having severe developmental disabilities (e.g., Iwata, Dorsey, Slifer, Bauman, & Richman, 1982).

Functional behavioral assessments have been endorsed by several organizations including the National Association of State Directors of Education (NASDE), National Association of School Psychologists (NASP), and National Institutes of Health (NIH). According to the IDEA (2004), functional behavioral assessments must be conducted by school personnel if a student receiving special education services is (a) assigned to an alternative placement for behavior that poses a threat to the individual or others; (b) assigned to an alternative setting for 45 days resulting from drug or weapons violations; or (c) suspended (or placed in an alternative setting) for more than 10 days or if the suspension constitutes a change in placement (Drasgow & Yell, 2001; Kern, Hilt, & Gresham, 2004). Despite the research support of functional behavioral assessment, questions remain as to whether evidence is sufficient to require FABIs for students with or at risk for EBD or aggressive behavior in naturalistic settings (e.g., Quinn et al., 2001; Sasso, Conroy, Stichter, & Fox, 2001).

In the next section, we present the findings of our systematic review of the literature examining the efficacy of FABIs with students who have a history of aggressive behavior. While it is beyond the scope of this chapter to provide a systematic application of the core quality indicators for single-case methodology as recommended by R. H. Horner and colleagues (2005) to

the articles identified, we will discuss (a) participant characteristics and instructional setting; (b) purpose of the studies conducted; (c) intervention components; (d) research design and dependent variables; (e) functional assessment tools and identified function; (f) components related to valid inference making and level of support; and (g) student outcomes.

Research Base

For the 31 articles reviewed, data are reported for 61 participants who met inclusion criteria (e.g., school-aged students, students presenting with aggressive behavior, studies conducted since 1988, studies that used at least two methods associated with functional behavioral assessment, intervention was function-based; see Appendix 7.2 at the end of this chapter for more details). Consistent with other reviews (e.g., Lane, Bruhn, Crnobori, & Sewell, 2009; Lane, Kalberg, & Shepcaro, 2009; Lane, Umbreit, & Beebe-Frankenberger, 1999; Quinn et al., 2001), the majority of participants were elementary-age (72%) students, and most were male (80%). Ethnicity was reported for only 28 students (46%), five of whom were Hispanic English Language Learners (see Appendix 7.2).

In terms of students' disability status, the majority of students were receiving special education services for emotional disturbances, other health impairments, and comorbid disorders. However, 20 were typically developing students, 2 of whom had been identified as at risk according to systematic screening data (see Kamps, Wendland, & Culpepper, 2006; Lane, Weisenbach, et al., 2007) and one of whom had a mild hearing loss (Liaupsin, Umbreit, Ferro, Urso, & Upreti, 2006). The majority of interventions were conducted with special education students in special education classrooms on general education campuses, self-contained schools, and alternative learning centers. However, it is important to note that 47% of the FABIs conducted since 2007 assessed students in the general education classrooms in public education schools.

Purpose

The purpose of the studies published has shifted somewhat over time. As expected, earlier studies were focused more on issues of efficacy, in the sense that they addressed questions pertaining to whether or not these procedures could work beyond clinical settings with individuals who did not have developmental disabilities (e.g., Knapczyk, 1988, 1992; Umbreit, 1995). Studies continued in this vein, exploring the utility of FABIs conducted in segregated schools for adolescents with EBD (e.g., Penno et al., 2000; Stahr, Cushing, Lane, & Fox,

2006), self-contained classrooms (e.g., Dunlap, White, Vera, Wilson, & Panacek, 1996; Kern, Delaney, Clarke, Dunlap, & Childs, 2001), traditional general education classrooms (e.g., Grandy & Peck, 1997; Todd, Horner, & Sugai, 1999), and inclusive settings (e.g., Umbreit, 1995). In time, the purpose of the studies began to shift beyond exploring efficacy in different settings to exploring the level of support necessary to implement FABIs in naturalistic contexts (e.g., Kamps et al., 2006; Lane, Barton-Arwood, et al., 2007; Lane, Weisenbach, et al., 2007).

Intervention

Although all interventions were function based, interventions contained a range of components. In general, most interventions contained antecedent adjustments. For example, several studies included components related to instructional accommodations or modifications (e.g., Burke, Hagan-Burke, & Sugai, 2003; Kern, Delaney, et al., 2001), and some included an instructional component (e.g., video modeling) to teach alternative responses to aggression (e.g., Knapczyk, 1992). In addition, some interventions incorporated self-management components (e.g., Todd et al., 1999; B. W. Smith & Sugai, 2000). Several studies explicitly mentioned three components: (a) antecedent adjustments, (b) increased reinforcement for the replacement behavior (e.g., differential rates of reinforcement of alternative behavior), and (c) extinction of the target behavior (e.g., Kennedy et al., 2001). The range of intervention components included in these studies reflects the individualized nature of FABIs.

Design and Dependent Variables

All of the 31 studies reviewed were single-case designs, of which 14 studies employed multiple baseline designs, 12 studies used some variation of an ABAB design, and two studies used alternating treatment designs. One study used a withdrawal design for one participant and a multiple baseline for another participant (Lane, Barton-Arwood, Spencer, & Kalberg, 2007). Two other studies involved combinations of these designs such as a multiple baseline across two settings with a withdrawal component (Stahr et al., 2006; Todd et al., 1999).

Very few studies explicitly monitored aggressive behavior as a student outcome measure (e.g., Knapczyk, 1988, 1992). The vast majority of behaviors monitored focused on target behaviors that occurred earlier in the acting-out cycle, such as disruption (e.g., Grandy & Peck, 1997; Umbreit, 1995), noncompliance (e.g., Fairbanks, Sugai, Guardino, & Lathrop, 2007), inappropriate touching (e.g., Lane, Barton-Arwood, et al., 2007), and off-task behaviors (Y. Lee, Sugai, & Horner, 1999), as well as

more global measures of problem behavior. Global measures focused on multiple behaviors in the response class such as making noises, talking to peers, and playing with other materials (e.g., Kennedy et al., 2001; Todd et al., 1999). Replacement behaviors often focused on academic-related behaviors such as task engagement, productivity, and accuracy of work completed (e.g., Burke et al., 2003; Filter & Horner, 2009; Kern, Delaney, et al., 2001; Penno et al., 2000; Preciado, Horner, & Baker, 2009; B. W. Smith & Sugai, 2000; Trussell, Lewis, & Stichter, 2008). Other studies focused on other academic-enabling skills such as hand raising, appropriate responding, and appropriate requests for breaks (e.g., Turton, Umbreit, Liaupsin, & Bartley, 2007; Wright-Gallo, Higbee, Reagon, & Davey, 2006). A few studies monitored students' social interactions (e.g., Christensen, Young, & Marchant, 2004; Knapczyk, 1988, 1992; Lane, Weisenbach, et al., 2007).

Functional Assessment Tools

Researchers used a wide range of tools to identify the function of the target behaviors of interest. In the 31 studies reviewed, the most common tools used were teacher interviews (29 studies), direct observation (predominately ABC data collection, 27 studies), and then student interviews (20 studies). Twelve studies conducted school record searches to gain information.

In terms of maintaining functions for the students in this review, 27 students' behaviors were maintained by some form of attention (e.g., peer, teacher, or combined), and 19 were maintained by escape from task demands. For other students, behavior served a dual function of escape from task and teacher attention. In the study by Kamps et al. (2006), for example, the behavior served three functions: accessing peer attention, accessing sensory stimulation, and escaping task demands.

Components Related to Valid Inference Making

In terms of reliability of the dependent variables examined, all 31 studies mentioned and reported interobserver agreement or other relevant reliability information for at least one variable. However, treatment integrity received less attention, with only 18 studies mentioning and reporting the extent to which the intervention was implemented as intended. In looking across the time frame during which these studies were published, treatment integrity data became more the rule than the exception, with 14 of 18 studies published between 2004 and 2009 including treatment integrity. Similarly, social validity was measured (at least anecdotally) and reported for 18 of the 31 studies, again becoming a relatively standard practice beginning in 2002 (R. E. March & Horner, 2002). A total of 12 studies mentioned and reported treatment integrity and social validity (see Table 7.2).

Outcomes

Although it is beyond the scope of this chapter to provide a detailed discussion of student outcomes for each of these ideographic interventions, the majority of the studies established a clear functional relation between the introduction of the intervention (when implemented with fidelity) and changes in student outcome measures. This relationship was true in the earlier studies, when the research teams were responsible for all facets of this multiple-step procedure (e.g., Umbreit, 1995; Umbreit et al., 2004), as well as in more recent research, when teachers assumed more active roles in this process with less-intensive support from local universities (e.g., Kamps et al., 2006; Lane, Barton-Arwood, et al., 2007; Lane, Weisenbach, et al., 2007). The evidence also supports the additional benefit of FABIs relative to nonfunctional assessment-based interventions in increasing task engagement and decreasing problem behavior (Filter & Horner, 2009; Trussell et al., 2008). Moreover, evidence also suggests that FABIs can play a role not only in improving decorum and social interactions (e.g., Lane, Weisenbach, et al., 2007), but also in improved academic outcomes, as evidenced by increases in completed and correct tasks (e.g., Preciado et al., 2009). Finally, social validity data were generally favorable, with the majority of parties indicating that these interventions, although labor intensive, did meet (and in some cases exceed) expectations.

Discussion

As we discussed at the onset of this chapter, aggressive behavior is a hallmark characteristic of students with antisocial behavior patterns and one of the most challenging behaviors to address within and beyond the school setting. Because it is difficult to teach students replacement behaviors that are more reliable and efficient than aggression, it is prudent to intervene at two junctures. First, we recommend intervening at initial school entry, when students are most amenable to intervention efforts before aggressive behavior patterns become highly stable and nonresponsive to intervention efforts (much like interventions for chronic diseases such as diabetes; Kazdin, 1987). Second, we recommend intervening early in the acting-out cycle before aggression is exhibited; the goal here is to respond effectively to lower levels of undesirable behaviors (e.g., disruption, noncompliance, coercion) before behavior escalates into aggression. To address these two objectives, we recommend FSS, a manualized intervention,

to address the first charge and FABIs to meet the second charge. The evidence reviewed in the chapter supports the efficacy of using both practices. Each approach, however, has identifiable strengths and limitations that are important to consider.

First Step to Success: Strengths and Considerations

One strength of FSS is that it is a manualized program involving the school and home contexts as pivotal factors for change. FSS provides explicit instructions to guide intervention training, implementation, and evaluation. It includes clear directions as well as all necessary materials for consultants, teachers, and parents (implementation guide, consultant guide, parent handbook, treatment fidelity-monitoring sheets for the classroom-based component, and even the stopwatch). For many interventions, a barrier to successful implementation is a lack of clarity about procedures related to intervention components. Explicit procedures may provide needed structure to key interventionists and enhance treatment fidelity, which is important to meaningful, lasting change—a long-standing goal of all intervention work (Baer, Wolfe, & Risley, 1968). The use of a consultant also provides much-needed support during start up, when barriers may prevent teachers and parents from initiating and sustaining implementation. Fading of this support to the teacher also programs for maintenance of the intervention within the context of the classroom.

Although social validity data suggest that some teachers view FSS to be too labor intensive, we encourage potential users to consider the costs—financially, emotionally, and otherwise—of dealing with the consequences of antisocial behavior for administrators, teachers, parents, students, and society as a whole (see Kauffman & Brigham, 2009). Fortunately, direction has been offered to guide feasible, effective implementation of FSS. For example, Overton et al. (2002) have provided the following points to consider before implementing FSS: (a) results appear to be somewhat less favorable in terms of success with students repeating kindergarten; (b) beginning teachers may struggle to implement the intervention with high fidelity; and (c) characteristics of the consultant influence intervention success, with consultants who lack training in teaching or counseling experiencing less success than consultants who have such training. Also, Diken and Rutherford (2005) suggested that FSS may be less efficacious for students residing in highly chaotic home environments that require more extensive intervention supports than those in more stable homes. Yet, regardless of these challenges, FSS has yielded meaningful changes for many students, as determined by high-quality single-case and group design studies. Thus, we recommend FSS as an evidence-based practice to reverse and reduce risk on initial school entry.

Functional Assessment-Based Interventions: Strengths and Considerations

One strength of FABI is that it is a highly ideographic process that allows for a customized, tertiary prevention effort to design, implement, and evaluate interventions based on the reasons why problem behaviors occur. This is a respectful approach that involves an individualized instructional approach to behavior, ultimately providing students with a more reliable, efficient method of accessing or avoiding relevant conditions (i.e., attention; activities, tasks, or tangibles; and sensory experiences). Such an intervention establishes the student as an effective learner who can acquire more desirable behaviors by modifying antecedent conditions, adjusting reinforcement rates, and using procedures to extinguish undesirable behaviors (Umbreit et al., 2007).

One of the challenges of FABIs is that, in contrast to FSS, it is not a manualized program, making fidelity of the intervention process at times challenging. Systematic approaches are now available for conducting functional assessments. Such approaches include specific guidelines for analyzing data collected from functional assessment tools and procedures, selecting an intervention method that is linked to the function of the target behavior with explicit instructions to guide intervention design, and constructing legally defensible designs to test the intervention effects that include the core components needed to draw accurate conclusions regarding intervention outcomes (Umbreit et al., 2007). Practices used by researchers and practitioners exhibit considerable variability (Sasso et al., 2001), however, which makes synthesis and evaluation activities (e.g., those attempted in this chapter) challenging.

Another challenge associated with FABIs, which is also true for FSS, pertains to social validity. Namely, the costs of conducting FABIs with respect to personnel time to learn the procedures and to develop fluency in the required skills to implement the practice are substantial. However, given the alternative of not intervening, we view the costs as warranted.

Despite these challenges, sufficient evidence suggests that FABIs are an effective, socially valid practice for intervening early in the acting-out cycle. Results from this review indicate FABIs are effective in decreasing problem behaviors that occur earlier in the cycle before aggression (whether physical, verbal, or directed toward property) occurs. Given the deleterious consequences associated with aggression, particularly as students become older, this is encouraging.

Recommendations

We conclude by offering recommendations to researchers and practitioners. First, to our esteemed colleagues, we thank you for the work that has been conducted to prevent the development of antisocial behavior. We are encouraged by the presence of FSS and FABI. And we encourage future inquiry with current practices and in development of new practices.

We recommend scaling up studies such as those funded by the Institute for Educational Sciences to determine how to best build district's and school's capacities to implement these practices. In particular, we encourage studies to determine how best to enable school-site personnel to implement and sustain these practices in isolation from university support (Lane, Kalberg, & Shepcaro, 2009). Additional inquiry to examine the efficacy and effectiveness of these practices when implemented with students whose culture is not the majority to established generalizability is also warranted (Cooper et al., 2007). Furthermore, because so many students (especially those with early-onset antisocial behaviors; Moffitt, 1993) have already developed their aggression skills as a highly effective, efficient component in their behavioral repertoire, we encourage additional inquiry to identify other secondary and tertiary levels of prevention to manage students who regularly display aggressive behaviors.

To those practitioners working with students who have acquired highly successful repertoires of aggressive and coercive behaviors, we understand and respect the significant challenges you face on a daily basis. Because it is extremely difficult to teach students a replacement behavior that is more reliable and efficient than aggression, we strongly encourage practitioners to intervene early in the student's educational experiences before these behavior patterns become firmly engrained and to intervene early in the acting-out cycle by identifying and preventing behaviors that precede aggressive outbursts. While intervention efforts such as FSS and FABI may be time-consuming, we contend that these procedures are more effective than less-comprehensive interventions (e.g., those that do not involve the families in the early years) and those interventions that do not take into account the communicative function of behavior.

Summary

In this chapter, we reviewed two highly effective practices to prevent and respond to aggressive behavior patterns: FSS and FABI. We provided a review of research studies investigating the efficacy of each practice. Appendixes 7.1 and 7.2 summarize the findings of our literature review of the research base for FSS and FABI, respectively.

Appendix 7.1

Summary of Studies Reviewed for Preventing Aggression: First Step to Success

Author	Participant Characteristics and Instructional Setting	Intervention Components	Outcomes
H. M. Walker, Kavanagh, Stiller, Golly, Severson, & Feil (1998)	$N = 46$; M ($n = 74\%$); Age NS; Ethnicity NS; Grades K and follow-up to 1; SLD ($n = 5$), SLI ($n = 4$), SED ($n = 2$); School and home.	1. ESP 2. CLASS 3. Home base	Significant differences between treatment and control for 4 of 5 measures for both clinical and nonclinical samples. Increases in AET and adaptive behavior and decreases in maladaptive behavior and aggression for the experimental group.
Golly, Stiller, & Walker (1998)	$N = 20$; M ($n = 19$), F ($n = 1$), Age NS; Ethnicity, C ($n = 19$), NA ($n = 1$); Grade K; Typical; School and home.	1. ESP 2. CLASS 3. Home base	Significant effects in the experimental group for adaptive, maladaptive, academic engaged time, and aggression from pre-test to post-test. No effects found for withdrawn behavior.
Golly, Sprague, Walker, Beard, & Gorham (2000)	$N = 4$ (2 sets of twins); M; Age 5; Ethnicity, C; Grade K; Typical; School and home.	1. All for S1 S2 2. Only school component for S3 S4	Initial decreases in problem behavior initially with slight variability after. Immediate increases in academic engaged time with variability for S4. S1 and S2 did not complete the program.
Overton, McKenzie, King, & Osborne (2002)	$N = 22$; 16 completed; M ($n = 16$), F ($n = 6$); Age 5–6; Ethnicity, C ($n = 5$), AA ($n = 7$), AA and C ($n = 5$), H ($n = 1$), NA ($n = 3$), NA and C ($n = 1$); Grade K; Typical; School and home.	1. SRSS 2. CLASS 3. Home base	Behavioral improvement was significant, but variable. Academic engaged time increased and maintained. Internalizing behavior did not significantly decrease per parent or teacher reports. Externalizing behavior decreased per parent and teacher reports. Aggression decreased per parent, but not teacher.
Diken & Rutherford (2005)	$N = 4$; M ($n = 3$); Age 5–7; Ethnicity, NA; Grade K ($n = 2$) and Grade 1 ($n = 2$); Typical Elementary school of a Southwestern Indian tribe in Arizona and home.	1. SRSS 2. CLASS 3. Home base	Social play behaviors increased for all participants with reductions in variability for S4. Nonsocial play behaviors decreased for S1–S3 with decreased variability for S4. Parent ratings of problem behavior decreased for most. Teacher ratings of class-wide problem behavior indicated little change.
Lien-Thorne & Kamps (2005)	$N = 3$; M ($n = 2$); Age 7–8; Grades 1–2; Ethnicity, C ($n = 2$), AA ($n = 1$); Label, ADHD (S1: SPED); School and home.	1. SSBD 2. CLASS 3. Home base	Academic engagement increased, and inappropriate behaviors decreased and maintained. Variability across participants in post-test measures of risk with little change.
D. R. Carter & Horner (2007)	$N = 1$; M; Age 6; Ethnicity, C; Grade 1; Typical; School and home.	1. CLASS with FABI	Initial decreases in problem behavior from 37% to 3% during the coaching phases of FSS with continued low levels during the teacher phase of FSS plus FABI. Problem behavior increased when FABI was removed.

Author	Participant Characteristics and Instructional Setting	Intervention Components	Outcomes
Seeley, Small, Walker, Feil, Severson, Golly, & Forness (2009)	$N = 42$ (Treatment = 23; Control = 19); M ($n = 39$); Age 6–8; Ethnicity, H ($n = 30$), NS ($n = 12$); Grades 1–3; ADHD ($n = 42$); School and home.	1. SSBD: Stages 1 and 2 2. CLASS 3. Home base	Significant effects on school-based measures of ADHD and disruptive behavior symptoms, social functioning, and academic performance. Effects of home-based assessments of problem behavior and social skills were nonsignificant.
H. M. Walker, Seeley, Small, Severson, Graham, Feil, Serna, Golly, & Forness (2009)	$N = 200$ (Treatment: 101; Usual care 99); M ($n = 73\%$); Ethnicity, C ($n = 24.5\%$), H ($n = 57\%$), NA ($n = 4.5\%$), A/PI ($n = 0.5\%$), AA ($n = 3\%$), NS ($n = 6\%$); Grade 1 ($n = 83$), Grade 2 ($n = 69$), Grade 3 ($n = 48$). School and home.	1. SSBD: Stages 1 and 2 2. CLASS 3. Home base	Significant gains in problem behavior for treatment (effect sizes: $d = 0.62$ to 0.73). Statistically significant gains for treatment across functional domains with an effect size of $d = 0.54$. Significant gains for treatment on academic competence and academic engaged time, but comparison group had significant gains on Letter–Word ID with no difference between groups on ORF.

Note: A/PI = Asian/Pacific Islander; AA = African American; ADHD = Attention Deficit Hyperactivity Disorder; C = Caucasian; CLASS = Contingencies for Learning Academic and Social Skills (Hops & Walker, 1988); ESP = Early Screening Project (H. M. Walker, Severson, & Feil, 1994); F = Female; FABI = Functional Assessment-Based Intervention; WJ-III = Woodcock-Johnson-III (Woodcock, McGrew, & Mather, 2001); FSS = First Step to Success (H. M. Walker, Stiller, Golly, Kavanagh, Severson, & Feil, 1997); H = Hispanic; M = Male; *N* = Number; NA = Native American; NS = Not Specified; ORF = Oral Reading Fluency; S = Student; SED = Seriously Emotionally Disturbed; SLD = Specific Learning Disability; SLI = Speech/Language Impairment; SRSS = Student Risk Screening Scale (Drummond, 1994); SSBD = Systematic Screener for Behavior Disorders (H. M. Walker & Severson, 1992).

Appendix 7.2

Summary of Studies Reviewed for Preventing Aggression: Functional Assessment-Based Interventions

Author	Participant Characteristics and Instructional Setting	Intervention Components	Outcomes
Knapczyk (1988)	S1 Mark; M; Age 13; Ethnicity NS; Grade 7; SPED S2 William; M; Age 14; Ethnicity NS; Grade 8; SPED Public school, special education, part time	Modeling and rehearsal procedures to teach alternative replacement behaviors (social skills).	Functional relation between introduction of intervention and (a) reduction in aggressive behavior, (b) increased initiation–participation events, and (c) decreased initiation–nonparticipation events.
Knapczyk (1992)	*Experiment 1:* S1 Warren; M; Age 16; Ethnicity NS; Grade 10; SPED BD *Experiment 2:* S2 Lonnie; M; Age 15; Ethnicity NS; Grade 9; SPED BD S3 Kenton; M; Age 15; Ethnicity NS; Grade 9; SPED BD S4 Philip; M; Age 16; Ethnicity NS; Grade 10; SPED BD Two rural high schools for students with EBD	Video modeling and behavioral rehearsal to develop alternative responses to aggression. Experiment 1—individually administered; Experiment 2—small-group training sessions.	When participants substituted alternative responses for aggressive responses following the treatment, decreases occurred in the frequency of aggressive behavior and antecedent events associated with the behavior.
Umbreit (1995)	Corey; M; Age 8; Ethnicity NS; Grade, 3; ADHD Public school, general education classroom	1. Independent assignments 2. Cooperative groups without friends 3. Brief breaks 4. Ignore disruption	Functional relation established between the introduction of the intervention and decreases in disruptive behavior in all three inclusive general education classes.
Dunlap, White, Vera, Wilson, & Panacek (1996)	S1 Michael; M; Age 7; Ethnicity NS; Grade 2; SED S2 Gizelle; F; Age 9; Ethnicity NS; Grade 4; SED S3 Ann; F; Age 7; Ethnicity NS; Grade 1: SED Typical public school; EBD classrooms	Individualized, multicomponent plan of curricular modifications.	Functional relation established for all participants demonstrating that task engagement increased and disruptive behavior decreased following the implementation of each intervention.

Author	Participant Characteristics and Instructional Setting	Intervention Components	Outcomes
Grandy & Peck (1997)	S1 M; Age 6; Grade 1; Ethnicity NS; Typical Suburban elementary school (K–3), general education	Self-management with fading: participant self-recording; contingent; experimenter attention.	A functional relation was evident between the introduction of the intervention and decreases in disruptive behavior across three settings.
Y. Lee, Sugai, & Horner (1999)	S1 Bill; M; Age 9; Ethnicity NS; Grade 3; EBD S2 Matt; M; Age 9; Ethnicity NS; Grade 3; Label EBD, ADHD Elementary school; Special education self-contained classroom	Component skill instruction on difficult math tasks.	Reductions in problem behavior with inconsistent results based on type of math problem. Reductions in off-task behavior are inconsistent based on the type of math problem. Increases in accuracy but inconsistent across math problem.
Todd, Horner, & Sugai (1999)	S1 Kyle; M; Age 9; Ethnicity NS; Grade 4; LD, physical disability Elementary school; general education classroom (blended 3–4)	Self-monitoring, self-evaluation, and self-recruitment of reinforcement.	Functional relation between the intervention and decrease in problem behaviors, increase in on-task, increase in work completion, increased teacher praise, and increased teacher views of performance.
Penno, Frank, & Wacker (2000)	S1 Andy; M; Age 13; Ethnicity NS; Grade NS; Typical S2 Nick; M; Age 14; Ethnicity NS; Grade NS; ADHD S3 Josh; M; Age 14; Ethnicity NS; Grade NS; LD, BD, ADHD State-funded segregated school for adolescents with EBD	S1: Completing assignments with computer and peer tutor. S2: Shortened assignments and peer tutor. S3: Self-monitoring and working 1:1 with staff.	For 2 students; 2+ modifications resulted in (a) improved productivity and accuracy; (b) decreased behavior problems. Increases in (a) percentage of items completed for S1 and S2 and (b) percent correct for S1 across, (c) number of problems completed for S3.
B. W. Smith & Sugai (2000)	Stu; M; Age NS; Ethnicity NS; Grade 7; Special Education, EBD Self-contained behavioral classroom	Self-management.	Increases in on-task behavior for first intervention phase with slower increases in second. Decreases in off-task during initial intervention, variable performance during second intervention.
Kennedy, Long, Jolivette, Cox, Tang, & Thompson (2001)	S1 Charles; M; Age 8; Ethnicity, C; Grade 4; Labels: Tourette's syndrome, ADHD, SED S2 Mickey; M; Age 6; Ethnicity, C; Grade 1; ADHD S3 Jolanda; F; Age 6; Ethnicity, AA; Grade 1; Typical S1 SPED resource S2 and S3: General education	Individualized PBS plans including antecedent adjustments, reinforcement, and extinction.	When interventions were implemented with integrity, problem behaviors were reduced and general education participation was either maintained or increased as problem behaviors decreased (one demonstration one replication for each DV).

Author	Participant Characteristics and Instructional Setting	Intervention Components	Outcomes
Kern, Delaney, Clarke, Dunlap, & Childs (2001)	S1 Benjamin; M; Age 11; Ethnicity NS; Grade 5; ADHD, EBD S2 Art; M; Age 11; Ethnicity NS; Grade 5; ED Self-contained classroom for student with EBD	S1 Choice of 3 media to complete the assignment. S1 and S2 Complete assignments using a preferred medium.	S1 preferred medium and choice of medium were both associated with increased engagement and decreased disruption behavior. Interesting assignments were associated with higher levels of engagement and decreased disruptive behavior. S2 preferred medium was associated with higher rates of engagement and lower rates of disruptive behavior and increased number of words written.
R. E. March & Horner (2002)	S1 Andy; M; Age 13; Ethnicity NS; Grade 7; SPED, NS S2 Bill; M; Age 13; Ethnicity NS; Grade 7; Typical S3 Cathy; F; 12; Ethnicity NS; Grade 6; SPED, general education middle school	1. Setting event procedures 2. Antecedent procedures 3. Teaching new skills 4. Consequence procedures	Decreases in level and variability of problem behavior across participants. Increases in academic engagement found across participants.
Burke, Hagan-Burke, & Sugai (2003)	Mario; M; Age NS; Grade 3; Ethnicity NS, ELL; LD Suburban elementary school (K–5), general education classroom	Intervention: preteaching vocabulary concepts.	Functional relation between preteaching vocabulary and on-task behaviors.
Christensen, Young, & Marchant (2004)	S1 Justin; M; Age 8; Ethnicity, C; Grade 3; referred Instructional setting: urban elementary school; third-grade general education classroom	Alternative behaviors/ skill development; self-monitoring; peer and teacher reinforcement; peer mediators.	Functional relationship was established between the introduction of the intervention package and improved socially appropriate classroom behavior.
Maag & Larson (2004)	S1 Allen; M; Age NS; Ethnicity NS; Grade 5; ED; Instructional Setting: general education class S2 Bruce; M; Age NS; Ethnicity NS; Grade 5; SLD Instructional Setting: general education class	S1 Preferred seating. S2 Contingent verbal praise.	Partial evidence (one demonstration; one replication) to suggest a functional relation between introduction of the intervention and decreases in problem behavior for both students.
Newcomer & Lewis (2004)	S1 Matthew; M; Age 9; Ethnicity NS; Grade 3; OHI S2 Emma; F; Age 11; Ethnicity NS; Grade 5; Typical Suburban, elementary school, general education class	Function based: S1: Antecedent, consequence, and instructional manipulations. S2: Instruction in appropriate replacement behaviors, teacher pleaser behaviors; Non-function based: Topography.	Partial evidence of a functional relation in support of function-based interventions; however, comparative data across (a) B and C phases revealed a slight level change during C phase for S2 and (b) A and B phases also revealed improvement.
Umbreit, Lane, & Dejud (2004)	S1 Jason; M; Age 10; Ethnicity, C; Grade 4; Typical Instructional setting: General education classroom at a public elementary school	Providing more challenging academic tasks to meet the ability level of the participant.	A functional relation was established between intervention implementation (challenging tasks) and academic engagement.

Author	Participant Characteristics and Instructional Setting	Intervention Components	Outcomes
Kamps, Wendland, & Culpepper (2006)	Patricia; F; Age 7; Ethnicity, AA; Grade 2; at risk (SSBD, DIBELS) Urban, culturally diverse charter elementary school classroom	*Group Instruction:* 1. Teacher attention, points 2. Self-management 3. Reminders *Independent Seat Work:* 1. Modeling 2. Help tickets 3. Social attention	S1: Functional relation established, with disruptive behavior decreasing and on-task behavior increasing during intervention for independent and group instruction as compared to initial assessments.
Liaupsin, Umbreit, Ferro, Urso, & Upreti (2006)	Fiona; F; Age 14; Ethnicity, C; Grade 7; Typical, mild, unilateral hearing loss Charter school that focused on athletics and academics	1. Antecedent adjustments 2. Reinforcement 3. Extinction	Introduction of the intervention was associated with increases in on-task behavior in both settings; one demonstration and one replication for each setting.
Lo & Cartledge (2006)	S1 Ted; M; Age 7; Ethnicity, AA; Grade 2; Typical S2 Adam; M; Age 8; Ethnicity, AA; Grade 2; Typical S3 Chad; M; Age 9; Ethnicity, AA; Grade 4; ADHD, SPED S4 Sam; M; Age 9; Ethnicity, AA; Grade 4; ADHD SEDPublic elementary school (P–5) S1 2nd grade Gen Ed S2 2/3 Gen Ed S3 Resource room for language arts (21%–50%) S4 51%–60% in SED resource room	*Intervention Components:* 1. Skill training 2. DRA 3. DRI 4. Self-monitor desired and replacement behaviors	Functional relation between introduction of the intervention and reductions in all participants' levels of off-task behavior. AAR behavior data revealed slight improvements in appropriate behavior and decreases in inappropriate behavior for S1 and S2. S3 demonstrated no changes in AAR but IAR declined to a low, stable level during implementation and maintenance. S4 showed inconsistent changes in IAR but AAR increased.
Wright-Gallo, Higbee, Reagon, & Davey (2006)	S1 Mike; M; Age 14.5; Ethnicity NS; Grade NS; SPED; EBD S2 Tim; M; Age 12.75; Ethnicity NS; Grade NS; SPED; EBD Public middle school self-contained special education classroom for students with EBD	Differential reinforcement of alternative behavior.	For both participants, there was one demonstration and one replication of experimental effect demonstrating lower rates of disruptive behavior during treatment (following the functional analysis).
Stahr, Cushing, Lane, & Fox (2006)	Shawn; M; Age 9; Ethnicity, AA; Grade 4; ADHD, internalizing (anxiety), and a SLI; OHI Self-contained school for students with EBD in a large metropolitan city	1. Teaching help seeking 2. Self-monitoring 3. Planned ignoring	A functional relation was established between intervention implementation and increased on-task time during language arts and math.

Author	Participant Characteristics and Instructional Setting	Intervention Components	Outcomes
Fairbanks, Sugai, Guardino, & Lathrop (2007)	S1 Blair; F; Age 7–8; Ethnicity, C; Grade 2; Typical S2 Ben; M; Age 7–8; Ethnicity, C; Grade 2; Typical S3 Marcellus; M; Age 7–8; Ethnicity, C; Grade 2; Typical S4 Olivia; F; Age 7–8; Ethnicity, C; Grade 2; LD General education classroom	Originally CICO, then FABI that included antecedent and reinforcement adjustments with clear consequences for infractions, review of expectations.	Mean intervals with problem behavior were reduced during function-based phases for all participants as compared to baseline and CICO phases.
Lane, Barton-Arwood, Spencer, & Kalberg (2007)	S1 John; M; Age 7; Ethnicity NS; Grade 2; ADHD S2 Thomas; M; Age 6; Ethnicity NS; Grade K; ADHD, OCD, special education—OHI S1 Private school for high-incidence disabilities S2 General education kindergarten, public elementary	*S1:* Curricular modifications Self-monitoring *S2:* Antecedent adjustments Consequence adjustments	S1: Functional relation between introduction of the intervention and interruptions. S2: Functional relation not established between introduction of the intervention and inappropriate touches (number of mediation changes). Replacement behaviors were used inconsistently for both students.
Lane, Smither, Huseman, Guffey, & Fox (2007)	S1 Harry; M; Age 6; Ethnicity, C; Grade K; Typical General education classroom in an inclusive school district in Middle TN	*Intervention Components:* 1. Self-monitoring 2. Differential reinforcement 3. Positive scanning	Possible functional relation; (one demonstration, one replication); improvements in disruption and academic engaged time were associated with the intervention despite some variability in treatment fidelity.
Lane, Weisenbach, Phillips, & Wehby (2007)	S1 Margaret; Age 7; Ethnicity NS; Grade 2; Typical, at risk per screening Inclusive, general education public schools in middle TN	*Method 1 and 2:* 1. Antecedent adjustments (teach and prompt desired behavior) 2. Reinforcement 3. Extinction	A functional relation existed between the introduction of the intervention and increases in Margaret's PSI and decreases in her NSI.
Turton, Umbreit, Liaupsin, & Bartley (2007)	S1 Saida; F; Age 16; Ethnicity, Black African (Bermudian); Grade 10; ED and LD Alternative high school for students with SED; received noncategorical special education services	Antecedent adjustments Reinforcement for replacement behavior; extinction of target behavior	Functional relation established between the introduction and increases in appropriate responses. The intervention was rated as socially valid by the teacher, Saida, and her peers.
Wood, Umbreit, Liaupsin, & Gresham (2007)	Josh; Age 8; Ethnicity NS; Grade 3; Typical General education	*Method 3:* 1. Adjust the antecedents 2. Adjust the contingencies 3. Extinction	Equivocal results produced by the intervention; the level of on-task behavior parallels the teacher's level of implementation.

Author	Participant Characteristics and Instructional Setting	Intervention Components	Outcomes
Trussell, Lewis, & Stichter (2008)	S1 Larry; Age 11; Ethnicity, AA; Grade 5; ED and SLD S2 Dave; Age 8; Ethnicity, AA; Grade 3; ED S3 ED; Jack; Age 7; Ethnicity, AA; Grade 1; ED Midwest school district, at an alternative public school	Targeted Classroom vs. Interventions FABI	S1, S2, and S3: Targeted classroom interventions decreased problem behaviors, which decreased further when individualized interventions based on the function were implemented.
Preciado, Horner, & Baker (2009)	S1 Juan; M; Age NS; Ethnicity, Latino ELL; Grade 2; Typical S2 Julia; F; Age NS; Ethnicity, Latina ELL; Grade 3; Typical S3 Jose; M; Age NS; Ethnicity, Latino ELL; Grade 2; LD S4 Javier; M; Age NS; Ethnicity, Latino ELL; Grade 4; Typical General education classes	Intervention: Language-matched instructional priming (LMIP)	Functional relation for S1, S2, and S3 between the introduction of the language-matched instructional priming and decreases in problem behavior, increases in engagement, increases in completed and correct tasks. Results for S4 were variable. Increased DIBELS and IDEL scores.
Filter & Horner (2009)	S1 Brett; M; Age NS; Ethnicity, C; Grade 4; LD S2 Dylan; M; Age NS; Ethnicity, C; Grade 4; ADHD (not in special education) General education classrooms	Functional-based academic Intervention compared to non-function-based interventions (S1 reading; S2 math)	Functional relation between the academic variables and the problem behaviors; S1 and S2 engaged in lower levels of problem behavior and higher levels of task engagement during function-based intervention than non-function-based interventions.

Note: A/PI = Asian/Pacific Islander; AA = African American; AAR = Appropriate Attention Recruitment; ADHD = Attention Deficit Hyperactivity Disorder; ADHDH = Attention Deficit Hyperactivity Disorder, Hyperactive type; BD = Behavior Disorder; C= Caucasian; CBM = Curriculum-Based Measurement; CICO = Check In/Check Out; DIBELS = Dynamic Indicators of Basic Early Literacy Skills; DRA = Differential Reinforcement of Alternative Behavior; DRI = Differential Reinforcement of Incompatible Behavior; EBD = Emotional/ Behavioral Disorder; ED = Emotional Disturbance; ELL = English Language Learner; F = Female; FABI = Functional Assessment-Based Intervention; FBA = Functional Behavioral Assessment; H = Hispanic; IAR = Inappropriate Attention Recruitment; IDEL = Indicadores Dinamicos del Exito en la Lectura (Good, Bank, & Watson, 2003); LD = Learning Disability; M = Male; NA = Native American; NS = Not Specified; NSI = Negative Social Interactions; OCD = Obsessive/Compulsive Disorder; OHI = Other Health Impairment; PSI = Positive Social Interactions; S = Student; SED = Seriously Emotionally Disturbed; SLD = Specific Learning Disability; SLI = Speech/Language Impaired; SPED = Special Education; TN = Tennessee.

CHAPTER 8

Research-Based Practices for Social Behavior:
Social Skills Training, Replacement Behavior Training, and Positive Peer Reporting

Frank M. Gresham, Lisa Libster, and **Keri Menesses** | *Louisiana State University*

C hildren and youth with emotional, behavioral, and social difficulties present substantial challenges to schools, teachers, parents, and peers. These challenges cut across disciplinary, instructional, and interpersonal domains and frequently create chaotic home, school, and classroom environments. The social, emotional, and behavioral characteristics of children with or at risk for behavior difficulties often overwhelm the capacity of schools to effectively accommodate these students' instructional and disciplinary needs. Schools are charged with teaching an increasingly diverse student population in terms of prevailing attitudes and beliefs, behavior styles, race and ethnicity, language, socioeconomic levels, and risk status (H. M. Walker, Ramsey, & Gresham, 2004). Additionally, pressures for higher academic standards and outcomes for all students currently are approaching nearly unattainable levels, particularly for students with behavioral challenges. Students bringing these behavioral challenges to school often create turbulent classroom and school environments, thereby disrupting the learning and achievement of other students.

Children with or at risk for behavior difficulties experience significant difficulties in the development and maintenance of satisfactory interpersonal relationships, exhibition of prosocial behavior patterns, and social acceptance by peers and teachers (Gresham, 1997, 1998; Maag, 2005, 2006; H. M. Walker et al., 2004). These social competence deficits can lead to short-term, intermediate, and long-term difficulties in the domains of educational, psychological, and vocational spheres of functioning (Kupersmidt, Coie, & Dodge, 1990; Newcomb, Bukowski, & Pattee, 1993; Parker & Asher, 1987). The fact that most children with or at risk for behavior difficulties exhibit severe social competence deficits dictates that we design and implement effective intervention strategies to remediate these children's interpersonal difficulties.

In this chapter we describe and critique three evidence-based practices designed to alter the social behavior of children and adolescents. Specifically, we review the following interventions: (a) social skills training, (b) replacement behavior training, and (c) positive peer reporting. We describe these practices within the context of a multitiered model of intervention delivery (universal, selected, and intensive) and point to directions for future research for each practice. Before reviewing each practice, we briefly review the risk and protective factors in relation to students' developing behavioral difficulties, provide a conceptualization of social competence, and provide a discussion of classification of specific types of social skills deficits. This discussion should provide a context for understanding how each of the three intervention practices addresses different aspects of social behavioral functioning.

Risk and Protective Factors in Serious Behavior Disorders

H. M. Walker and Severson (2002) suggested that children and youth having characteristics of behavioral difficulties or disorders are at risk for a host of negative developmental outcomes, many of which place these individuals on destructive pathways often leading to unfortunate consequences such as school failure and dropout, alcohol and substance abuse, delinquency, social rejection, and violent and destructive behavior patterns. These risk factors interact in complex ways, and it is unlikely that a single risk factor is responsible for the development of behavior difficulties in a particular individual. Given that single risk factors may predict multiple outcomes and that a great deal of overlap occurs among behavioral markers, interventions focusing on risk reduction of interacting risk factors may have direct effects on multiple outcomes (Coie & Dodge, 1983; Dryfoos, 1990). Researchers typically find a nonlinear relationship among risk factors and outcomes, suggesting that a single risk factor may have a small effect, but researchers also find that rates of students identified with serious behavior disorders (SBDs) increase rapidly and exponentially with the accumulation of additional risk factors (Rutter, 1979; Sameroff, Seifer, Barocas, Zax, & Greenspan, 1987).

More germane to the present chapter, H. M. Walker and Severson (2002) identified a number of risk and protective factors specifically within the realm of social competence that could be targeted for intervention efforts. In particular, poor problem solving, poor social skills, lack of empathy, bullying, and peer rejection represent important risk factors for students who may develop behavior disorders. A recent synthesis of the meta-analytic literature of the risk and protective factor literature also found that controversial, rejected, and neglected sociometric statuses as well as poor social skills were significant risk factors for children and youth with externalizing (e.g., noncompliance, aggression, or coercive behaviors) and internalizing (e.g., social withdrawal, anxiety, or depression) behavior concerns (Crews et al., 2007).

Although children and youth with behavioral difficulties have a number of social competence risk factors, a number of protective factors buffer the negative outcomes created by risk factors. Protective factors are variables that reduce the likelihood of maladaptive outcomes, given conditions of risk. Protective factors in the realm of social competence include social-cognitive skills, prosocial behavior patterns, and peer acceptance. In a meta-analytic synthesis, Crews et al. (2007) found that positive play activities, popular sociometric status, and prosocial behavior patterns served as significant protective factors for individuals with both externalizing and internalizing behavior patterns.

This brief review of the risk and protective factor literature indicates that individuals with characteristics of SBD experience a number of risk factors that interact in complex ways to produce negative developmental trajectories. Unfortunately, many of these risk factors are immutable and are not amenable to change by schools. On the positive side, a number of risk factors, particularly within the realm of social competence, can be targeted for intervention by schools. Moreover, the literature has demonstrated that many behaviors that make up the construct of social competence serve as important protective factors that buffer the pernicious effects of risk factors associated with behavioral difficulties. This chapter reviews three strategies designed to teach social skills to children and youth who are at risk for or who have behavioral concerns.

Conceptualization of Social Competence

Since the 1990s, we have seen an explosion of professional interest and investment in the development of children's social competence in general and those of at-risk students in particular (Elksnin & Elksnin, 2006; Gresham & Elliott, 1990; Maag, 2006; Merrell & Gimpel, 1998). An important distinction in the theoretical conceptualization of social behavior is the distinction between the concepts of *social skill* and *social competence*. Social skills are a specific class of behaviors that an individual exhibits in order to complete a social task. Social tasks might include things such as peer-group entry, having a conversation, making friends, and playing a game with peers. Social competence, in contrast, is an evaluative term based on judgments (given certain criteria) that an individual has performed a social task adequately. These judgments are made by social agents with whom the individual interacts within natural environments (e.g., school, home, community). Given this conceptualization, social skills are specific behaviors exhibited in specific situations that lead to judgments by others that these behaviors were competent or incompetent in accomplishing social tasks.

Gresham (1986) suggested that evaluations of social competence might be based on three criteria: (a) relevant judgments of an individual's social behavior (e.g., by peers, teachers, parents); (b) evaluations of social behavior relative to explicit, pre-established criteria (e.g., number of steps successfully completed in the performance of a social task); and (c) behavioral performances relative to a normative standard (e.g., scores on social skills rating scales). It is important to note that social behaviors, in and of themselves, cannot be considered "socially skilled" apart from their impact on the judgments of social agents in a given social environment.

Definitions of Social Skills

Numerous definitions of social skills have been developed since the 1980s. Merrell and Gimpel (1998) identified at least 15 definitions of social skills that have appeared in the professional literature. Despite these myriad definitions, social skills are perhaps best conceptualized as a behavioral *response class,* because specific social behaviors are grouped under the generic category of "social skill." Conceptually, social skills make up a set of competencies that (a) facilitate the initiation and maintenance of positive social relationships, (b) contribute to peer acceptance and friendship development, (c) result in satisfactory school adjustment, and (d) allow for individuals to cope with and adapt to the demands of the social environment (Gresham, 1998, 2002a). For purposes of the current chapter, social skills can be defined as socially acceptable learned behaviors that enable an individual to interact effectively with others and to avoid or escape unacceptable behaviors that result in negative social interactions with others (Gresham & Elliott, 1984, 1990, 2008).

A useful way of conceptualizing social skills is based on the concept of *social validity* (Kazdin, 1977; M. M. Wolf, 1978). In this approach, social skills can be defined as social behaviors occurring in specific situations that result in important social outcomes for children and youth (Gresham, 1983, 1986). Socially important outcomes are those that key social agents (peers, teachers, parents) consider significant, adaptive, and functional within specific settings. Put differently, socially important outcomes are those that make a difference in individuals' adaptation both to societal expectations and to the behavioral demands of specific environments in which they function (H. M. Walker, Forness, et al., 1998).

What are socially important outcomes? Research has shown that some of the most socially important outcomes for children and youth include peer acceptance (Newcomb et al., 1993; Parker & Asher, 1987), academic achievement, and school adjustment (DiPerma, Volpe, & Elliott, 2002; Hersh & Walker, 1983; H. M. Walker, Irvin, Noell, & Singer, 1992), as well as teacher and parent acceptance (Gresham, 2002c; Gresham & Elliott, 1990). It is well established that children who are poorly accepted or rejected by peers, who have few friendships, and who adjust poorly to schooling are at much greater risk for lifelong maladaptive outcomes. Parker and Asher (1987) showed that children having difficulties in peer relationships often demonstrate a behavior pattern that can be described as antisocial or aggressive and characterized by repeated school norm violations. This behavior pattern is characteristic of many children with or at risk for SBD. In the absence of effective interventions, this behavior pattern is likely to continue and morph into more virulent and resistant forms of maladaptive behavior (Patterson, DeBaryshe, & Ramsey, 1989; Reid, 1993; H. M. Walker et al., 2004).

Social Skills as Academic Enablers

Researchers have documented meaningful and predictive relationships between children's social behaviors and their long-term academic achievement (DiPerma & Elliott, 2002; DiPerma et al., 2002; Malecki & Elliott, 2002; Wentzel, 1993). The notion of *academic enablers* evolved from the work of researchers who explored the relationship between students' nonacademic behaviors (e.g., social skills and motivation) and their academic achievement (Gresham & Elliott, 1990; Malecki, 1998; Wentzel, 1993; Wigfield & Karpathian, 1991). DiPerma and Elliott (2000) distinguished between academic skills and academic enablers. Academic skills are viewed as the basic and complex skills that are the primary focus of academic instruction. In contrast, academic enablers are attitudes and behaviors that allow a student to participate in and ultimately benefit from academic instruction in the classroom. Research using the Academic Competence Evaluation Scales (ACES; DiPerma & Elliott, 2000) showed that academic enablers were moderately related to students' academic achievement as measured by standardized tests (*Mdn r* = 0.50). In a major longitudinal study, Caprara and colleagues found that social skills of third graders as assessed by teachers were better predictors of eighth-grade academic achievement than achievement test results in third grade (Caprara, Barbaranelli, Pastorelli, Bandura, & Zimbardo, 2000). Even stronger findings were reported by Malecki and Elliott (2002), who showed that social skills correlated approximately 0.70 with end-of-year academic achievement as measured by high-stakes tests. It thus appears that social skills are vitally important academic enablers for children in schools.

Classification of Social Skills Deficits

Another important conceptual feature of social skills that has direct implications for the design and delivery of social skills intervention programs is the distinction between social skills acquisition deficits and social skills performance deficits (Gresham, 1981a, 1981b). This distinction is important because different intervention approaches in remediating social skills deficits are required, and different settings (e.g., general education classroom vs. pullout groups) are indicated, for different tiers of intervention (universal, selected, or targeted/intensive).

Acquisition deficits result from either the absence of knowledge about how to perform a given social skill, an inability to fluently enact a sequence of social behaviors, or difficulty in knowing which social skill is appropriate in specific situations (Gresham, 1981a, 2002a). Based on the preceding conceptualization, acquisition deficits can result from deficits in social-cognitive abilities, difficulties in integrating fluent response patterns, or deficits in appropriate discrimination of social situations. Acquisition deficits can be characterized as "can't do" problems because the child cannot perform a given social skill under the most optimal conditions of motivation.

Performance deficits can be conceptualized as the failure to perform a given social skill at acceptable levels even though the child knows how to perform the social skill. These types of social skills deficits can be thought of as "won't do" problems; the child knows what to do, but does not want to perform a particular social skill. These types of social skills deficits can best be thought of as motivational or performance issues rather than learning or acquisition issues.

Competing Problem Behaviors

Another important component in the conceptualization of social skills deficits is the notion of *competing problem behaviors* (Gresham & Elliott, 1990). Competing problem behaviors effectively compete with, interfere with, or "block" either the acquisition or performance of a given social skill. Competing problem behaviors can be broadly classified as either externalizing behavior patterns or internalizing behavior patterns. For example, a child with a history of noncompliant, oppositional, and coercive behavior may never learn prosocial behavioral alternatives such as sharing, cooperation, and self-control because of the absence of opportunities to learn these behaviors caused by the competing function of these aversive behaviors (Eddy, Reid, & Curry, 2002). Similarly, a child with a history of social anxiety, social withdrawal, and shyness may never learn appropriate social behaviors because of withdrawal from the peer group, thereby creating an absence of the opportunities to learn peer-related social skills (Gresham, Van, & Cook, 2006).

In the sections that follow, we introduce three strategies designed to teach social skills to children and youth who are at risk for or who have SBD: (a) social skills training, (b) replacement behavior training, and (c) positive peer reporting.

Social Skills Training

The importance of social competence for children and youth with SBD has been translated into various service-delivery and instructional approaches to remediate deficits in social competence functioning. One of the most popular of these approaches is *social skills training* (SST), which is designed to remediate children's acquisition and performance deficits and to reduce or eliminate competing problem behaviors (Gresham, Sugai, & Horner, 2001). See Figure 8.1 for a list of steps used in most SST programs. An important question to be answered is whether or not SST is efficacious in

Figure 8.1 Social skills training: treatment integrity checklist.

1. Tell/Coach
   a. Define the skill.
   b. Give examples of the skill.
   c. Discuss steps to perform the skill.
   d. Tell students why the skill is important.
2. Show/Model
   a. Use videos or live modeling to show exemplars and nonexemplars of the skill.
   b. Discuss reasons why models are positive or negative examples of performing the skill.
3. Do/Behavioral Rehearsal
   a. Review skill steps.
   b. Allow students to role-play positive and negative examples of the skill.
   c. Give feedback on student performance.
   d. Discuss reasons why role-plays are positive or negative examples of performing the skill.
4. Practice
   a. Rehearse skill in role-plays.
   b. Encourage students to practice skill in multiple settings.
   c. Assign homework to further encourage practice.
5. Monitor Progress
   a. Ask students to consider how well they perform the skill.
   b. Periodically monitor progress in applying the skill.
6. Generalize
   a. Discuss situations in which the skill should be performed.
   b. Brainstorm ways to improve the skill.
   c. Discuss advanced applications of the skill (e.g., situations that may require modifying the skill).
   d. Discuss when it is easy/difficult to perform the skill.
   e. Review the skill.

remediating social skills deficits. Several narrative and meta-analytic reviews have addressed this question, with some reviews yielding conflicting conclusions.

Narrative Reviews

At least 12 narrative reviews of the SST literature using both group and single-case experimental designs have been conducted since the 1980s (Ager & Cole, 1991; Coleman, Wheeler, & Webber, 1993; Gresham, 1981b, 1985; Hollinger, 1987; Landrum & Lloyd, 1992; Mathur & Rutherford, 1991; R. McIntosh, Vaughn, & Zaragoza, 1991; Olmeda & Kauffman, 2003; Schloss, Schloss, Wood, & Kiel, 1986; Templeton, 1990; Zaragoza, Vaughn, & McIntosh, 1991). These narrative reviews reached the following general conclusions about the efficacy of SST: (a) The most effective SST strategies appear to be some combination of modeling, coaching behavioral rehearsal, and procedures derived from applied behavior analysis; (b) evidence for cognitive-behavioral procedures (e.g., social problem solving, self-instruction) is generally weaker, particularly on direct measures of social behavior in naturalistic settings; and (c) by far the greatest weakness in the SST literature is the absence of consistent, durable gains in prosocial behaviors across situations, settings, and over time (maintenance).

Meta-Analytic Reviews

Eight meta-analyses of the SST literature have been conducted since 1985 (Ang & Hughes, 2001; Beelmann, Pfingsten, & Losel, 1994; C. R. Cook et al., 2008; Gresham, Cook, Crews, & Kern, 2004; Losel & Beelmann, 2003; Quinn, Kavale, Mathur, Rutherford, & Forness, 1999; Schneider, 1992; Schneider & Byrne, 1985). It should be noted that the Gresham et al. (2004) and C. R. Cook et al. (2008) meta-analyses were syntheses of the above six meta-analyses (i.e., they were "mega"-analyses). These meta-analyses focused on children and youth with behavioral difficulties, involved 338 studies, and included over 25,000 children and youth between the ages of 3 and 18 years. We reserve our discussion of the Quinn et al. (1999) meta-analysis for a later section of this chapter because of its methodological problems.

Based on the above-cited meta-analyses, the definition of the construct of social skills appears to be consistent for research synthesis purposes. The meta-analyses suggested that the social skills construct can be divided into three major categories: social interaction, prosocial behavior, and social-cognitive skills. Correlates of social skills fall into two categories: problem behavior (externalizing and internalizing) and academic achievement/performance. These social skills categories and correlates are consistent with other work in the area of social skills conducted

by a number of researchers (Caldarella & Merrell, 1997; Coie, Dodge, & Coppotelli, 1982; Dodge, 1986; Gresham, 2002a; Gresham & Elliott, 2008; H. M. Walker & McConnell, 1995; H. M. Walker et al., 1992).

Gresham et al. (2004) summarized five of the meta-analyses and found a grand mean effect size $r = 0.29$ (range, 0.19–0.40) and Cohen's $d = 0.60$ (range, 0.47–0.89). Using the binomial effect size display (BESD), these data suggest that approximately 65% of the participants in the SST groups improved their social skills compared to only 35% of individuals in the control groups. The BESD shows the effect of group membership (i.e., treatment vs. control students) on the success rate of a given outcome. The BESD is a 2×2 contingency table with the columns representing group status and rows representing success and non-success rates (Rosenthal, Rosnow, & Rubin, 2000). Using Cohen's (1977) conventional standards, an effect size of this magnitude would be considered "medium." Considering these five meta-analyses, it is clear that SST produces practically significant changes in social behavior based on percentages of participants in SST groups that show improvement.

In a subsequent meta-analytic synthesis, C. R. Cook et al. (2008) extended the findings of Gresham et al. (2004) by examining the efficacy of SST with secondary-age students (ages 11 to 19 years). These authors analyzed data from five meta-analyses that involved secondary-age students with or at risk for SBD (Ang & Hughes, 2001; Beelmann et al., 1994; Durlak, Fuhrman, & Lampman, 1991; Losel & Beelmann, 2003; Schneider & Byrne, 1985). Because secondary grades entail both middle and high school students, as well as the fact that youth as young as 11 years of age attend middle school, age 11 was used to demarcate secondary from elementary students. The overall weighted mean effect size across the five meta-analyses was $r = 0.32$, $d = 0.63$ (range = 0.41–0.92). An effect size of this magnitude indicates a medium effect size for SST according to Cohen's (1977) guidelines. Using the BESD, almost two thirds (66%) of secondary-age students improve with SST compared to only 34% of control students.

The majority of studies analyzed across the meta-analyses included random assignment to intervention conditions, which is the most rigorous procedure that can be employed to ensure the internal validity of a particular intervention. Moreover, the five meta-analyses clearly showed that SST produces *practically* important changes in social behavior according to percentage of youth in the SST groups who showed improvement relative to controls.

These findings also support the external validity of SST for students with behavioral difficulties. That is, all five meta-analyses reviewed showed that SST was an effective intervention for students representative of the SBD population. These findings suggest that SST would likely be an effective intervention for students with emotional and/or behavioral problems beyond those included in different meta-analyses—that evidence in the meta-analyses supports generalization across sample characteristics. That is, across the meta-analyses, SST programs were implemented with students with different types of behavioral issues, and comparison of effect size indices suggested similar benefits of SST for individuals with different social, emotional, and behavioral problems.

Quinn et al. (1999) Meta-Analysis

The Quinn et al. meta-analysis of 35 studies is particularly relevant to the SBD population because it was reported to be based entirely on students labeled as emotionally disturbed (ED) under IDEA (1999). Unfortunately, it appears that the 35 studies in this meta-analysis did not meet the more stringent inclusion criteria of the previously described meta-analyses (Christoff, Scott, Kelley, Schlundt, Baer, & Kelly, 1985; Goldstein & Ferrell, 1987) by requiring a control group and either an experimental or quasi-experimental design. Therefore, the results of the Quinn et al. report, an overall mean effect size of $r = 0.10$ ($d = 0.199$) across the 35 studies, are questioned. Using a BESD, an effect size of $r = 0.10$ suggests that 55% of the participants in the SST groups improved and 45% of the controls improved. However, the Quinn et al. effect size of $r = 0.10$ is far below the average effect size of $r = 0.29$ reported in the meta-analyses reviewed earlier. What explains this divergence in the magnitude of effect sizes between the Quinn et al. and other meta-analyses? One influence on effect size estimation is the nature of the dependent measures on which the effect size is based. Approximately 22% of the effect sizes were based on measures of academic achievement ($r = 0.03$). Although academic competence is an important correlate of social competence, aggregation of academic achievement effect sizes in the overall effect for SST is questionable. Moreover, an additional eight effect sizes were based on personality test measures ($r = 0.06$). Thus, almost 40% of the effect size estimates were based on outcome variables that SST was never intended to impact. It appears that many of the effect sizes calculated in the Quinn et al. meta-analysis are tainted theoretically by construct irrelevant variance (see Messick, 1995). Therefore, the meta-analysis performed by Quinn et al. does not appear to be representative of the true population effect size for SST.

Replacement Behavior Training

Replacement Behavior Training (RBT) is an intensive intervention and is designed primarily for students who are weak responders to other intervention strategies. RBT is designed to remediate resistant social skills performance deficits that are accompanied by well-entrenched competing problem behaviors by identifying positive replacement behaviors that serve the same behavioral function as the problem behavior, and to actively teach the student to use the positive replacement behavior instead. RBT requires a functional behavioral assessment (FBA) and a competing behavioral pathways conceptualization of the relationship between prosocial behavior and competing problem behavior (Sugai, Horner, & Gresham, 2002). See Figure 8.2 for a list of steps used in most RBT programs.

Competing Problem Behaviors

Social skills performance deficits are due primarily to motivational variables rather than a lack of knowledge or learning concerning how to enact a particular social skill. One of the most conceptually powerful and empirically established learning principles used to explain the relationship between social skills performance deficits and competing problem behaviors is the *Matching Law* (Herrnstein, 1961, 1970). The Matching Law states that the relative rate of any given behavior matches the relative rate of reinforcement for that behavior. In other words, response rate *matches* reinforcement rate.

Figure 8.2 Replacement Behavior Training: treatment integrity checklist.

1. Identify the problem behavior that will be replaced.
2. Conduct a functional behavioral assessment to determine the function of the problem behavior.
3. Identify a positive behavior that will serve to replace the problem behavior.
   a. This behavior must already be in the student's repertoire (i.e., the student already exhibits the behavior to some degree).
   b. This behavior cannot be more effortful to exhibit than the problem behavior.
   c. The behavior must occur at a rate sufficient to come into contact with contingencies.
   d. The behavior is likely to contact natural contingencies such that the behavior will continue to be reinforced when the intervention is withdrawn.
4. Identify rewards that will effectively reinforce the occurrence of the positive behavior.
   a. Consider applying the same type of reinforcement that was identified as maintaining the problem behavior to the positive replacement behavior.
5. Consistently and immediately deliver reinforcement each time the positive behavior occurs.
6. Consistently withhold reinforcement during occurrences of the problem behavior.

Matching is studied in a concurrent schedules of reinforcement paradigm, which refers to an experimental arrangement in which two or more responses are reinforced according to two or more simultaneous, but quantitatively different, schedules of reinforcement (i.e., concurrently).

Matching involves *"choice behavior"* in that behaviors having a higher rate of reinforcement will be "chosen" more frequently than behaviors reinforced at lower rates. For example, if aggressive behavior is reinforced, on average, every 3 times it occurs (variable ratio 3 or VR-3 schedule of reinforcement) and prosocial behavior is reinforced, on average, every 15 times it occurs (VR-15 schedule of reinforcement), the Matching Law would predict that, on average, aggressive behavior will be chosen (i.e., performed) five times more frequently than prosocial behavior based on the ratio between the two concurrent schedules of reinforcement (15/3 = 5). Research in naturalistic settings has consistently shown that behavior observed under concurrent schedules of reinforcement closely follow the Matching Law (Martens, 1992; Martens & Houk, 1989; Martens, Lochner, & Kelly, 1992; J. Snyder & Stoolmiller, 2002).

Maag (2005) suggested that one way to decrease competing problem behaviors is to teach *positive replacement behaviors,* or Replacement Behavior Training (RBT). RBT may help solve many of the problems described in the social skills training literature such as poor generalization and maintenance, modest effect sizes, and social invalidity of target behavior selection (C. R. Cook et al., 2008; Gresham, 1998; Gresham et al., 2004). RBT seeks to identify *functionally equivalent* prosocial behaviors to replace the competing problem behaviors. Two or more behaviors are functionally equivalent if they produce similar amounts of reinforcement from the environment (R. H. Horner & Billingsley, 1988).

Conceptualization of RBT

Why does RBT work, and what explains its utility in teaching positive replacement behaviors? RBT is based on the principle of *differential reinforcement,* which requires the reinforcement of one response class and withholding or reducing the amount of reinforcement for another response class (J. O. Cooper, Heron, & Heward, 2007). For example, using differential reinforcement, a student may be reinforced when he asks for an item in a pleasant voice but ignored when he makes a request in an aggressive tone. Although several forms of differential reinforcement exist, two forms are the most frequently used in RBT: *differential reinforcement of alternative behavior* (DRA) and *differential reinforcement of incompatible behavior* (DRI). Both DRA and DRI have the effects of strengthening the behavior that is the desired

alternative to or is incompatible with the problem behavior (e.g., appropriate social skills) and simultaneously weakening problem behavior (e.g., aggression).

There are three basic steps in implementing DRA or DRI to increase prosocial behavior and to decrease competing problem behaviors. First, a prosocial alternative or incompatible behavior must be identified to effectively compete with the problem behavior. This prosocial behavior must meet the following criteria: it already exists in the student's repertoire, requires equal or less effort than the competing problem behavior, occurs at a rate that would allow for it to be reinforced, and is likely to be reinforced after the intervention is withdrawn (J. O. Cooper et al., 2007). The second step in using DRA/DRI is to identify and deliver reinforcers for prosocial behaviors that can be delivered immediately and consistently. J. O. Cooper et al. suggest that the magnitude or quality of the reinforcer for behavior is probably less important than its *consistent* delivery and control. The third step in this process is to systematically and consistently withhold reinforcement for the competing problem behavior. In other words, you would "thin" the schedule of reinforcement for problem behavior, which would make the ratio of reinforcement for prosocial behavior and problem behavior greater, thereby inducing the principle of the Matching Law.

A study by Gresham and colleagues demonstrates using DRA to teach social skills in a school setting (Gresham et al., 2006). Four students were taught social skills over a period of 20 weeks, which involved a combination of SST and DRA interventions in the classroom. The SST procedures were delivered in a small-group pullout setting using four basic instruction variables of coaching, modeling, behavioral rehearsal, and performance feedback (see Elliott & Gresham, 1991). All students were classified as having social skills acquisition deficits before the study. The DRA intervention (RBT) consisted of four steps: (a) identify the reinforcer for the competing problem behavior (social attention); (b) identify the reinforcer for the replacement behavior (social attention); (c) specify the DRA time interval (DRA-5 minutes); and (d) eliminate the reinforcer for the competing behavior, and deliver the reinforcer for the replacement behavior instead.

The Gresham et al. (2006) study indicated that students receiving SST and DRA interventions exhibited relatively large decreases in competing problem behaviors and improvement on a measure of teacher-rated social skills (Gresham & Elliott, 1990). These results suggest that a higher intensity or "dosage" of SST than has been reported in the literature produces larger effects on measures of target behaviors and social validation than lower-intensity SST interventions produce. This "dose effect" would seem to argue for simply providing more SST to achieve positive outcomes. Treatment integrity levels, however, may also moderate these findings. The effect of treatment integrity has not been studied extensively in the SST literature.

Positive Peer Reporting

Positive Peer Reporting (PPR) is a peer-mediated social skills intervention used to improve the quality of social interactions and the social status of socially rejected or neglected children. It has been effectively applied with children ages 4 to 16 in a variety of settings including general and special education classrooms and a residential treatment center (Bowers, Cook, Jensen, Snyder, & McEachern, 2008; Bowers, Woods, Carolyn, & Friman, 2000; Ervin, Johnston, & Friman, 1998; Ervin, Miller, & Friman, 1996; Hoff & Ronk, 2006; Johnson-Gros & Shriver, 2006; K. M. Jones, Young, & Friman, 2000; Moroz & Jones, 2002). In PPR, classmates are informed they will be able to earn rewards for reporting a specific classmate's prosocial behavior during a daily reporting session. Next, they are taught to recognize and report prosocial behavior. Examples and nonexamples are provided as models of appropriate praise statements, which must be positive, specific, and genuine. The classmates are then prompted to generate their own examples, and positive or corrective feedback is provided. Finally, the type of reinforcement (e.g., token/points for a class-wide reward or preferred activities/items for individual reporters) is chosen and delivered for each appropriate praise statement reported during the daily reporting session. Treatment effects are monitored through direct observation of social interactions and by sociometric data, such as peer ratings and nominations, which are used to assess changes in peer acceptance. See Figure 8.3 for a list of steps used in most PPR programs.

The goal of PPR is to enhance reinforcement for the selected child's prosocial behaviors by having peers verbally acknowledge these appropriate behaviors and, thereby, increase the performance of similar behaviors in the future. Rather than targeting specific skills, prosocial behaviors are conceptualized as a functional response class in that any positive social behavior can be reported and reinforced (C. H. Skinner, Neddenriep, Robinson, Ervin, & Jones, 2002). This intervention is designed to remediate performance deficits by increasing reinforcement contingent on behaviors already in the child's repertoire but performed infrequently, rather than teaching specific behaviors (i.e., social skills acquisition deficits).

PPR is thought to produce socially valid outcomes by restructuring classroom social ecologies (K. M. Jones et al., 2000; Moroz & Jones, 2002; C. H. Skinner et al., 2002). Research indicates teachers devote more time and

Figure 8.3   Positive Peer Reporting: treatment integrity checklist.

Pre-intervention

1. Inform students that they will be playing a game in which they can earn rewards for noticing and reporting prosocial or "friendly" behavior.
2. Discuss the meaning of prosocial behavior:
   a. Provide examples and nonexamples.
3. Have students provide examples of prosocial behavior, giving positive or corrective feedback.
4. Explain the rules of the game:
   a. A target student will be selected.
   b. Pay attention to the target student during the course of the day.
   c. During a specific period each day, students can earn points toward a reward for reporting instances in which the target student exhibited prosocial behaviors.
5. Determine rewards:
   a. Consider class-wide rewards.
   b. Set a goal for the total number of positive statements.

Intervention

At the beginning of the school day:

1. Remind the class who the target student is for the day.
2. Remind the class to look for positive behaviors displayed by the target student throughout the day or during a certain class period.

During the reporting session:

1. Ask students to raise their hands if they observed the target student displaying positive behavior.
2. Call on students to make praise statements.
3. Give the class a point/token for each appropriate comment reported.
4. Tell the class how many points/tokens they earned today, and remind them of the final goal.
5. Administer rewards when the goal is obtained.

resources responding to disruptive rather than appropriate behavior and have 60% to 90% more interactions with students who have behavior problems (R. H. Thompson, White, & Morgan, 1982). The pattern of interactions establishes an ecology wherein classmates are more likely to attend to and report inappropriate behaviors, a practice that may encourage excessively negative peer evaluations of the students with behavior problems, leading to their social rejection. It should be recalled from our earlier discussion that peer rejection and social isolation are well-established risk factors for the development of SBD (Crews et al., 2007; H. M. Walker & Severson, 2002).

Therefore, in typical classroom ecologies, the children in greatest need of practice with social skills are provided with the fewest opportunities to do so. PPR addresses these issues by explicitly modifying existing contingencies; the selected student's prosocial behaviors are reinforced, whereas classmates receive reinforcement for reporting the student's positive behavior (C. H. Skinner et al., 2002). In addition, PPR influences the social ecology by encouraging classmates to form more positive perceptions of the selected child, thereby establishing protective factors against SBD and related adverse outcomes.

Next, PPR capitalizes on incidental teaching; peers are more likely to notice prosocial behaviors as they naturally occur. A teacher or parent may not observe the occurrence of the behavior due to numerous environmental demands. Prosocial behaviors exhibited by the socially isolated child are more likely noticed by peers, and PPR provides a way for peers to provide reinforcement during the reporting session. Also, the intervention is operating across all times and settings. As peers notice and report incidental prosocial behaviors that occur in novel settings, these behaviors are "trapped" and are more likely to occur in the future (Stokes & Baer, 1977). Moreover, because peer-meditated reinforcement can serve as a type of natural reinforcement contingency (Kohler & Greenwood, 1986), treatment effects are more likely to generalize across settings (Stokes & Osnes, 1989).

Although generalization has been documented (Bowers et al., 2008: Libster, 2008; Morrison & Jones, 2007), researchers have mixed findings for the maintenance, or durability, of treatment gains over time (Bowers et al., 2008, Moroz & Jones, 2002). Bowers and colleagues (2008) assessed maintenance 15, 30, and 45 days after PPR was withdrawn and found that some participants showed maintenance throughout this entire duration, whereas others' gains appeared to deteriorate. Maintenance may need to be actively programmed. In fact, Bowers and colleagues (2008) suggest implementing PPR for a longer duration and/or providing periodic booster sessions, which may enhance the durability of treatment effects.

Literature Review

Grieger, Kauffman, and Grieger (1976) were the first to use peer reporting procedures as a class-wide intervention to improve the social behavior of kindergarteners. Ervin and colleagues (1996) further refined PPR as a dependent contingency to improve the social interactions and peer acceptance of a socially rejected girl in a middle school classroom. Studies conducted at the Nebraska Girls and Boys Town program further established the efficacy of PPR procedures across educational and residential treatment center settings (Bowers, McGinnis,

Friman, & Ervin, 1999; Bowers et al., 2008; Ervin et al., 1998; K. M. Jones et al., 2000).

Other investigators have successfully applied PPR in a variety of settings and with other populations. Hoff and Ronk (2006) used PPR to improve the quality of social interactions in a special education classroom for children with cognitive delays. Johnson-Gros and Shriver (2006) used a combination of PPR and compliance-training procedures to achieve similar effects in a preschool classroom. Finally, Moroz and Jones (2002) demonstrated the efficacy of PPR in elementary school general education classrooms.

Although a complete narrative review of studies is beyond the scope of this chapter (see Johnson-Gros & Shriver, 2006, and Hoff & Ronk, 2006, for reviews), we will highlight Ervin and colleagues (1996), who targeted the social behavior and peer acceptance of Allison, a socially rejected girl in a middle school classroom. At the end of math class, classmates could earn points (exchanged for privileges) for reporting specific instances in which Allison engaged in prosocial behaviors. Allison's peer interactions during an interactive part of class were directly observed and coded as positive, negative, or neutral. At baseline, Allison engaged in high levels of negative interactions and low levels of positive interactions. When the intervention was introduced, negative interactions immediately ceased to near zero, and a corresponding increase in positive interactions was noted. Behavior returned to near baseline levels on treatment removal, and attained previous levels when treatment was reinstated.

Moreover, Ervin et al. (1996) found the intervention produced changes in Allison's social acceptance. Classmates were asked to rate how much they enjoyed working and playing with Allison, and, following the use of PPR, a slight gain in Allison's peer ratings occurred. This finding has been replicated across many, but not all, participants in subsequent PPR studies (Bowers et al., 2000; K. M. Jones et al., 2000). Although improvements in social acceptance are uniformly small, few interventions produce immediate improvements in social acceptance (Bowers et al., 1999; Coie & Dodge, 1983; DuPaul & Eckert, 1994). However, it is important to note that even small changes may indicate practically important treatment effects (Gresham & Lopez, 1996; Hawkins, 1991).

Class-Wide Applications

PPR can be conceptualized as a selected intervention in which a few students are specifically targeted; however, PPR has also been successfully applied as a primary or universal class-wide intervention (Hoff & Ronk, 2006; Morrison & Jones, 2007). In the class-wide variation, there is no selected student; rather, students may report the positive behaviors of any classmate. Morrison and Jones (2007) found class-wide PPR was effective in reducing disruptive events in the classroom, as well as in untrained settings (e.g., lunchroom, during transitions). In addition, fewer students were identified as socially isolated after the intervention, evidencing the beneficial effects of PPR on peer acceptance.

Current research suggests that PPR may be effective for children with a range of social difficulties. However, as with any intervention, PPR will not be universally effective or maintainable for some children (Bowers et al., 2008; Libster, 2008; Moroz & Jones, 2002). Differential treatment effects may be due to externalizing or internalizing competing problem behaviors and may require more individualized interventions, such as RBT. Another reason that some students may not benefit or maintain benefits may be the differences in the social ecologies in which children function. Some children may be surrounded by peers who initiate interactions even if the child does not; other children may initiate positive interactions independently. Although hypotheses have been proposed, determining moderators of the effectiveness of PPR will require future systematic research (Bowers et al., 2008; Libster, 2008; Moroz & Jones, 2002).

Conclusions

This chapter discussed the role of social competence in designing and implementing interventions for students with or at risk for severe behavioral difficulties. A conceptualization of social competence was provided in which the concepts of social skills, social tasks, and social competence were delineated. In this view, social skills were seen as specific behaviors, which, when successfully performed, allow for individuals to successfully accomplish specific social tasks. Social tasks were conceptualized as a *response class,* which includes a group of social behaviors (responses) having different topographies that produce the same effect on the environment (J. O. Cooper et al., 2007). Social competence was seen as *judgments* by significant social agents (e.g., peers, teachers, parents) that these social tasks were successfully accomplished.

An important distinction was made between social skills acquisition deficits versus social skills performance deficits. Acquisition deficits indicate that the individual does not have a particular social skill. These acquisition deficits might arise from deficits in social-cognitive abilities, difficulties in integrating social behavior patterns in a fluent manner, or deficits in appropriate discrimination of social situations. Acquisition deficits therefore require direct instruction of social behavior using evidence-based strategies of modeling, coaching, behavioral rehearsal, and performance feedback (Gresham & Elliott, 2008).

This chapter reviewed six meta-analyses of the SST literature that involved 338 studies and over 25,000 children and youth ages 3 to 18 years. These meta-analyses assumed that students receiving SST have primarily acquisition rather than performance deficits (Gresham et al., 2004). Five of the six meta-analyses showed an average effect size of $d = 0.60$, which indicates that 65% of students who receive SST improve compared to 35% of students who do not receive such training. An effect size of this magnitude is considered to be medium and indicates that most children receiving SST will benefit from this intervention.

The other type of social skills deficit can be classified as performance deficits in which the student fails to perform a particular social skill at acceptable levels even though the student knows how to perform the social skill. Such deficits can be viewed as "won't do" problems and can be best conceptualized as motivational or performance deficits rather than learning or acquisition deficits. PPR is an intervention that is well-suited for the remediation of social skills performance deficits because it assumes that the student knows how to and does perform a specific social skill. PPR is based on the notion that a student's peers notice and report on the student's successful performance of social skills. PPR is based on the principle of social attention as a reinforcer for successful social skills performances. It also takes advantage of the principle of incidental teaching, which allows for the immediate reinforcement of prosocial behavior patterns.

RBT is based on differential reinforcement (DRA or DRI) and incorporates another response class (competing problem behavior) into the social skills intervention process. We used Herrnstein's notion of the Matching Law to explain how and why RBT reduces competing problem behaviors and increases socially skilled behaviors. RBT requires an FBA to determine the function of the competing problem behavior and to identify a socially skilled alternative or incompatible behavior that will serve the same function.

References

Abrams, L., Flood, J., & Phelps, L. (2006). Psychopharmacology in the schools. *Psychology in the Schools, 43,* 493–501.

Achenbach, T. M. (1991). *Integrative guide for the 1991 CBCL/4-18, YRS, & TRF profiles.* Burlington: University of Vermont, Department of Psychiatry.

Ager, C., & Cole, C. (1991). A review of cognitive-behavioral interventions for children and adolescents with behavioral disorders. *Behavioral Disorders, 16,* 276–287.

Algozzine, B. (1977). The emotionally disturbed child: Disturbed or disturbing. *Journal of Abnormal Child Psychology, 5,* 205–211.

American Psychiatric Association. (1994). *Diagnostic and statistical manual of mental disorders* (4th ed.). Washington, DC: American Psychiatric Publishing.

American Psychiatric Association. (2000). *Diagnostic and statistical manual of mental disorders* (4th ed.). Washington, DC: Author.

American Psychological Association [APA] Board of Educational Affairs Task Force on Classroom Violence Directed Against Teachers. (2011). *Understanding and preventing violence directed against teachers.* American Psychological Association. Retrieved from http://www.apa.org/ed/schools/cpse/activities/classroom-violence.aspx

Ang, R., & Hughes, J. (2001). Differential benefits of skills training with antisocial youth based on group composition: A meta-analytic investigation. *School Psychology Review, 31,* 164–185.

Ardoin, S. P., Martens, B. K., & Wolfe, L. A. (1999). Using high-probability instruction sequences with fading to increase student compliance during transitions. *Journal of Applied Behavior Analysis, 32,* 339–351.

Arunachalam, V. (2001). The science behind tradition. *Current Science, 80,* 1272–1275.

Austin, J. L., & Agar, G. (2005). Helping young children follow their teachers' directions: The utility of high-probability command sequences in pre-K and kindergarten classrooms. *Education and Treatment of Children, 28*(3), 222–236.

Baer, D., Wolfe, M., & Risley, T. (1968). Some current dimensions of applied behavior analysis. *Journal of Applied Behavior Analysis, 1,* 91–97.

Baker, J. A., Clark, T. P., Maier, K. S., & Viger, S. (2008). The differential influence of instructional context on the academic engagement of students with behavior problems. *Teaching and Teacher Education, 24,* 1876–1883.

Bambara, L. M., Koger, F., Katzer, T., & Davenport, T. A. (1995). Embedding choice in the context of daily routines: An experimental case study. *Journal of the Association for Persons with Severe Handicaps, 20,* 185–195.

Banda, D. R., & Kubina, R. M., Jr. (2006). The effects of a high-probability request sequencing technique in enhancing transition behaviors. *Education and Treatment of Children, 29*(3), 507–516.

Bandura, A. (1976). Self-reinforcement: Theoretical and methodological considerations. *Behaviorism, 4*(2), 135–155.

Bandura, A. (1979). Self-efficacy: Toward a unifying theory of behavioral change. *Psychological Review, 84,* 191–215.

Bandura, A. (1993). Perceived self-efficacy in cognitive development and functioning. *Educational Psychologist, 28,* 117–148.

Barney, T., Klovin, I., & Bhate, S. R. (1981). School phobia: A therapeutic trial with clomipramine and short-term outcome. *British Journal of Psychiatry, 138,* 110–122.

Barrish, H., Saunders, M., & Wolf, M. M. (1969). Good Behavior Game: Effects of individual contingencies for group consequences on disruptive behavior in a classroom. *Journal of Applied Behavior Analysis, 2,* 119–124.

Beck, A. T., Rush, A. J., Shaw, B. F., & Emery, G. (1979). *Cognitive therapy of depression.* New York: Guilford Press.

Beelmann, A., Pfingsten, U., & Losel, F. (1994). Effects of training social competence in children: A meta-analysis of recent evaluation studies. *Journal of Clinical Child Psychology, 23,* 260–271.

Belfiore, P. J., Basile, S. P., & Lee, D. L. (2008). Using a high-probability sequence to increase classroom compliance: The role of behavioral momentum. *Journal of Behavioral Education, 17,* 160–171.

Belfiore, P. J., Lee, D. L., Scheeler, M. C., & Klein, D. (2002). Implications of behavioral momentum and academic achievement for students with behavior disorders: Theory, application, and practice. *Psychology in the Schools, 39*(2), 171–179.

Belfiore, P. J., Lee, D. L., Vargas, A. U., & Skinner, C. H. (1997). Effects of high-preference single-digit mathematics problem completion on multiple-digit mathematics problem performance. *Journal of Applied Behavior Analysis, 30*, 327–330.

Bernhardt, A., & Forehand, R. (1975). The effects of labeled and unlabeled praise upon lower and middle class children. *Journal of Experimental Child Psychology, 19*, 536–543.

Bernstein, G. A., Borchardt, C. M., Perwin, A. R., Crosby, R. D., Kushner, M. G., Thuras, P. D., et al. (2000). Imipramine plus cognitive behavioral therapy in treatment of school refusal. *Journal of the American Academy of Child and Adolescent Psychiatry, 39*, 276–283.

Bernstein, G. A., Garfinkel, B. D., & Borchardt, C. M. (1990). Comparative studies of pharmachotherapy for school refusal. *Journal of the American Academy of Child and Adolescent Psychiatry, 29*, 773–781.

Biederman, J. (1987). Clonazepam in the treatment of prepubertal children with panic-like symptoms. *Journal of Clinical Psychiatry, 1*, 38–41.

Biglan, A., & Dow, M.G. (1981). Toward a second-generation model: A problem-specific approach. In L. P. Rehm (Ed.), *Behavior therapy for depression: Present status and future directions* (pp. 97–131). New York: Academic Press.

Birmaher, B., Axelson, D. A., Monk, K., Kalas, C., Clark, D. B., Ehmann, M., et al. (2003). Fluoxetine for the treatment of childhood anxiety disorders. *Journal of the American Academy of Child and Adolescent Psychiatry, 42*, 415–423.

Blick, D. W., & Test, D. W. (1987). Effects of self-recording on high-school students' on-task behavior. *Learning Disability Quarterly, 10*, 203–213.

Boardman, A. G., Arguelles, M. E., Vaughn, S., Hughes, M. T., & Klingner, J. (2005). Special education teachers' views of research-based practices. *Journal of Special Education, 39*, 168–180.

Bowers, F., Cook, C.R., Jensen, M.E., Snyder, T., & McEachern, A. (2008). Generalization and maintenance of positive peer reporting intervention for peer-rejected youth. *International Journal of Cognitive Behavior Therapy, 4*, 230–246.

Bowers, F. E., McGinnis, J. C., Friman, P. C., & Ervin, R. A. (1999). Merging research and practice: The example of positive peer reporting applied to social rejection. *Education and Treatment of Children, 22*, 218–226.

Bowers, F. E., Woods, D. W., Carolyn, W. D., & Friman, P. C. (2000). Using positive peer reporting to improve the social interactions and acceptance of socially isolated adolescents in residential care: A systematic replication. *Journal of Applied Behavioral Analysis, 33*, 239–242.

Braconnier, A., Le Coent, R., & Cohen, D. (2003). Paroxine versus clomipramine in adolescents with severe major depression: A double-blind, randomized, multicenter trial. *Journal of the American Academy of Child and Adolescent Psychiatry, 42*, 22–29.

Brent, D. A., Holder, D., Kolko D. J., Birmaher, B., Baugher, M., & Roth, C., et al. (1997). A clinical psychotherapy trial for adolescent depression comparing cognitive, family, and supportive therapy. *Archives of General Psychiatry, 54*, 877–885.

Bronfenbrenner, U. (1979). *The ecology of human development.* Cambridge, MA: Harvard University Press.

Brophy, J., & Good, T. L. (1986). Teacher behavior and student achievement. In M. C. Wittrock (Ed.), *Handbook of research on teaching* (3rd ed., pp. 328–375). New York: Macmillan.

Brouwers, A., & Tomic, W. (2000). A longitudinal study of teacher burnout and perceived self-efficacy in classroom management. *Teaching and Teacher Education, 16*, 239–253.

Bullock, C., & Normand, M. P. (2006). The effects of a high-probability instruction sequence and response-independent reinforcer delivery on child compliance. *Journal of Applied Behavior Analysis, 39*(4), 495–499.

Burke, M., Hagan-Burke, S., & Sugai, G. (2003). The efficacy of function-based interventions for students with learning disabilities who exhibit escape-motivated behaviors: Preliminary results from a single-case experiment. *Learning Disability Quarterly, 26*, 15–25.

Burns, B. J., Costello, E. J., Angold, A., Tweed, D., Stangle, D., Farmer, E. M. Z., et al. (1995). Children's mental health service use across service sectors. *Health Affairs, 14*, 148–159.

Burns, M. K., & Ysseldyke, J. E. (2009). Reported prevalence of evidence-based instructional practices in special education. *Journal of Special Education, 43*, 3–11.

Caldarella, P., & Merrell, K. (1997). Common dimensions of social skills in children and adolescents: taxonomy of positive social behaviors. *School Psychology Review, 26*, 265–279.

Callahan, K., & Radenmacher, J. A. (1999). Using self-management strategies to increase the on-task behavior of a student with autism. *Journal of Positive Behavior Interventions, 1*, 117–122.

Caprara, G., Barbaranelli, C., Pastorelli, C., Bandura, A., & Zimbardo, P. (2000). Prosocial foundations of children's academic achievement. *Psychological Science, 11*, 302–305.

Cardemil, E. V., Reivich, K. J., & Seligman, E. P. (2002). The prevention of depressive symptoms in low-income minority middle school students. *Prevention and Treatment, 5*, 8–38.

Carlson, J. I., Luiselli, J. K., Slyman, A., & Markowski, A. (2008). Choice-making as intervention for public disrobing children with developmental disabilities. *Journal of Positive Behavior Intervention, 10*, 86–90.

Carnine, D. W. (1976). Effects of two teacher-presentation rates on off-task behavior, answering correctly, and participation. *Journal of Applied Behavior Analysis, 9*, 199–206.

Carnine, D. (1997). Bridging the research-to-practice gap. *Exceptional Children, 63*, 513–521.

Carr, E. G., & Carlson, J. I. (1993). Reduction of severe behavior problems in the community using multicomponent treatment approach. *Journal of Applied Behavior Analysis, 26*, 157–172.

Carr, J. E., Nicolson, A. C., & Higbee, T. S. (2000). Evaluation of a brief multiple-stimulus preference assessment in a naturalistic context. *Journal of Applied Behavior Analysis, 33*, 353–357.

Carter, D. R., & Horner, R. H. (2007). Adding functional behavioral assessment to First Step to Success. *Journal of Positive Behavior Interventions, 9*, 229–238.

Carter, E. W., Sisco, L. G., Brown, L., Brickham, D., & Al-Khabbaz, Z. A. (2008). Peer interactions and academic engagement of youth with developmental disabilities in inclusive middle and high school classrooms. *American Journal on Mental Retardation, 113*, 479–494.

Chabris, C., & Simons, D. (2010). *The invisible gorilla: And other ways our intuitions deceive us*. New York: Crown.

Chambless, D. L., & Hollon, S. D. (1998). Defining empirically supported therapies. *Journal of Consulting and Clinical Psychology, 66*, 7–18.

Chard, D. J., Cook, B. G., & Tankersley, M. (2013). *Research-based strategies for improving outcomes in academics*. Upper Saddle River, NJ: Pearson.

Chard, D. J., Ketterlin-Geller, L. R., Baker, S. K., Doabler, C., & Apichatabutra, C. (2009). Repeated reading interventions for students with learning disabilities: Status of the evidence. *Exceptional Children, 75*, 263–281.

Cheney, D., Blum, C., & Walker, B. (2004). An analysis of leadership teams' perceptions of positive behavior support and the outcomes of typically developing and at-risk students in their schools. *Assessment for Effective Intervention, 30*, 7–24.

Cheney, D., Flower, A., & Templeton, T. (2008). Applying response to intervention metrics in the social domain for students at risk for developing emotional and behavioral disorders, *Journal of Special Education, 42*, 108–126.

Christensen, L., Young, K., & Marchant, M. (2004). The effects of a peer-mediated positive behavior support program on socially appropriate classroom behavior. *Education and Treatment of Children, 27*, 199–234.

Christoff, K. A., Scott, W. O. N., Kelley, M. L., Schlundt, D., Baer, G., & Kelly, J. A. (1985). Social skills and social problem-solving for shy young adolescents. *Behavior Therapy, 16*, 468–477.

Clarke-Edmands, S. (2004). *S.P.I.R.E.®*. Cambridge, MA: Educators Publishing Service.

Clonan, S., McDougal, J., Clark, K., & Davison, S. (2007). Use of office discipline referrals in school-wide decision making: A practical example. *Psychology in the Schools, 44*(1), 19–27.

Cohen, J. (1977). *Statistical power analysis for the behavioral sciences* (rev. ed.). New York: Academic Press.

Coie, J. D., & Dodge, K. A. (1983). Continuities and changes in children's social status: A five-year longitudinal study. *Merrill-Palmer Quarterly, 29*, 261–282.

Coie, J., Dodge, K., & Coppotelli, H. (1982). Dimensions and types of social status: A cross-age perspective. *Developmental Psychology, 18*, 557–570.

Cole, C. L., & Levinson, T. R. (2002). Effects of within-activity choices on the challenging behavior of children with severe developmental disabilities. *Journal of Positive Behavior Interventions, 4*, 29–37.

Coleman, M., Wheeler, L., & Webber, J. (1993). Research on interpersonal problem-solving training: A review. *Remedial and Special Education, 14*, 25–36.

Collins, K. A., Westra, H. A., Dozois, D. J., & Burns, D. D. (2004). Gaps in accessing treatment for anxiety and depression: Challenges for the delivery of care. *Clinical Psychology Review, 24*, 583–616.

Colvin, G. (2004). *Managing the cycle of acting-out behavior in the classroom*. Eugene, OR: Behavior Associates.

Colvin, G., Sugai, G., Good, R. H., III, & Lee, Y. Y. (1997). Using active supervision and precorrection to improve transition behaviors in an elementary school. *School Psychology Quarterly, 12*, 344–363.

Colvin, G., Sugai, G., & Patching, B. (1993). Pre-correction: An instructional approach for managing predictable problem behaviors. *Intervention in School and Clinic, 28*, 143–150.

Committee for Children. (2007). *Second steps violence prevention*. Seattle, WA: Author.

Connell, M. C., & Carta, J. J. (1993). Building independence during in-class transitions: Teaching in-class transition skills to preschoolers with developmental delays through choral-response-based self-assessment and contingent praise. *Education and Treatment of Children, 16*(2), 160–174.

Conroy, M. A., Sutherland, K. S., Snyder, A., Al-Hendaawi, M., & Vo, A. (2009). Creating a positive classroom atmosphere: Teachers' use of effective praise and feedback. *Beyond Behavior, 18*, 18–26.

Conroy, M. A., Sutherland, K. S., Snyder, A. L., & Marsh, S. (2008). Classwide interventions: Effective instruction makes a difference. *Teaching Exceptional Children, 40*(6), 24–30.

Cook, B. G., Landrum, T. J., Tankersley, M., Kauffman, J. M. (2003). Bringing research to bear on practice: Effecting evidence-based instruction for students with emotional or behavioral disorders. *Education and Treatment of Children, 26*, 325–361.

Cook, B. G., & Schirmer, B. R. (2006). An overview and analysis of the role of evidence-based practices in special education. In B. G. Cook & B. R. Schirmer (Eds.), *What is special about special education: The role of evidence-based practices* (pp. 175–185). Austin, TX: Pro-Ed.

Cook, B. G., & Smith, G. J. (2012). Leadership and instruction: Evidence-based practices in special education. In J. B. Crockett, B. S. Billingsley, & M. L. Boscardin (Eds.), *Handbook of leadership and administration for special education*. London: Routledge.

Cook, B. G., & Tankersley, M. (Eds.). (2013). *Research-based practices in special education*. Upper Saddle River, NJ: Pearson.

Cook, B. G., Tankersley, M., Cook, L., & Landrum, T. J. (2008). Evidence-based practices in special education: Some practical considerations. *Intervention in School & Clinic, 44*(2), 69–75.

Cook, B. G., Tankersley, M., & Harjusola-Webb, S. (2008). Evidence-based special education and professional wisdom: Putting it all together. *Intervention in School and Clinic, 44*, 105–111.

Cook, C. R., Gresham, F. M., Kern, L., Barreras, R.B., Thornton, S., & Crews, S. D. (2008). Social skills training with secondary EBD students: A review and analysis of the meta-analytic literature. *Journal of Emotional and Behavioral Disorders, 16*, 131–144.

Cook, L., Cook, B. G., Landrum, T. J., & Tankersley, M. (2008). Examining the role of group experimental research in establishing evidenced-based practices. *Intervention in School & Clinic, 44*(2), 76–82.

Cook, T. D., Habib, F. N., Phillips, M., Settersten, R. A., Shagle, S. C., & Degimencioglu, S. M. (1999). Comer's school development program in Prince George's County, Maryland: A theory-based evaluation. *American Educational Research Journal, 36,* 543–597.

Cooper, J. O., Heron, T. E., & Heward, W. L. (2007). *Applied behavior analysis* (2nd ed.). Upper Saddle River, NJ: Merrill/Pearson.

Costello, E. J., Erkanli, A., & Angold, A. (2006). Is there an epidemic of child or adolescent depression? *Journal of Child Psychology and Psychiatry, 47,* 1263–1271.

Council for Exceptional Children. (2009). *What every special educator must know: Ethics, standards, and guidelines* (6th ed.). Arlington, VA: Council for Exceptional Children.

Coyle, C., & Cole, P. (2004). A videotaped self-modeling and self-monitoring treatment program to decrease off-task behavior in children with autism. *Journal of Intellectual & Developmental Disability, 29,* 3–15.

Crews, S. D., Bender, H., Gresham, F. M., Kern, L., Vanderwood, M., & Cook, C. R. (2007). Risk and protective factors of emotional and/or behavioral disorders in children and adolescents: A "mega"-analytic synthesis. *Behavioral Disorders, 32,* 64–77.

Crone, D. A., Horner, R. H., & Hawken, L. S. (2004). *Responding to problem behavior in schools: The behavior education program.* New York: Guilford.

Cullinan, D., & Sabornie, E. J. (2004). Characteristics of emotional disturbance in middle and high school students. *Journal of Emotional and Behavioral Disorders, 12,* 157–167.

Curry, J. F. (2001). Specific psychotherapies for childhood and adolescent depression. *Biological Psychiatry, 49,* 1091–1100.

Dacy, B. J. S., Nihalani, P. K., Cestone, C. M., & Robinson, D. H. (2011). (Lack of) support for prescriptive statements in teacher education textbooks. *The Journal of Educational Research, 104,* 1–6.

Dammann, J. E., & Vaughn, S. (2001). Science and sanity in special education. *Behavioral Disorders, 27,* 21–29.

Darch, C., & Gersten, R. (1985). The effects of teacher presentation rate and praise on LD students' oral reading performance. *British Journal of Educational Psychology, 55,* 295–303.

Darch, C. B., & Thorpe, H. W. (1977). The principal game: A group consequence procedure to increase classroom on-task behavior. *Psychology in the Schools, 14,* 341–347.

Darveaux, D. X. (1984). The good behavior game plus merit: Controlling disruptive behavior and improving student motivation. *School Psychology Review, 13,* 510–514.

Dattilo, J., & Rusch, F. R. (1985). Effects of choice on leisure participation for persons with severe handicaps. *The Association for Persons with Severe Handicaps, 10,* 194–199.

Davies, G., McMahon, R., Flessati, E., & Tiedemann, G. (1984). Verbal rationales and modeling as adjuncts to a parenting technique for child compliance. *Child Development, 55,* 1290–1298.

Davis, C. A., Brady, M. P., Hamilton, R., McEvoy, M. A., & Williams, R. E. (1994). Effects of high-probability requests on the social interactions of young children with severe disabilities. *Journal of Applied Behavior Analysis, 27*(4), 619–637.

Davis, C. A., Brady, M. P., Williams, R. E., & Hamilton, R. (1992). Effects of high-probability requests on the acquisition and generalization of responses to requests in young children with behavior disorders. *Journal of Applied Behavior Analysis, 25*(4), 905–916.

Davis, C. A., & Reichle, J. E. (1996). Variant and invariant high-probability requests: Increasing appropriate behaviors in children with emotional-behavioral disorders. *Journal of Applied Behavior Analysis, 29*(4), 471–482.

Davis, C. A., Reichle, J. E., & Southard, K. L. (2001). High-probability requests and preferred item as a distracter: Increasing successful transitions in children with problem behavior. *Education and Treatment of Children, 23*(4), 423–440.

DeBaryshe, D., Patterson, G., & Capaldi, D. (1993). A performance model for academic achievement in early adolescent boys. *Developmental Psychology, 29,* 795–804.

Deno, S. L. (2006). Developments in curriculum-based measurement. In B. G. Cook & B. R. Schirmer (Eds.), *What is special about special education: The role of evidence-based practices* (pp. 100–112). Austin, TX: Pro-Ed.

Depry, R. L., & Sugai, G. (2002). The effect of active supervision and pre-correction on minor behavioral incidents in a sixth grade general education classroom. *Journal of Behavioral Education, 11,* 255–267.

Dickson, D. (2003). Let's not get too romantic about traditional knowledge. *Science Development Network.* Retrieved from http://www.scidev.net/en/editorials/lets-not-get-too-romantic-about-traditional-knowl.html

DiGangi, S. A., Maag, J. W., & Rutherford, R. B. (1991). Self-graphing of on-task behavior: Enhancing the reactive effects of self-monitoring on on-task behavior and academic performance. *Learning Disability Quarterly, 14,* 221–230.

Diken, I. H., & Rutherford, R. B. (2005). First Step to Success Early Intervention Program: A study of effectiveness with Native-American children. *Education and Treatment of Children, 28,* 444–465.

Dinkes, R., Kemp, J., & Baum, K. (2009). *Indicators of School Crime and Safety: 2008* (NCES 2009–022/NCJ 226343). Washington, DC: National Center for Education Statistics, Institute of Education Sciences, U.S. Department of Education, and Bureau of Justice Statistics, Office of Justice Programs, U.S. Department of Justice.

Dinkes, R., Kemp, J., Baum, K., & Snyder, T. (2008). *Indicators of school crime and safety: 2008.* Washington, DC: National Center for Education Statistics, Institute of Education Sciences, U.S. Department of Education, and Bureau of Justice Statistics, Office of Justice Programs, U.S. Department of Justice.

DiPerma, J., & Elliott, S.N. (2000). *Academic competence evaluation scales.* San Antonio, TX: Psychological Corporation.

DiPerma, J., & Elliott, S. N. (2002). Promoting academic enablers to improve student achievement: An introduction to the mini-series. *School Psychology Review, 31,* 293–297.

DiPerma, J. C., Volpe, R. J., & Elliott, S. N. (2002). A model of academic enablers and elementary reading/language arts achievement. *School Psychology Review, 31,* 298–312.

Dishion, T. J., & Patterson, G. R. (2006). The development and ecology of antisocial behavior in children and adolescents. In D. Cicchetti & D. J. Cohen (Eds.), *Developmental psychopathology* (2nd ed., pp. 503–541). Hoboken, NJ: Wiley.

Dodge, K. (1986). A social information processing model of social competence in children. In M. Perlmutter (Ed.), *Minnesota symposium on child psychology* (Vol. 18, pp. 77–125). Hillsdale, NJ: Erlbaum.

Downing, J. A. (2002). Individualized behavior contracts. *Intervention in School and Clinic, 37,* 168–172.

Doyle, W. (1986). Classroom organization and management. In M. C. Wittrock (Ed.), *Handbook of research on teaching* (3rd ed., pp. 392–431). New York: Macmillan.

Drasgow, E., & Yell, M. L. (2001). Functional behavioral assessments: Legal requirements and challenges. *The School Psychology Review, 30,* 239–251.

Drummond, T. (1994). *The Student Risk Screening Scale (SRSS).* Grants Pass, OR: Josephine County Mental Health Program.

Dryfoos, J. (1990). *Adolescents at risk: Prevalence and prevention.* New York: Oxford University Press.

Ducharme, J. M., Atkinson, L., & Poulton, L. (2001). Errorless compliance training with physically abusive mothers: A single-case approach. *Child Abuse and Neglect, 6,* 855–868.

Ducharme, J. M., & DiAdamo, C. (2005). An errorless approach to management of child noncompliance in a special education setting. *School Psychology Review, 34,* 107–115.

Ducharme, J. M., DiPadova, T., & Ashworth, M. (2010). Errorless compliance training to reduce extreme conduct problems and intrusive control strategies in home and school settings. *Clinical Case Studies, 9,* 16.

Ducharme, J. M., & Drain, T. (2004). Errorless academic compliance training: Improving generalized cooperation with parental requests in children with autism. *Journal of the American Academy of Child and Adolescent Psychiatry, 43,* 469–487.

Ducharme, J. M., & Harris, K. (2005). Errorless embedding for children with on-task and conduct difficulties: Rapport-based, success-focused intervention in the classroom. *Behavior Therapy, 36,* 213–222.

Ducharme, J., Harris, K., Milligan, K., & Pontes, E. (2003). Sequential evaluation of reinforced compliance and graduated request delivery for the treatment of noncompliance in children with developmental disabilities. *Journal of Autism and Developmental Disabilities, 33,* 519–526.

Ducharme, J., & Popynick, M. (1993). Errorless compliance to parental requests: Treatment effects and generalization. *Behavior Therapy, 24,* 209–226.

Ducharme, J., Popynick, M., Pontes, E., & Steele, S. (1996). Errorless compliance to parental requests: Group parent training with parent observation data and long-term follow-up. *Behavior Therapy, 27,* 353–372.

Ducharme, J., Sanjuan, E., & Drain, T. (2007). Errorless compliance training: Success-focused behaviors treatment of children with Asperger syndrome. *Behavior Modification, 31,* 329–346.

Ducharme, J. M., & Worling, D. E. (1994). Behavioral momentum and stimulus fading in the acquisition and maintenance of child compliance in the home. *Journal of Applied Behavior Analysis, 27*(4), 639–647.

Dunlap, G., DePerczel, M., Clarke, S., Wilson, D., Wright, S., et al. (1994). Choice making to promote adaptive behavior for students with emotional and behavioral challenges. *Journal of Applied Behavior Analysis, 27,* 505–518.

Dunlap, G., White, R., Vera, A., Wilson, D., & Panacek, L. (1996). The effects of multi-component, assessment-based curricular modifications on the classroom behavior of children with emotional and behavioral disorders. *Journal of Behavioral Education, 6,* 481–500.

DuPaul, G. J., & Eckert, T. L. (1994). The effects of social skills curricula: Now you see them, now you don't. *School Psychology Quarterly, 9,* 113–132.

Durlak, J. A., Fuhrman, T., & Lampman, C. (1991). Effectiveness of cognitive-behavior therapy for maladapting children: A meta-analysis. *Psychological Bulletin, 110,* 204–214.

Dweck, C. S. (2007). The perils and promises of praise. *Educational Leadership, 65*(2), 34–39.

Dwyer, K. P., Osher, D., & Warger, W. (1998). *Early warning, timely response: A guide to safe schools.* Washington, DC: U.S. Department of Education.

Dyer, K. (1987). The competition of autistic stereotyped behavior with usual and specially assessed reinforcers. *Research in Developmental Disabilities, 8,* 607–626.

Dyer, K., Dunlap, G., & Winterling, V. (1990). Effects of choice making on the serious problem behaviors of students with severe handicaps. *Journal of Applied Behavior Analysis, 23,* 515–524.

Eddy, J. M., Reid, J. B., & Curry, V. (2002). The etiology of youth antisocial behavior, delinquency and violence and a public health approach to prevention. In M. Shinn, H. Walker, & G. Stoner (Eds.), *Interventions for academic and behavior problems: II. Preventive and remedial approaches.* Bethesda, MD: National Association for School Psychologists.

Elksnin, L., & Elksnin, N. (2006). *Teaching social-emotional skills at school and home.* Denver: Love Publishing.

Elliott, S. N., & Gresham, F. M. (1991). *Social skills intervention guide.* Bloomington, MN: Pearson Assessments.

Elliott, S. N., & Gresham, F. M. (2007). *Social skills improvement system: Classwide intervention program.* Bloomington, MN: Pearson Assessments.

Embry, D. D. (2002). The Good Behavior Game: A best practice candidate as a universal behavioral vaccine. *Clinical Child and Family Psychology Review, 5,* 273–297.

Emslie, G., Heiligenstein, J. H., Wagner, K. D., Hoog, S. L., Ernest, D. E., Brown, E., et al. (2002). Fluoxetine for acute treatment of depression in children and adolescents: A placebo-controlled randomized clinical trial. *Journal of the American Academy of Child and Adolescent Psychiatry, 41,* 1205–1215.

Engelmann, S., & Colvin, G. (1983). *Generalized compliance training: A direct-instruction program for managing severe behavior problems.* Austin: Pro-Ed.

Epstein, M. H., & Walker, H. M. (2002). Special education: Best practices and First Step to Success. In B. J. Burns & K. Hoagwood (Eds.), *Community treatment for youth: Evidence-based interventions for severe emotional and behavioral disorders* (pp. 179–197). New York: Oxford University Press.

Ervin, R. A., Johnston, E. S., & Friman, P.C. (1998). Positive peer reporting to improve the social interactions of a socially rejected girl. *Proven Practice: Prevention and Remediation Solutions for Schools, 1,* 17–21.

Ervin, R. A., Miller, P. M., & Friman, P. C. (1996). Feed the hungry bee: Using positive peer reports to improve the social interactions and acceptance of a socially rejected girl in residential care. *Journal of Applied Behavior Analysis, 29,* 251–253.

Ervin, R. A., Schaughency, E., Goodman, S. D., McGlinchey, M. T., & Matthews, A. (2006). Merging research and practice agendas to address reading and behavior school-wide. *School Psychology Review 35,* 198–223.

Evans, I. M., & Meyer, L. H. (1990). Toward a science in support of meaningful outcomes: A response to Horner et al. *Journal of the Association for Persons with Severe Handicaps, 15,* 133–135.

Evans, M. D., Hollon, S. D., DeRubeis, R. J., Piasecki, J. M., Grove, W. M., Garvey, M. J., et al. (1992). Differential relapse following cognitive therapy and pharmacotherapy for depression. *Archives of General Psychiatry, 49,* 802–808.

Fairbanks, S., Sugai, G., Guardino, D., & Lathrop, M. (2007). Response to intervention: Examining classroom behavior support in second grade. *Exceptional Children, 73,* 288–310.

Filter, K. J., & Horner, R. H. (2009). Function-based academic interventions for problem behavior. *Education and Treatment of Children, 32,* 1–19.

Fishbein, J. E., & Wasik, B. H. (1981). Effect of the Good Behavior Game on disruptive library behavior. *Journal of Applied Behavior Analysis, 14,* 89–93.

Fisher, W. W., Adelinis, J. D., Thompson, R. H., Worsdell, A. S., & Zarcone, J. R. (1998). Functional analysis and treatment of destructive behavior maintained by termination of "don't" (and symmetrical "do") requests. *Journal of Applied Behavior Analysis, 31*(3), 339–356.

Fitzpatrick, M., & Knowlton, E. (2009). Bringing evidence-based self-directed intervention practices to the trenches for students with emotional and behavioral disorders. *Preventing School Failure, 53,* 253–266.

Ford, A., Olmi, J., Edwards, R., & Tingstrom, D. (2001). The sequential introduction of compliance training components with elementary-aged children in general education classroom settings. *School Psychology Quarterly, 16,* 142–157.

Forehand, R., & McMahon, R. (1981). *Helping the non-compliant child.* New York: Guilford Press.

Forehand, R., & Scarboro, M. (1975). An analysis of children's oppositional behavior. *Journal of Abnormal Child Psychology, 3,* 27–31.

Forehand, R., Wells, K., & Sturgis, E. (1978). Predictors of child non-compliant behaviors in the home. *Journal of Consulting and Clinical Psychology, 46,* 179.

Forness, S. R., Freeman, S. F., & Paparella, T. (2006). Recent randomized clinical trials comparing behavioral interventions and psychopharmacologic treatments for students with EBD. *Behavioral Disorders, 31,* 284–296.

Freedman, D. H. (2010). *Wrong: Why experts keep failing us—and how to know when not to trust them.* New York: Little, Brown.

Frey, K. S., Hirschstein, M. K., & Guzzo, B. A. (2000). Second step: Preventing aggression by promoting social competence. *Journal of Emotional and Behavioral Disorders, 8,* 102–112.

Gable, R. A., Hester, P. H., Rock, M. L., & Hughes, K. G. (2009). Back to basics: Rules, praise, ignoring, and reprimands revisited. *Intervention in School and Clinic, 44,* 195–205.

Gast, D. L. (2010). *Single subject research in behavioral sciences.* New York: Routledge.

Geller, B., Reising, D., Leonard, H. L., Riddle, M. A., & Walsh, B. T. (1999). Critical review of tricyclic antidepressant use in children and adolescents. *Journal of the American Academy of Child and Adolescent Psychiatry, 38,* 513–516.

Gersten, R., Fuchs, L. S., Compton, D., Coyne, M., Greenwood, C., & Innocenti, M. S. (2005). Quality indicators for group experimental and quasi-experimental research in special education. *Exceptional Children, 71,* 149–164.

Gillham, J. E., Shatte, A. J., & Freres, D. R. (2000). Preventing depression: A review of cognitive-behavioral and family interventions. *Applied & Preventive Psychology, 9,* 63–88.

Gilliam, W. S., & Shahar, G. (2006). Prekindergarten expulsion and suspension: Rates and predictors in one state. *Infants and Young Children, 19,* 228–245.

Gittelman-Klein, R., & Klein, D. F. (1971). Controlled imipramine treatment of school phobia. *Archives of General Psychiatry, 25,* 204–207.

Goldstein, H., & Ferrell, D. R. (1987). Augmenting communicative interaction between handicapped and nonhandicapped preschool children. *Journal of Speech and Hearing Disorders, 52,* 200–211.

Golly, A., Sprague, J., Walker, H. M., Beard, K., & Gorham, G. (2000). The First Step to Success program: An analysis of outcomes with identical twins across multiple baselines. *Behavioral Disorders, 25,* 170–182.

Golly, A. M., Stiller, B., & Walker, H. M. (1998). First Step to Success: Replication and social validation of an early intervention program. *Journal of Emotional and Behavioral Disorders, 6,* 243–250.

Good, R. H., Bank, N., & Watson, J. M. (Eds.). (2003). *Indicadores dinamicos del exito en la lectura* [Dynamic indicators of basic early literacy skills]. Eugene, OR: Institute for the Development of Educational Achievement.

Goodman, R. (1997). The Strengths and Difficulties Questionnaire: A research note. *Journal of Child Psychology and Psychiatry, 38,* 581–586.

Goodman, R. (2001). Psychometric properties of the Strengths and Difficulties Questionnaire (SDQ). *Journal of the American Academy of Child and Adolescent Psychiatry, 40,* 1337–1345.

Goodman, R., Meltzer, H., & Bailey, V. (1998). The Strengths and Difficulties Questionnaire: A pilot study on the validity of the self-report version. *European Child and Adolescent Psychiatry, 7,* 125–130.

Gottfredson, D. C., Gottfredson, G. D., & Hybl, L. G. (1993). Managing adolescent behavior: A multiyear, multischool study. *American Educational Research Journal, 30,* 179–215.

Graae, F., Milner, J., Rizzotto, L., & Klein, R. G. (1994). Clonazepam in childhood anxiety disorders. *Journal of the American Academy of Child and Adolescent Psychiatry, 33,* 372–376.

Grandy, S. E., & Peck, S. M. (1997). The use of functional assessment and self-management with a first grader. *Family Behavior Therapy, 19,* 29–43.

Greenwood, C. R., & Abbott, M. (2001). The research-to-practice gap in special education. *Teacher Education and Special Education, 24,* 276–289.

Greenwood, C. R., Hart, B., Walker, D., & Risley, T. (1994). The opportunity to respond and academic performance revisited: A behavioral theory of developmental retardation and its prevention. In R. Gardner, D. M. Sainato, J. O. Cooper, T. E. Heron, W. L. Heward, J. W. Eshleman, & T. A. Grossi (Eds.), *Behavior analysis in education: Focus on measurably superior instruction* (pp. 213–223). Pacific Grove, CA: Brooks/ Cole.

Greenwood, C. R., Horton, B. T., & Utley, C. A. (2002). Academic engagement: Current perspectives on research and practice. *School Psychology Review, 31,* 328–349.

Gresham, F. M. (1981a). Assessment of children's social skills. *Journal of School Psychology, 19,* 120–134.

Gresham, F. M. (1981b). Social skills training with handicapped children: A review. *Review of Educational Research, 51,* 139–176.

Gresham, F. M. (1983). Social validity in the assessment of children's social skills: Establishing standards for social competency. *Journal of Psychoeducational Assessment, 1,* 297–307.

Gresham, F. M. (1985). Utility of cognitive-behavioral procedures for social skills training with children: A critical review. *Journal of Abnormal Child Psychology, 13,* 411–423.

Gresham, F. M. (1986). Conceptual issues in the assessment of social competence in children. In P. Strain, M. Guralnick, & H. Walker (Eds.), *Children's social behavior: Development, assessment, and modification* (pp. 143–180). New York: Academic Press.

Gresham, F. M. (1989). Assessment of treatment integrity in school consultation and prereferral intervention. *School Psychology Review, 18,* 37–50.

Gresham, F. M. (1997). Social competence and students with behavior disorders: Where we've been, where we are, and where we should go. *Education and Treatment of Children, 20,* 233–250.

Gresham, F. M., (1998). Social skills training: Should we raze, remodel, or rebuild? *Behavioral Disorders, 24,* 19–25.

Gresham, F. M. (2002a). Best practices in social skills training. In A. Thomas & J. Grimes (Eds.), *Best practices in school psychology* (4th ed., pp. 1029–1040). Bethesda, MD: National Association of School Psychologists.

Gresham, F. M. (2002b). Responsiveness to intervention: An alternative approach to learning disabilities. In R. Bradley, L. Danielson, & D. Hallahan (Eds.), *Identification of learning disabilities: Research to practice.* Mahwah, NJ: Erlbaum.

Gresham, F. M. (2002c). Teaching social skills to high-risk children and youth: Preventive and remedial strategies. In M. Shinn, H. Walker, & G. Stoner (Eds.), *Interventions for academic and behavior problems: Preventive and remedial approaches* (2nd ed., pp. 403–432). Bethesda, MD: National Association of School Psychologists.

Gresham, F. M., Cook, C. R., Crews, S. D., & Kern, L. (2004). Social skills training for children and youth with emotional and behavioral disorders: Validity considerations and future directions. *Behavioral Disorders, 30,* 32–46.

Gresham, F. M., & Elliot, S. N. (1984). Assessment and classification of children's social skills: A review of methods and issues. *School Psychology Review, 13,* 292–301.

Gresham, F. M., & Elliott, S. N. (1990). *Social Skills Rating System.* Bloomington, MN: Pearson Assessments.

Gresham, F. M., & Elliott, S. N. (2008). *Social Skills Improvement System-Rating Scales.* Bloomington, MN: Pearson Assessments.

Gresham, F. M., & Gansle, K. A. (1992). Misguided assumptions of DSM-III-R: Implications for school psychological practice. *School Psychology Quarterly, 7,* 79–95.

Gresham, F. M., Gansle, K. A., & Noell, G. H. (1993). Treatment integrity in applied behavior analysis with children. *Journal of Applied Behavior Analysis, 26,* 257–263.

Gresham, F. M., & Kern, L. (2004). Internalizing behavior problems in children and adolescents. In R. Rutherford, M. M. Quinn, & S. R. Mather (Eds.), *Handbook of research in emotional and behavioral disorders* (pp. 262–281). New York: The Guilford Press.

Gresham, F. M., & Lopez, M. F. (1996). Social validation: A unifying concept for school-based consultation research and practice. *School Psychology Quarterly, 11,* 204–227.

Gresham, F. M., Sugai, G., & Horner, R. (2001). Interpreting outcomes of social skills training for students with high-risk disabilities. *Exceptional Children, 67,* 331–344.

Gresham, F. M., Sugai, G., Horner, R., Quinn, M., & McInerney, M. (1998). *Classroom and schoolwide practices that support students' social competence: A synthesis of research.* Washington, DC: Office of Special Education Programs.

Gresham, F. M., Van, M. B., & Cook, C. R. (2006). Social skills training for teaching replacement behaviors: Remediation of acquisition deficits for at-risk children. *Behavioral Disorders, 30,* 32–46.

Grieger, T., Kauffman, J. M., & Grieger, R. M. (1976). Effects of peer reporting on cooperative play and aggression of kindergarten children. *Journal of School Psychology, 14,* 307–313.

Gulchak, D. (2008). Using a mobile hand-held computer to teach a student with an emotional and behavioral disorder to self-monitor attention. *Education and Treatment of Children, 31,* 567–581.

Gunter, P. L., Hummel, J. H., & Venn, M. L. (1998). Are effective academic instructional practices used to teach students with behavior disorders? *Beyond Behavior, 9,* 5–11.

Gunter, P. L., & Sutherland, K. S. (2005). Active student responding. In G. Sugai & R. Horner (Eds.), *Encyclopedia of behavior modification and cognitive behavior therapy: Vol. 3. Educational applications* (pp. 1131–1132). Thousand Oaks, CA: Sage.

Haager, D., & Klinger, J. (2005). *Differentiating instruction in inclusive classrooms: The special educator's guide.* Upper Saddle River, NJ: Pearson Education.

Hains, A. A. (1992). Comparison of cognitive-behavioral stress management techniques with adolescent boys. *Journal of Counseling and Development, 70,* 600–605.

Hains, A. A., & Szyjakowski, M. (1990). A cognitive stress-reduction intervention program for adolescents. *Journal of Counseling Psychology, 37,* 79–84.

Hallahan, D. P., & Sapona, R. (1983). Self-monitoring of attention within learning disabled children: Past research and current issues. *Journal of Learning Disabilities, 16,* 616–620.

Hammen, C., & Rudolph, R. D. (1996). Childhood depression. In E. J. Mash & R. A. Barkley (Eds.), *Child psychopathology* (pp.153–195). New York: Guilford Press

Harchik, A. E., & Putzier, V. S. (1990). The use of high-probability requests to increase compliance with instructions to take medication. *Journal of the Association for Persons with Severe Handicaps (JASH), 15*(1), 40-43.

Harrington, R., Whittaker, J., & Shoebridge, P. (1998). Psychological treatment of depression in children and adolescents: A review of treatment research. *British Journal of Psychiatry, 173,* 291–298.

Harris, K. R. (1982). Cognitive-behavior modification: Applications with exceptional students. *Focus on Exceptional Children, 15,* 1–16.

Harris, K. R. Graham, S., Mason, L. H., & Friedlander, B. (2008). *POWERFUL writing strategies for all students.* Baltimore, MD: Brookes

Harris, L. (1991). *The Metropolitan Life Survey of the American Teacher, 1991, The first year: New teachers' expectations and ideals.* New York: Metropolitan Life Insurance Company.

Hawken, L. S., MacLeod, S. K., & Rawlings, L. (2007). Effects of the behavior education program (BEP) on office discipline referrals of elementary school students. *Journal of Positive Behavior Interventions, 9,* 94–102.

Hawkins, R. (1991). Is social validity what we are interested in? Argument for a functional approach. *Journal of Applied Behavior Analysis, 24,* 205–213.

Haydon, T., Mancil, G. R., & Van Loan, C. (2009). Using opportunities to respond in a general education classroom: A case study. *Education and Treatment of Children, 32,* 267–278.

Haydon, T., & Scott, T. M. (2008). Using common sense in common settings: Active supervision and pre-correction in the morning gym. *Intervention in School and Clinic, 43,* 283–290.

Haynes, R. S., Derby, K. M., McLaughlin, T. F., & Weber, K. P. (2002). A comparison of forced-choice preferences assessment procedures using a parent and novel therapist. *Journal of Positive Behavior Interventions, 4,* 176–181.

Henderlong, J., & Lepper, M. R. (2002). The effects of praise on children's intrinsic motivation: A review and synthesis. *Psychological Bulletin, 128,* 774–795.

Henggeler, S. W., Mihalic, S. F., Rone, L., Thomas, C., & Timmons-Mitchell, J. (1998). *Multisystemic therapy: Blueprints for violence prevention, Book Six* (D. S. Elliott, Series Editor). Boulder, CO: Center for the Study and Prevention of Violence, Institute of Behavioral Science, University of Colorado.

Herrnstein, R. J. (1961). Relative and absolute strength of response as a function of frequency of reinforcement. *Journal of the Experimental Analysis of Behavior, 4,* 267–272.

Herrnstein, R. J. (1970). On the law of effect. *Journal of the Experimental Analysis of Behavior, 13,* 243–266.

Hersh, R., & Walker, H. M. (1983). Great expectations: Making schools effective for all students. *Policy Studies Review, 2,* 147–188.

Hess, F., & Petrilli, M. (2006). *No Child Left Behind primer.* New York: Peter Lang.

Heward, W. L. (1994). Three "low tech" strategies for increasing the frequency of active student response during group instruction. In R. Gardner, III, D. M. Sainato, J. O. Cooper, T. E. Heron, W. L. Heward, J. Eshleman, & T. A. Grossi (Eds.), *Behavior analysis in education: Focus on measurably superior instruction* (pp. 283–320). Pacific Grove, CA: Brooks/Cole.

Hilt-Panahon, A., Kern, L., Divatia, A., & Gresham, F. (2007). School-based interventions for students with or at-risk for depression: A review of the literature. *Advances in School Mental Health Promotion, 1,* 32–41.

Hobbs, S., Forehand, R., & Murray, R. (1978). Effects of various durations of timeout on the noncompliant behavior of children. *Behavior Therapy, 9,* 652–656.

Hoff, K. E., & DuPaul, G. J. (1998). Reducing disruptive behavior in general education classrooms: The use of self-management strategies. *School Psychology Review, 27,* 290–303.

Hoff, K. E., & Ronk, M. J. (2006). Increasing pro-social interactions using peers: Extension of positive peer-reporting methods. *Journal of Evidenced-Based Practices for Schools, 7,* 27–42.

Hogue, A., Henderson, C. E., Dauber, S., Barajas, P. C., Fried, A., & Liddle, H. A. (2008). Treatment adherence, competence, and outcome in individual and family therapy for adolescent behavior problems. *Journal of Consulting and Clinical Psychology, 76,* 544–555.

Hollinger, J. (1987). Social skills for behaviorally disordered children as preparation for mainstreaming: Theory, practice, and new directions. *Remedial and Special Education, 8,* 17–27.

Hops, H., & Walker, H. M. (1988). CLASS: Contingencies for learning academic and social skills. Seattle, WA: Educational Achievement Systems.

Horner, R. H. (2000). Positive behavior supports. In M. L. Wehmeyer & J. R. Patton (Eds.), *Mental retardation in the 21st century* (pp. 181–196). Austin, TX: Pro-Ed.

Horner, R., & Billingsley, F. (1988). The effects of competing behavior on the generalization and maintenance of adaptive behavior in applied settings. In R. Horner, G. Dunlap, & R. Koegel (Eds.), *Generalization and maintenance: Lifestyle changes in applied settings* (pp. 197–220). Baltimore: Brookes.

Horner, R. H., Carr, E. G., Halle, J., McGee, G., Odom, S., & Wolery, M. (2005). The use of single-subject research to identify evidence-based practice in special education. *Exceptional Children, 71,* 165–179.

Horner, R. H., Day, H. M., Sprague, J. R., O'Brien, M., & Heathfield, L. T. (1991). Interspersed requests: A nonaversive procedure for reducing aggression and self-injury during instruction. *Journal of Applied Behavior Analysis, 24*(2), 265–278.

Horner, R. H. & Sugai, G. (2000). School-wide behavior support: An emerging initiative. *Journal of Positive Behavior Interventions, 2,* 231–232.

Horner, R., Sugai, G., Smolkowski, K., Eber, L., Nakasato, J., Todd, A., et al. (2009). A randomized, wait-list controlled effectiveness trial assessing school-wide positive behavior support in elementary schools. *Journal of Positive Behavior Interventions, 11*(3), 133–144.

Horner, R. H., Todd, A. W., Lewis-Palmer, T., Irvin, L. K., Sugai, G., & Boland, J. B. (2004). The school-wide evaluation tool (SET): A research instrument for assessing school-wide positive behavior support. *Journal of Positive Behavior Interventions, 6,* 3–12.

Houlihan, D., & Brandon, P. K. (1996). Compliant in a moment: A commentary on Nevin. *Journal of Applied Behavior Analysis, 29*(4), 549–555.

Houlihan, D., Jacobson, L., & Brandon, P. K. (1994). Replication of a high-probability request sequence with varied interprompt times in a preschool setting. *Journal of Applied Behavior Analysis, 27*(4), 737–738.

Houlihan, D., & Jones, R. N. (1990). Exploring the reinforcement of compliance with do and don't requests and their side effects: A partial replication and extension. *Psychological Reports, 67,* 439–448.

Individuals with Disabilities Education Act of 1997, Pub. L. No. 105-17, 105 Stat. 37.

Individuals with Disabilities Education Improvement Act of 2004, 20 U.S.C. § 1415 *et seq.* (2004).

Iwata, B. A., Dorsey, M. F., Slifer, K. J., Bauman, K. E., & Richman, G. S. (1982). Toward a functional analysis of self-injury. *Analysis and Intervention in Developmental Disabilities, 2,* 3–20.

Jacobsen, E. (1938). *Progressive relaxation.* Chicago: University of Chicago Press.

Jaycox, L. H., Reivich, K. J., Gillham, J., & Seligman, M. E. P. (1994). Prevention of depressive symptoms in school children. *Behaviour Research and Therapy, 32,* 801–816.

Johnson, S. M., Wahl, G., Martin, S., & Johansson, S. (1973). How deviant is the normal child: A behavioral analysis of the preschool child and his family. In R. D. Rubin, J. P. Brady, & J. D. Henderson (Eds.), *Advances in behavioral therapy (Vol. 4).* New York: Academic Press.

Johnson-Gros, K. N., & Shriver, M. D. (2006). Compliance training and positive peer reporting with a 4-year old in a preschool classroom. *Journal of Evidence-Based Practices for Schools, 7,* 167–185.

Jolivette, K., McCormick, K., McLaren, E., & Steed, E. A. (2009). Opportunities for young children to make choices in a model interdisciplinary and inclusive preschool program. *Infants and Young Children, 22,* 279–289.

Jolivette, K., Ridgely, R., & White, A. (2002). Choice-making strategies: Information for families. *Center for Effective Collaboration and Practice.* Retrieved from http://cecp.air.org/familybriefs/docs/choice_at_home/pdf

Jolivette, K., Stichter, J. P., & McCormick, K. M. (2002). Making choices—improving behavior—engaging in learning. *Teaching Exceptional Children, 34,* 24–29.

Jolivette, K., Stichter, J. P., Sibilisky, S., Scott, T. M., & Ridgely, R. (2002). Naturally occurring opportunities for preschool children with or without disabilities to make choices. *Education and Treatment of Children, 25,* 396–414.

Jolivette, K., Wehby, J. H., Canale, J., & Massey, N. G. (2001). Effects of choice-making opportunities on the behavior of students with emotional and behavioral disorders. *Behavioral Disorders, 26,* 131–145.

Jones, K. M., Young, M. M., & Friman, P. C. (2000). Increasing peer praise of socially rejected delinquent youth: Effects on cooperation and acceptance. *School Psychology Quarterly, 15,* 30–39.

Jones, M. L. (2009). A study of novice special educators' views of evidence-based practices. *Teacher Education and Special Education, 32*(2), 101–120.

Kahn, J. S., Kehle, T. J., Jenson, W. R., & Clark, E. (1990). Comparison of cognitive-behavioral, relaxation, and self-modeling interventions for depression among middle-school students. *School Psychology Review, 19,* 196–211.

Kalberg, J. R., Lane, K. L., & Lambert, W. (2012). The utility of conflict resolution and social skills interventions with middle school students at risk for antisocial behavior: A methodological illustration. *Remedial and Special Education, 33,* 23–38.

Kalberg, J. R., Lane, K. L., & Menzies, H. M. (2010). Using systematic screening procedures to identify students who are nonresponsive to primary prevention efforts: Integrating academic and behavioral measures. *Education and Treatment of Children, 33,* 561–584.

Kamins, M. L., & Dweck, C. S. (1999). Person versus process praise and criticism: Implications for contingent self-worth and coping. *Developmental Psychology, 35,* 835–847.

Kamphaus, R. W., & Reynolds, C. R. (2007). *BASC-2 behavior and emotional screening system (BASC-2 BESS).* San Antonio, TX: Pearson.

Kamps, D., Wendland, M., & Culpepper, M. (2006). Active teacher participation in functional behavior assessment for students with emotional and behavior disorders in general education classrooms. *Behavioral Disorders, 31*, 128–146.

Kartub, D. T., Taylor-Greene, S., March, R. E., & Horner, R. H. (2000). Reducing hallway noise: A systems approach. *Journal of Positive Behavior Intervention, 2,* 179–182.

Kauffman, J. M. (1996). Research to practice issues. *Behavioral Disorders, 22*, 55–60.

Kauffman, J. M. (2001). *Characteristics of emotional and behavioral disorders of children and youth* (7th ed.). Upper Saddle River, NJ: Merrill/Pearson.

Kauffman, J. M. (2010). *The tragicomedy of public education: Laughing and crying, thinking and fixing.* Verona, Wisconsin: Full Court Press.

Kauffman, J. M., & Brigham, F. J., (2009). *Working with troubled children.* Verona, WI: Full Court Press.

Kauffman, J. M., & Landrum, T. (2009). *Characteristics of emotional and behavioral disorders of children and youth* (8th ed.). Upper Saddle River, NJ: Merrill/Pearson.

Kazdin, A. (1977). Assessing the clinical or applied significance of behavior change through social validation. *Behavior Modification, 1,* 427–452.

Kazdin, A. E. (1987). Treatment of antisocial behavior in children: Current status and future directions. *American Psychological Association, 102,* 187–203.

Kazdin, A. E., & Marciano, P. L. (1998). Childhood and adolescent depression. In E. J. Mash & R. A. Barkley (Eds.), *Treatment of childhood disorders* (2nd ed, pp. 211–248). New York: Guilford Press.

Kellam, S., Ling, X., Merisca, R., Brown, C. H., & Ialongo, N. (1998). The effect of the level of aggression in the first grade classroom on the course and malleability of aggressive behavior into middle school. *Development and Psychopathology, 10*, 165–185.

Keller, M. B., Neal, R. D., Strober, M., Klein, R. G., Kutcher, S. P., Birmaher, B., et al. (2001). Efficacy of paroxetine in the treatment of adolescent major depression: A randomized, controlled trial. *Journal of the American Academy of Child and Adolescent Psychiatry, 40*, 762–772.

Kemp, C., & Carter, M. (2006). Active and passive task related behavior, direction following and the inclusion of children with disabilities. *Education and Training in Developmental Disabilities, 41*, 14–27.

Kendall, P. C., Stark, K. D., & Adam, T. (1990). Cognitive deficit or cognitive distortion of childhood depression. *Journal of abnormal childhood psychology, 18*(3), 255–270.

Kennedy C. H., Itkonen, T., & Lindquist K. (1995). Comparing interspersed requests and social comments as antecedents for increasing student compliance. *Journal of Applied Behavior Analysis, 28*, 97–98.

Kennedy, C. H., Long, T., Jolivette, K., Cox, J., Tang, J., & Thompson, T. (2001). Facilitating general education participation for students with behavior problems by linking positive behavior supports and person-centered planning. *Journal of Emotional and Behavioral Disorders, 9*, 161–171.

Kern, L., Bambara, L., & Fogt, J. (2002). Classwide curricular modification to improve the behavior of students with emotional and behavioral disorders. *Behavioral Disorders, 27*, 317–326.

Kern, L., Childs, K. E., Dunlap, G., Clarke, S., & Falk, G. D. (1994). Using assessment-based curricular intervention to improve the classroom behavior of a student with emotional and behavioral challenges. *Journal of Applied Behavior Analysis, 27*, 7–19.

Kern, L., & Clemens, N. H. (2007). Antecedent strategies to promote appropriate classroom behavior. *Psychology in the Schools, 44*, 65–75.

Kern, L., Delaney, B., Clarke, S., Dunlap, G., & Childs, K. (2001). Improving classroom behavior of students with emotional and behavioral disorders using individualized curricular modifications. *Journal of Emotional and Behavioral Disorders, 9*, 239–247.

Kern, L., DuPaul, G. J., Volpe, R., Sokol, N., Lutz, J. G., Arbolino, L., et al. (2007). Multi-setting assessment-based intervention for young children at-risk for ADHD: Initial effects on academic and behavioral functioning. *School Psychology Review, 36*(2), 237-255.

Kern, L., Hilt, A., & Gresham, F. (2004). An evaluation of the functional behavioral assessment process used with students with or at risk for emotional and behavioral disorders. *Education and Treatment of Children, 27*, 440-–452.

Kern, L., Mantegna, M. E., Vorndran, C. M., Bailin, D., & Hilt, A. (2001). Choice of task sequence to reduce problem behaviors. *Journal of Positive Behavior Interventions, 3*, 3–10.

Kern, L., & Manz, P. (2004). A look at current validity issues of school-wide behavior support. *Behavioral Disorders, 30*, 47–59.

Kern, L., & State, T. M. (2009). Incorporating choice and preferred activities into classwide instruction. *Beyond Behavior, 18*, 3–11.

Killu, K., Sainato, D. M., Davis, C. A., Ospelt, H., & Paul, J. N. (1998). Effects of high-probability request sequences on preschoolers' compliance and disruptive behavior. *Journal of Behavioral Education, 8*(3), 347–368.

Klein, R. G., Koplewicz, H. S., & Kanner, A. (1992). Imipramine treatment of children with separation anxiety disorder. *Journal of the American Academy of Child and Adolescent Psychiatry, 31*, 21–28.

Klem, A. M., & Connell, J. P. (2004). Relationships matter: Linking teacher support to student engagement and achievement. *The Journal of School Health, 74*, 262–273.

Knapczyk, D. R. (1988). Reducing aggressive behaviors in special and regular class settings by training alternative social responses. *Behavioral Disorders, 14*, 27–39.

Knapczyk, D. R. (1992). Effects of developing alternative responses on the aggressive behavior of adolescents. *Behavioral Disorders, 17*, 247–263.

Kohler, F. W., & Greenwood, C. R. (1986). Toward a technology of generalization: The identification of natural contingencies of reinforcement. *The Behavior Analyst, 9*, 19–26.

Kotler, J., & McMahon, R. (2003). Compliance and noncompliance in anxious, aggressive, and socially competent children: The impact of the Child's Game. *Behavior Therapy, 35*, 495–512.

Kupersmidt, J., Coie, J., & Dodge, K. (1990). The role of peer relationships in the development of disorder. In S. Asher & J. Coie

(Eds.), *Peer rejection in childhood* (pp. 274–308). New York: Cambridge University Press.

Kutcher, S., & Mackenzie. S. (1988). Successful clonazepam treatment of adolescents with panic disorder. *Journal of Clinical Psychopharmacology, 8*, 299–301.

Ladd, G. W., Kochenderfer, B. J., & Coleman, C. C. (1997). Classroom peer acceptance, friendship, and victimization: Distinct relational systems that contribute uniquely to children's school adjustment. *Child Development, 68*(6), 1181–1197.

Lancioni, G. E., O'Reilly, M. F., & Emerson, E. (1996). A review of choice research with people with severe and profound developmental disabilities. *Research in Developmental Disabilities, 17*, 391–411.

Landrum, T. J., Cook, B. G., Tankersley, M. T., & Fitzgerald, S. (2002). Teachers' perceptions of the trustworthiness, useability, and accessibility of information from different sources. *Remedial and Special Education, 23*(1), 42–48.

Landrum, T. J., Cook, B. G., Tankersley, M., & Fitzgerald, S. (2007). Teacher perceptions of the usability of intervention information from personal versus data-based sources. *Education and Treatment of Children, 30*, 27–42.

Landrum, T., & Lloyd, J. (1992). Generalization in social behavior research with children and youth who have emotional or behavioral disorders. *Behavior Modification, 16*, 593–616.

Landrum, T. J., & McDuffie, K. A. (2010). Learning styles in the age of differentiated instruction. *Exceptionality, 18*, 6–17.

Landrum, T. J., & Tankersley, M. (2004). Science at the schoolhouse: An uninvited guest. *Journal of Learning Disabilities, 37*, 207–212.

Landrum, T. J., Tankersley, M., & Kauffman, J. M. (2003). What is special about special education for students with emotional and behavioral disorders? *Journal of Special Education, 37*, 148–156.

Lane, K. L. (2007). Identifying and supporting students at risk for emotional and behavioral disorders within multilevel models: Data driven approaches to conducting secondary interventions with an academic emphasis. *Education and Treatment of Children, 30*, 135–164.

Lane, K. L., Barton-Arwood, S. M., Spencer, J. L., & Kalberg, J. R. (2007). Teaching elementary school educators to design, implement, and evaluate functional assessment-based interventions: Successes and challenges. *Preventing School Failure, 51*, 35–46.

Lane, K. L., & Beebe-Frankenberger, M. (2004). *School-based interventions: The tools you need to succeed.* Upper Saddle River, NJ: Pearson Education.

Lane, K. L., Bruhn, A. L., Crnobori, M. L., & Sewell, A. L. (2009). Designing functional assessment-based interventions using a systematic approach: A promising practice for supporting challenging behavior (p. 341–370). In T. E. Scruggs & M. A. Mastropieri (Eds.), *Policy and practice: Advances in learning and behavioral disabilities* (vol. 22). Bingley, UK: Emerald.

Lane, K. L., Bruhn, A. L., Eisner, S. L., & Kalberg, J. R. (in press). Score reliability and validity of the Student Risk Screening Scale: A psychometrically-sound, feasible tool for use in urban middle schools. *Journal of Emotional and Behavioral Disorders.*

Lane, K. L., & Eisner, S. (2007). *Behavior screening at the elementary level.* Paper presented at Metropolitan Nashville Public Schools. Nashville, TN.

Lane, K. L., Harris, K., Graham, S., Driscoll, S. A., Sandmel, K., Morphy, P., Hebert, M., House, E., & Schatschneider, C. (2011). Self-regulated strategy development at tier-2 for second-grade students with writing and behavioral difficulties: A randomized control trial. *Journal of Research on Educational Effectiveness, 4*, 322–353.

Lane, K. L., Kalberg, J. E., Bruhn, A. L., Driscoll, S. A., Wehby, J. H., & Elliott, S. N. (2009). Assessing social validity of school-wide positive behavior support plans: Evidence for the reliability and structure of the Primary Intervention Rating Scale. *School Psychology Review, 38*, 135–144.

Lane, K. L., Kalberg, J. R., Bruhn, A. L., Mahoney, M. E., & Driscoll, S. A. (2008). Primary prevention programs at the elementary level: Issues of treatment integrity, systematic screening, and reinforcement. *Education and Treatment of Children, 31*, 465–494.

Lane, K. L., Kalberg, J. R., & Edwards, C. (2008). An examination of schoolwide interventions with primary level efforts conducted in elementary schools: Implications for school psychologists. In D. H. Molina (Ed.), *School psychology: 21st century issues and challenges* (pp. 253–278). New York: Nova Science.

Lane, K. L., Kalberg, J. R., & Menzies, H. M. (2009). *Developing schoolwide programs to prevent and manage problem behaviors: A step-by-step approach.* New York: Guilford Press.

Lane, K. L., Kalberg, J. R., Menzies, H. M., Bruhn, A., Eisner, S., & Crnobori, M. (2011). Using systematic screening data to assess risk and identify students for targeted supports: Illustrations across the K-12 continuum. *Remedial and Special Education, 32*, 39–54.

Lane, K. L., Kalberg, J. R., Parks, R. J., & Carter, E. W. (2008). Student Risks Screening Scale: Initial evidence for score reliability and validity at the high school level. *Journal of Emotional and Behavioral Disorders, 16*, 178–190.

Lane, K. L., Kalberg, J. R., & Shepcaro, J. C. (2009). An examination of quality indicators of function-based interventions for students with emotional or behavioral disorders attending middle and high schools. *Exceptional Children, 75*, 321–340.

Lane, K. L., & Menzies, H. M. (2002). The effects of a school-based primary intervention program: Preliminary outcomes. *Preventing School Failure, 47*, 26–32.

Lane, K. L., & Menzies, H. M. (2003). A school-wide intervention with primary and secondary levels of support for elementary students: Outcomes and considerations. *Education and Treatment of Children, 26*, 431–451.

Lane, K. L., & Menzies, H. M. (2005). Teacher-identified students with and without academic and behavioral concerns: Characteristics and responsiveness. *Behavioral Disorders, 31*, 65–83.

Lane, K. L., Menzies, H., Bruhn, A., & Crnobori, M. (2011). *Managing challenging behaviors in schools: Research-based strategies that work.* New York: Guilford Press.

Lane, K. L., Menzies, H. M., Oakes, W. P., & Kalberg, J. R. (2012). *Systematic screenings of behavior to support instruction: From preschool to high school.* New York: Guilford.

Lane, K. L., Robertson, E. J., & Graham-Bailey, M. A. L. (2006). An examination of school-wide interventions with primary level efforts conducted in secondary schools: Methodological considerations. In T. E. Scruggs & M. A. Mastropieri (Eds.), *Applications of research methodology: Advances in learning and behavioral disabilities* (vol. 19; pp. 157–199). Oxford, UK: Elsevier.

Lane, K. L., Robertson, E. J., & Wehby, J. H. (2002). *Primary Intervention Rating Scale.* Unpublished rating scale.

Lane, K. L., Smither, R., Huseman, R., Guffey, J., & Fox, J. (2007). A function-based intervention to decrease disruptive behavior and increase academic engagement. *Journal of Early and Intensive Behavioral Intervention, 3.4–4.1,* 348–364.

Lane, K. L., Umbreit, J., & Beebe-Frankenberger, M. (1999). A review of functional assessment research with students with or at-risk for emotional and behavioral disorders. *Journal of Positive Behavioral Interventions, 1,* 101–111.

Lane, K. L., & Wehby, J. (2002). Addressing antisocial behavior in the schools: A call for action. *Academic Exchange Quarterly, 6,* 4–9.

Lane, K. L., Wehby, J., Menzies, H. M., Doukas, G. L., Munton, S. M., & Gregg, R. M. (2003). Social skills instruction for students at risk for antisocial behavior: The effects of small-group instruction. *Behavioral Disorders, 28,* 229–248.

Lane, K. L., Wehby, J. H., Menzies, H. M., Gregg, R. M., Doukas, G. L., & Munton, S. M. (2002). Early literacy instruction for first-grade students at-risk for antisocial behavior. *Education and Treatment of Children, 25,* 438–458.

Lane, K. L., Wehby, J., Robertson, E. J., & Rogers, L. (2007). How do different types of high school students respond to positive behavior support programs? Characteristics and responsiveness of teacher-identified students. *Journal of Emotional and Behavioral Disorders, 15,* 3–20.

Lane, K. L., Weisenbach, J. L., Phillips, A., & Wehby, J. H. (2007). Designing, implementing, and evaluating function-based interventions using a systematic, feasible approach. *Behavioral Disorders, 32,* 122–139.

Lane, K. L., Wolery, M., Reichow, B., & Rogers, L. (2006). Describing baseline conditions: Suggestions for study reports. *Journal of Behavioral Education, 16,* 224–234.

Lannie, A. L., & McCurdy, B. L. (2007). Preventing disruptive behavior in the urban classroom: Effects of the Good Behavior Game on student and teacher behavior. *Education and Treatment of Children, 30,* 85–98.

Lee, D. L., Belfiore, P. J., & Ferko, D. (2006). Using pre and post low-p latency to assess behavioral momentum: A preliminary investigation. *Journal of Behavioral Education, 15*(4), 203–214.

Lee, D. L., & Laspe, A. K. (2003). Using high-probability request sequences to increase journal writing. *Journal of Behavioral Education, 12*(4), 261–273.

Lee, Y., Sugai, G., & Horner, R. H. (1999). Using an instructional intervention to reduce problem and off-task behaviors, *Journal of Positive Behavior Interventions, 1,* 195–204.

Leedy, A., Bates, P., & Safran, S. P. (2004). Bridging the research-to-practice gap: Improving hallway behavior using positive behavior supports. *Behavioral Disorders, 29,* 130–139.

Leff, S. S., Costigan, T., & Power, T. J. (2003). Using participatory research to develop a playground-based prevention program. *Journal of School Psychology, 42,* 3–21.

Lewinsohn, P. M. (1974). A behavioral approach to depression. In R. J. Friedman & M. M. Katz (Eds.), *The psychology of depression: Contemporary theory and research* (pp. 157–184). New York: Wiley.

Lewinsohn, P. M., Munoz, R., Youngren, M. A., & Zeiss, A. (1978). *Control your depression.* Upper Saddle River, NJ: Prentice-Hall.

Lewis, T. J., Colvin, G., & Sugai, G. (2000). The effects of pre-correction and active supervision on the recess behavior of elementary students. *Education and Treatment of Children, 23,* 109–121.

Lewis, T. J., Powers, L. J., Kelk, M. J., & Newcomer, L. L. (2002). Reducing problem behaviors on the playground: An investigation of the application of schoolwide positive behaviors supports. *Psychology in the Schools, 39,* 181–190.

Lewis, T. J., & Sugai, G. (1999). Effective behavior support: A systems approach to proactive schoolwide management. *Focus on Exceptional Children, 31,* 1–24.

Lewis, T. J., Sugai, G., & Colvin, G. (1998). Reducing problem behavior through a school-wide system of effective behavioral support: Investigation of a school-wide social skills training program and contextual intervention. *School Psychology Review, 27,* 446–459.

Liaupsin, C. J., Umbreit, J., Ferro, J. B., Urso, A., & Upreti, G. (2006). Improving academic engagement through systematic, function-based intervention. *Education and Treatment of Children, 29,* 573–591.

Libster, L. R. (2008). *The efficacy of positive peer reporting procedures for use with neglected-status students in general education classrooms.* Unpublished master's thesis, Louisiana State University.

Lien-Thorne, S., & Kamps, D. (2005). Replication study of the First Step to Success early intervention program. *Behavioral Disorders, 31,* 18–32.

Lloyd, J. W., Pullen, P. C., Tankersley, M., & Lloyd, P. A. (2006). Critical dimensions of experimental studies and research syntheses that help define effective practice. In B. G. Cook & B. R. Schirmer (Eds.), *What is special about special education? Examining the role of evidence-based practices* (pp. 136–153). Austin, TX: Pro-Ed.

Lo, Ya-yu., & Cartledge, G. (2006). FBA and BIP: Increasing the behavior adjustment of African American boys in schools. *Council for Children with Behavioral Disorders, 31,* 147–161.

Lohrmann-O'Rourke, S., Knoster, T., Sabatine, K., Smith, D., Horvath, B., &

Llewellyn, G. (2000). School-wide application of PBS in the Bangor area school district. *Journal of Positive Behavior Interventions, 2,* 238–240.

Losel, F., & Beelmann, A. (2003). Effects of child skills training in preventing antisocial behavior: A systematic review of randomized evaluations. *Annals AAPSS, 857,* 84–109.

Luiselli, J. K., Putnam, R. F., & Sunderland, M. (2002). Longitudinal evaluation of behavior support intervention in a public middle school. *Journal of Positive Behavior Intervention, 4,* 182–188.

Maag, J. W. (2004). *From theoretical implications to practical applications* (2nd ed.). Belmont, CA: Thompson Wadsworth.

Maag, J. W. (2005). Social skills training for youth with emotional and behavioral disorders and learning disabilities: Problems, conclusions, and suggestions. *Exceptionality, 13,* 155–172.

Maag, J. W. (2006). Social skills training for students with emotional and behavioral disorders; A review of reviews. *Behavioral Disorders, 32,* 5–17.

Maag, J. W., & Larson, P. J. (2004). Training a general education teacher to apply functional assessment. *Education and Treatment of Children, 27,* 26–36.

Maag, J. W., Reid, R., & DiGangi, S. A. (1993). Differential effects of self-monitoring, attention, accuracy, and productivity. *Journal of Applied Behavior Analysis, 26,* 329–344.

Mace, F. C. (1996). In pursuit of general behavioral relations. *Journal of Applied Behavior Analysis, 29,* 557–563.

Mace, F. C., Hock, M. L., Lalli, J. S., West, B. J., Belfiore, P. J., Pinter, E., & Brown, D. K. (1988). Behavioral momentum in the treatment of noncompliance. *Journal of Applied Behavior Analysis, 21*(2), 123–141.

Mace, F. C., Mauro, B. C., Boyajian, A. E., & Eckert, T. L. (1997). Effects of reinforcer quality on behavioral momentum: Coordinated applied and basic research. *Journal of Applied Behavior Analysis, 30,* 1–20.

MacMillan, D., Gresham, F., & Forness, S. (1996). Full inclusion: An empirical perspective. *Behavioral Disorders, 21,* 145–159.

Madelaine, A., & Wheldall, K. (2005). Identifying low-progress readers: Comparing teacher judgment with a curriculum-based measurement procedure. *International Journal of Disability, Development and Education, 52,* 33–42.

Madsen, C., Becker, W., & Thomas, D. (1968). Rules, praise, and ignoring: Elements of classroom elementary control. *Journal of Applied Behavior Analysis, 1,* 139–150.

Malecki, C. M. (1998). *The influence of elementary students' social behaviors on academic achievement.* Unpublished doctoral dissertation, University of Wisconsin-Madison.

Malecki, C. M., & Elliott, S. N. (2002). Children's social behaviors as predictors of academic achievement: A longitudinal analysis. *School Psychology Quarterly, 17,* 1–23.

Malouf, D. B., & Schiller, E. P. (1995). Practice and research in special education. *Exceptional Children, 61,* 414–424.

March, J. S., Biederman, J., Wolkow, R., Safferman, A., Mardekian, J., Cook, E. H., et al. (1998). Sertraline in children and adolescents with obsessive-compulsive disorder: A multicenter randomized controlled trial. *Journal of the American Medical Association, 280,* 1252–1293.

March, R. E., & Horner, R. H. (2002). Feasibility and contributions of functional behavioral assessment in schools. *Journal of Emotional and Behavioral Disorders, 10,* 158–170.

March, R., Lewis-Palmer, T., Brown, D., Crone, D., Todd, A.W., & Carr, E. (2000). *Functional assessment checklist for teachers and staff (FACTS).* Eugene, OR: University of Oregon, Educational and Community Supports.

Marr, M. B., Aduette, B., White, R., Ellis, E., & Algozzine, B. (2002). School-wide discipline and classroom ecology. *Special Services in the Schools, 18,* 55–72.

Martens, B. K. (1992). Contingency and choice: The implications of matching theory for classroom instruction. *Journal of Behavioral Education, 2,* 121–137.

Martens, B. K., & Houk, J. L. (1989). The application of Herrnstein's Law of Effect to disruptive and on-task behavior of a retarded adolescent girl. *Journal of the Experimental Analysis of Behavior, 51,* 17–27.

Martens, B. K., Lochner, D. G., & Kelly, S. Q. (1992). The effects of variable-interval reinforcement on academic engagement: A demonstration of matching theory. *Journal of Applied Behavior Analysis, 25,* 143–151.

Martin, A. J., Linfoot, K., & Stephenson, J. (1999). How teachers respond to concerns about misbehavior in their classroom. *Psychology in the Schools, 36,* 347–358.

Mathur, S., & Rutherford, R. (1991). Peer-mediated interventions promoting social skills for children and youth with behavioral disorders. *Education and Treatment of Children, 14,* 227–242.

May, S., Ard, W., III, Todd, A. W., Horner, R. H., Glasgow, A., Sugai, G., & Sprague, J. (2000). *School-wide Information System (SWIS ©).* Eugene, OR: University of Oregon, Educational and Community Supports.

Mayer, G. R. (1995). Preventing antisocial behavior in the schools. *Journal of Applied Behavior Analysis, 28,* 467–478.

Mayer, G. R., Butterworth, T., Nafpaktitis, M., & Sulzer-Azaroff, B. (1983). Preventing school vandalism and improving discipline: A three-year study. *Journal of Applied Behavior Analysis, 16,* 355–369.

McCauley, E., Burke, P., Mitchell, J. R., & Moss, S. (1988). Cognitive attributes of depression in children and adolescents. *Journal of Consulting and Clinical Psychology, 56*(6), 903–908.

McComas, J. J., Wacker, D. P., & Cooper, L. J. (1998). Increasing compliance with medical procedures: Application of the high-probability request procedure to a toddler. *Journal of Applied Behavior Analysis, 31*(2), 287–290.

McComas, J. J., Wacker, D. P., Cooper, L. J., Peck, S., Golonka, Z., Millard, T., & Richman, D. (2000). Effects of the high-probability request procedure: Patterns of responding to low-probability requests. *Journal of Developmental and Physical Disabilities, 12*(2), 157–171.

McCormick, K. M., Jolivette, K., & Ridgely, R. (2003). Choice making as an intervention strategy for young children. *Young Exceptional Children, 6,* 3–10.

McCurdy, B. L., Manella, M. C., & Eldridge, N. (2003). Positive behavior support in urban schools: Can we prevent the escalation of antisocial behavior? *Journal of Positive Behavior Interventions, 5,* 158–170.

McDonnell, A. (1993). Ethical considerations in teaching compliance to individuals with mental retardation. *Education and Training in Mental Retardation, 28,* 3-12.

McDougall, D. (1998). Research on self-management techniques used by students with disabilities in general education settings. *Remedial and Special Education, 19,* 310–320.

McIntosh, K., Campbell, A., Carter, D., & Zumbo, B. (2009). Concurrent validity of office discipline referrals and cut points used in schoolwide positive behavior support. *Behavioral Disorders, 34*(2), 100–113.

McIntosh, R., Vaughn, S., & Zaragoza, N. (1991). A review of social interventions for students with learning disabilities. *Journal of Learning Disabilities, 24,* 451–458.

McLaughlin, C. A., & Davis, C.A. (2010). *Using high-probability requests in the classroom to decrease challenging behaviors.* Paper presented at the International Conference on Autism, Intellectual Disabilities, and Other Developmental Disabilities. Maui, HI.

McLeod, B. D., Southam-Gerow, M. A., & Weisz, J. R. (2009). Conceptual and methodological issues in treatment integrity measurement. *School Psychology Review, 38,* 541–546.

McMahon, R., & Forehand, R. (2003) *Helping the noncompliant child: Family-based treatment for oppositional behavior* (2nd ed.). New York: Guilford Press.

McMahon, S. D., & Washburn, J. J. (2003). Violence prevention: An evaluation of program effects with urban African-American students. *Journal of Primary Prevention, 24,* 43–62.

McMaster, K. L., Fuchs, D., Saenz, L., Lemons, C., Kearns, D., Yen, L., . . . Fuchs, L. S. (2010). Scaling up PALS: The importance of implementing evidence-based practice with fidelity and flexibility.

New Times for DLD, 28(1), 1–3. Retrieved from http://www.teachingld.org/pdf/NewTimes_ScalingUpPals2010.pdf

Merrell, K. W. (2001). *Helping students overcome depression and anxiety: A practical guide.* New York: Guilford Press.

Merrell, K. W., & Gimpel, G. A. (1998). *Social skills of children and adolescents: Conceptualization, assessment, treatment.* Mahwah, NJ: Erlbaum.

Messick, S. (1995). Validity of psychological assessment: Validation of inferences from persons' responses and performances as scientific inquiry into score meaning. *American Psychologist, 50,* 741–179.

Metzler, C. W., Biglan, A., Rusby, J. C., & Sprague, J. R. (2001). Evaluation of a comprehensive behavior management program to improve school-wide positive behavior support. *Education and Treatment of Children, 24,* 448–479.

Meyer, L., & Evans, I. (1989). *Nonaversive intervention for behavior problems: A manual for home and community.* Baltimore, MD: Brookes.

Miller, M. J., Lane, K. L., & Wehby, J. (2005). Social skills instruction for students with high incidence disabilities: An effective, efficient approach for addressing acquisition deficits. *Preventing School Failure, 49,* 27–40.

Moffitt, T. E. (1993). Adolescence-limited and life-course-persistent antisocial behavior: A developmental taxonomy. *Psychological Review, 100,* 674–701.

Mooney, P., Ryan, J., Uhing, B., Reid, R., & Epstein, M. (2005). A review of self-management interventions targeting academic outcomes for students with emotional and behavioral disorders. *Journal of Behavioral Education, 14,* 203–221.

Morgan, P. (2006). Increasing task engagement using preference or choice-making: Some behavioral and methodological factors affecting their efficacy as classroom interventions. *Remedial and Special Education, 27,* 176–187.

Moroz, K. B., & Jones, K. M. (2002). The effects of positive peer reporting on children's social involvement.

School Psychology Review, 31, 235–245.

Morrison, J. Q., & Jones, K. M. (2007). The effects of positive peer reporting as a class-wide positive behavioral support. *Journal of Behavioral Education, 16,* 111–124.

Mostert, M. P. (Ed.). (2010). Empirically unsupported interventions in special education [special issue]. *Exceptionality, 18*(1).

Mostert, M. P., & Crockett, J. B. (2000). Reclaiming the history of special education for more effective practice. *Exceptionality, 8,* 133–143.

Neef, N. A., Shafer, M. S., Egel, A. L., Cataldo, M. F., & Parrish, J. M. (1983). The class specific effects of compliance training with *do* and *don't* requests: Analogue analysis and classroom application. *Journal of Applied Behavior Analysis, 16,* 81–99.

Neiman, S., & DeVoe, J. F. (2009). *Crime, violence, discipline, and safety in U.S. public schools: Findings from the school survey on crime and safety: 2007–08* (NCES 2009-326). Washington, DC: National Center for Education Statistics, Institute of Education Sciences, U.S. Department of Education.

Nelson, J. R. (1996). Designing schools to meet the needs of students who exhibit disruptive behaviors. *Journal of Emotional and Behavioral Disorders, 4,* 147–161.

Nelson, J. R., Benner, G. J., Lane, K. L., & Smith, B. W. (2004). Academic achievement of K–12 students with emotional and behavioral disorders. *Exceptional Children, 71,* 59–73.

Nelson, J. R., Benner, G. J., Reid, R. C., Epstein, M. H., & Currin, D. (2002). The convergent validity of office discipline referrals with the CBCL-TRF. *Journal of Emotional and Behavioral Disorders, 10,* 181–188.

Nelson, J. R., Martella, R., & Galand, B. (1998). The effects of teaching school expectations and establishing a consistent consequence on formal office disciplinary actions. *Journal of Emotional and Behavioral Disorders, 6,* 153–161.

Nelson, J. R., Martella, R. M., & Marchand-Martella, N. (2002). Maximizing student learning: The effects of a comprehensive school-based program for preventing problem behaviors. *Journal of Emotional and Behavioral Disorders, 10,* 136–148.

Netzel, D. M., & Eber, L. (2003). Shifting from reactive to proactive discipline in an urban school district: A change in focus through PBIS implementation. *Journal of Positive Behavior Interventions, 5,* 71–79.

Nevin, J. A. (1996). The momentum of compliance. *Journal of Applied Behavior Analysis, 29,* 535–547.

Nevin, J. A., Mandell, C., & Atak, J. R. (1983). The analysis of behavioral momentum. *Journal of Applied Behavior Analysis, 39,* 49–59.

Newcomb, A., Bukowski, W., & Pattee, L. (1993). Children's peer relations: A meta-analytic review of popular, rejected, neglected, controversial, and average sociometric status. *Psychological Bulletin, 113,* 99–128.

Newcomer, L. L., & Lewis, T. J. (2004). Functional behavioral assessment: An investigation of assessment reliability and effectiveness of function-based interventions. *Journal of Emotional and Behavioral Disorders, 12,* 168–181.

Niesyn, M. (2009). Strategies for success: Evidence-based instructional practices for students with emotional and behavioral disorders. *Preventing School Failure, 53,* 227–233.

No Child Left Behind Act of 2001, 20 U.S.C. 70 § 6301 *et seq.* (2001).

Olmeda, R., & Kauffman, J. (2003). Sociocultural considerations in social skills research with African American students with emotional and behavioral disorders. *Journal of Developmental and Physical Disabilities, 15,* 101–121.

O'Neill, R., Horner, R., Albin, R., Sprague, J., Storey, K., & Newton, J. (1997). *Functional assessment and program development for problem behavior: A practical handbook.* Pacific Grove, CA: Brooks/Cole.

Overton, S., McKenzie, L., King, K., & Osborne, J. (2002). Replication of the First Step to Success model: A multiple-case study of implementation effectiveness. *Behavioral Disorders, 28*(1), 40–56.

Paine, S. C., Radicchi, J., Rosellini, L. C., Deutchman, L., & Darch, C. B. (1983). *Structuring your classroom for academic success.* Champaign, IL: Research Press.

Parker, J., & Asher, S. (1987). Peer relations and later personal adjustment: Are low-accepted children at-risk? *Psychological Bulletin, 102,* 357–389.

Parrish, J., Cataldo, M., Kolko, D., Neef, N., & Egel, A. (1986). Experimental analysis of response covariation among compliant and inappropriate behaviors. *Journal of Applied Behavior Analysis, 19,* 241–254.

Patterson, G. R. (1982). *Coercive family process.* Castalia: Eugene, OR.

Patterson, G. R., DeBaryshe, B. D., & Ramsey, E. (1989). A developmental perspective on antisocial behavior. *American Psychologist, 44,* 329–335.

Patterson, G. R., & Reid, J. B. (1973). Intervention for families of aggressive boys: A replication study. *Behavior Research and Therapy, 11,* 383–394.

Patterson, G. R., Reid, J. B., & Dishion, T. J. (1992). *Antisocial boys.* Castalia: Eugene, OR.

Patton, B., Jolivette., K., & Ramsey, M. (2006). Students with emotional and behavioral disorders can manage their own behavior: Implications for practice. *Teaching Exceptional Children, 39,* 14–21.

Paykel, E. S., Scott, J., Teasdale, J. D., Johnson, A. L., Garland, A., Moore, R., et al. (1999). Prevention of relapse in residual depression by cognitive therapy: A controlled trial. *Archives of General Psychiatry, 56,* 829–835.

Pearson Education. (2008). *AIMSweb.* Upper Saddle River, NJ: Author.

Pearson Scott Foresman. (Ed.). (2008). *Scott Foresman, Reading Street.* Glenview, IL: Pearson Education.

Peck, S. M., Wacker, D. P., Berg, W. K., Cooper, L. J., Brown, K. A., et al. (1996). Choice-making treatment of young children's severe behavior problems. *Journal of Applied Behavior Analysis, 29,* 263–290.

Pediatric OCD Treatment Study Team. (2004). Cognitive-behavior therapy, sertraline, and their combination for children and adolescents with obsessive-compulsive disorder: The pediatric OCD treatment study (POTS) randomized controlled trial. *Journal of the American Medical Association, 292*(16), 1969–1976.

Penno, D. A., Frank, A.R., & Wacker, D.P. (2000). Instructional accommodations

for adolescent students with severe emotional or behavioral disorders. *Behavioral Disorders, 25,* 325–343.

Piazza, C., Fisher, W., Hagopian, L., Bowman, L., & Toole, L. (1996). Using a choice assessment to predict reinforce effectiveness. *Journal of Applied Behavior Analysis, 29,* 1–9.

Poduska, J. M., Kellam, S. G., Wang, W., Brown, C. H., Ialongo, N. S., & Toyinbo, P. (2008). Impact of the Good Behavior Game, a universal classroom-based behavior intervention, on young adult service use for problems with emotions, behavior, or drugs or alcohol. *Drug and Alcohol Dependence, 95,* 529–545.

Prater, M. A., Hogan, S., & Miller, S. R. (1992). Using self-monitoring to improve on-task behavior and academic skills of an adolescent with mild handicaps across special and regular education settings. *Education & Treatment of Children, 15,* 43–55.

Preciado, J. A., Horner, R. H., & Baker, S. K. (2009). Using a function-based approach to decrease problem behaviors and increase academic engagement for Latino English language learners. *Journal of Special Education, 42,* 227–240.

Quinn, M. M., Gable, R. A., Fox, J., Rutherford, R. B., Van Acker, R., & Conroy, M. (2001). Putting quality functional assessment into practice in schools: A research agenda on behalf of E/BD students. *Education and Treatment of Children, 24,* 261–275.

Quinn, M., Kavale, K., Mathur, S., Rutherford, R., & Forness, S. (1999). A meta-analysis of social skill interventions for students with emotional and behavioral disorders. *Journal of Emotional and Behavioral Disorders, 7,* 54–64.

Ramsey, M. L., Jolivette, K., Patterson, D. P., & Kennedy, C. (2010). Using choice to increase time on-task, task completion, and accuracy for students with emotional/behavior disorders in a residential facility. *Education and Treatment of Children, 33*(1), 1–21.

Ray, K. P., Skinner, C. H., & Watson, T. S. (1999). Transferring stimulus control via momentum to increase compliance in a student with autism: A demonstration of collaborative consultation. *The School Psychology Review, 28*(4), 622–628.

Reid, J. B. (1993). Prevention of conduct disorder before and after school entry: Relating interventions to developmental findings. *Development and Psychopathology, 5,* 243–262.

Reiter, S., Kutcher, S., & Gardner, D. (1992). Anxiety disorders in children and adolescents: Clinical and related issues in pharmacological treatment. *Canadian Journal of Psychiatry, 37,* 432–438.

The Research Unit on Pediatric Psychopharmacology Anxiety Study Group. (2001). Fluvoxamine for the treatment of anxiety disorders in children and adolescents. *New England Journal of Medicine, 344,* 1279–1285.

The Research Unit on Pediatric Psychopharmacology Anxiety Study Group. (2002). Treatment of pediatric anxiety disorders: An open-label extension of the research units on pediatric psychopharmacology anxiety study. *Journal of Child and Adolescent Psychopharmacology, 12,* 175–188.

Reynolds, W. M., & Coats, K. I. (1986). A comparison of cognitive-behavioral therapy and relaxation training for the treatment of depression in adolescents. *Journal of Consulting and Clinical Psychology, 54,* 653–660.

Reynolds, W. M., & Stark, K. D. (1987). School-based intervention strategies for the treatment of depression in children and adolescents. In S. G. Forman (Ed.), *School-based affective and social intervention* (pp. 67–88). New York: Haworth Press.

Rhode, G., Jenson, W. R., & Reavis, H. K. (1992). *The tough kid book: Practical classroom applications.* Longmont, CO: Sopris West.

Rhode, G., Morgan, D. P., & Young, K. R. (1983). Generalization and maintenance of treatment gains of behaviorally disordered handicapped students from resource rooms to regular classroom using self-evaluation procedures. *Journal of Applied Behavior Analysis, 16,* 171–188.

Riddle, M. A., Geller, B., & Ryan, N. (1993). Case study: Another sudden death in a child treated with desipramine. *Journal of American Academy of Child and Adolescent Psychiatry, 32,* 792–797.

Roberts, L. M., Marshall, J., Nelson, R., & Albers, C. A. (2001). Curriculum-based assessment procedures embedded within functional behavioral assessments: Identifying escape-motivated behaviors in a general education classroom. *School Psychology Review, 30,* 264–272.

Roberts, M., McMahon, R., Forehand, R., & Humphreys, L. (1978). The effect of parental instruction-giving on child compliance. *Behavior Therapy, 9,* 793–798.

Robertson, E. J., & Lane, K. L. (2007). Supporting middle school students with academic and behavioral concerns within the context of a three-tiered model of support: Findings of a secondary prevention program. *Behavioral Disorders, 33,* 5–22.

Rock, M. L. (2005). Use of strategic self-monitoring to enhance academic engagement, productivity, and accuracy of students with and without exceptionalities. *Journal of Positive Behavior Interventions, 7,* 3–17.

Romaniuk, C., Miltenberger, R., Conyers, C., Jenner, N., Jurgens, M., & Ringenberg, C. (2002). The influence of activity choices on problem behaviors maintained by escape versus attention. *Journal of Applied Behavior Analysis, 35,* 349–362.

Romano, J. P., & Roll, D. (2000). Expanding the utility of behavior momentum for youth with developmental disabilities. *Behavioral Interventions, 15,* 99–111.

Rortverdt, A. K., & Miltenberger, R. G. (1994). Analysis of a high-probability instructional sequence and time-out in the treatment of child noncompliance. *Journal of Applied Behavior Analysis, 27*(2), 327–330.

Rosenbaum, M. S., & Drabman, R. S. (1979). Self-control training in the classroom: A review and critique. *Journal of Applied Behavior Analysis, 12,* 467–485.

Rosenthal, R., Rosnow, R. L., & Rubin, D. B. (2000). *Contrasts and effect sizes in behavioral research: A correlational approach.* New York: Cambridge University Press.

Rushton, J. L., Clark, S. J., & Freed, G. L. (2000). Primary care role in the management of childhood depression: A comparison of pediatricians and family care physicians. *Pediatrics, 105,* 957–962.

Russo, D. C., Cataldo, M. F., & Cushing, P. J. (1981). Compliance training and behavioral covariation in the treatment of multiple behavior problems. *Journal of Applied Behavior Analysis, 14*(3), 209–222.

Rutter, R. (1979). Protective factors in children's responses to stress and disadvantage. In M. W. Kent & J. E. Rolf (Eds.), *Primary prevention of psychopathology: Vol. 3. Social competence in children* (pp. 49–74). Hanover, NH: University Press of New England.

Rynn, M. A., Siqueland, L., & Rickels, K. (2001). Placebo-controlled trial of sertraline in the treatment of children with generalized anxiety disorder. *American Journal of Psychiatry. 158,* 2008–2014.

Safe and Drug-Free Schools and Communities Act of 1994, Pub. L. No. 103-382, 4001-4133, 108 Stat. 3518 (codified as amended at 20 U.S.C. 7101-7143 [2000]).

Sagan, C. (1996). *The demon-haunted world: Science as a candle in the dark.* New York: Ballantine Books.

Salend, S. J., Reynolds, C. J., & Coyle, E. M. (1989). Individualizing the Good Behavior Game across type and frequency of behavior with emotionally disturbed adolescents. *Behavior Modification, 13,* 108–126.

Sallee, F., Hilal, R., Dougherty, D., Beach, K., & Nesbitt, L. (1998). Platlet serotonin transporter in depressed children and adolescants: 3H-paroxetine platelet binding before and after sertraline. *Journal of the American Academy of Child and Adolescent Psychiatry, 37,* 777–784.

Sallee, F., Vrindavanam, N., Deas-Nesmith, D., Carson, S., & Sethuraman, G. (1997). Pulse intravenous clomipramine for depressed adolescents: Double-blind controlled trial. *American Journal of Psychiatry, 154,* 668–673.

Sameroff, A. J. (1983). Developmental systems: Contexts and evolution. In P. H. Mussen (Gen. Ed.) & W. Kessen (Vol. Ed.), *Handbook of child psychology: Vol 1. History, theory, and methods* (4th ed., pp. 237–294). New York: Wiley.

Sameroff, A. J., Seifer, R., Barocas, R., Zax, M., & Greenspan, R. (1987). Intelligence quotient scores of 4-year-old children: Social environmental risk factors. *Pediatrics, 79,* 343–350.

Sanchez-Fort, M. R., Brady, M. P., & Davis, C. A. (1995). Using high-probability requests to increase low-probability communication behavior in young children with severe disabilities. *Education and Training in Mental Retardation and Developmental Disabilities, 30*(2), 151–165.

Sandmel, K., Brindle, M., Harris, K., Lane, K., Graham, S., Nackel, J., Mathias, R., & Little, A. (2009). Making it work: Differentiating tier two self-regulated strategies development in writing in tandem with schoolwide positive behavioral support. *Focus on Exceptional Children, 42,* 22–33.

Santos, R. M., & Lignugaris-Kraft, B. (1999). The effects of direct questions on preschool children's responses to indirect requests. *Journal of Behavioral Education, 9,* 193–210.

Sasso, G., Conroy, M., Stichter, J., & Fox, J. (2001). Slowing down the bandwagon: The misapplication of functional assessment for students with emotional and behavioral disorders. *Behavioral Disorders, 26,* 282–296.

Satcher, D. (2001). *Youth violence: A report of the Surgeon General.* Washington, DC: Office of the Surgeon General, U.S. Department of Health & Human Services.

Sattler, J. M., & Hoge, R. D. (2006). *Assessment of children: Behavioral, social, and clinical foundations* (5th ed.). La Mesa, CA: Jerome M. Sattler.

Scarboro, M., & Forehand, R. (1975). Effects of response contingent isolation and ignoring on compliance and oppositional behavior of children. *Journal of Experimental Child Psychology, 19,* 252–264.

Schloss, P., Schloss, C., Wood, C., & Kiehl, W. (1986). A critical review of social skills research with behaviorally disordered students. *Behavioral Disorders, 12,* 1–14.

Schneider, B. (1992). Didactic methods for enhancing children's peer relationships. *Clinical Psychology Review, 12,* 363–382.

Schneider, B., & Byrne, B. (1985). Children's social skills training: A meta-analysis. In B. Schneider, K. Rubin, & J. Ledingham (Eds.), *Children's peer relations: Issues in assessment and intervention* (pp. 175–190). New York: Springer-Verlag.

Schoen, S. F. (1983). The status of compliance technology: Implications for programming. *The Journal of Special Education, 17,* 438–496.

Schumm, J. S., & Vaughn, S. (1995). General education teacher planning: What can students with learning disabilities expect? *Exceptional Children, 61,* 335–353.

Schunk, D. H. (2004). *Learning theories: An educational perspective.* Upper Saddle River, NJ: Pearson.

Scott, T. M. (2001). A schoolwide example of positive behavioral support. *Journal of Positive Behavior Interventions, 3,* 88–94.

Scott, T. M., & Barrett, S. B. (2004). Using staff and student time engaged in disciplinary procedures to evaluate the impact of school-side PBS. *Journal of Positive Behavior Interventions, 6,* 21–27.

Scruggs, T. M., & Mastropieri, M. A. (2000). The effectiveness of mnemonic instruction for students with learning and behavior problems: An update and research synthesis. *Journal of Behavioral Education, 10,* 163–173.

Seeley, J. R., Small, J. W., Walker, H. M., Feil, E. G., Severson, H. H., Golly, A. M., & Forness, S. R. (2009). Efficacy of the *First Step to Success* intervention for students with ADHD. *School Mental Health, 1,* 37–48.

Seybert, A., Dunlap, G., & Ferro, J. (1996). The effects of choice-making on the problem behaviors of high school students with intellectual disabilities. *Journal of Behavioral Education, 6,* 49–65.

Shapiro, J. P., Burgoon, J. D., Welker, C. J., & Clough, J. B. (2002). Evaluation of the peacemakers program: School-based violence prevention for students in grades four through eight. *Psychology in the Schools, 39,* 87–100.

Shermer, M. (2002). *Why people believe weird things.* New York: Henry Holt.

Shevin, M., & Klein, N. K. (1984). The importance of choice-making skills for students with severe disabilities. *Journal of the Association for Persons with Severe Handicaps, 9,* 159–166.

Shogren, K. A., Faggella-Luby, M. N., Bae, A. J., & Wehmeyer, M. L. (2004). The effect of choice-making as an intervention for problem behavior: A meta-analysis. *Journal of Positive Behavior Interventions, 6,* 228–237.

Shores, R. E., & Wehby, J. H. (1999). Analyzing social behavior of children with emotional and behavioral disorders in classrooms. *Journal of Emotional and Behavioral Disorders, 7,* 194–199.

Sigafoos, F., & Dempsey, R. (1992). Assessing choice making among children with multiple disabilities. *Journal of Applied Behavior Analysis, 25,* 747–755.

Sigafoos, J., Roberts, D., Couzens, D., & Kerr, M. (1993). Providing opportunities for choice-making and turn-taking to adults with multiple disabilities. *Journal of Developmental and Physical Disabilities, 5,* 297–310.

Simeon, J., & Ferguson, B. (1987). Alprazolam effects in children with anxiety disorders. *Canadian Journal Psychiatry, 32,* 570–574.

Singer, G. H., Singer, J., & Horner, R. H. (1987). Using pretask requests to increase the probability of compliance for students with severe disabilities. *Journal of the Association for Persons with Severe Handicaps, 12,* 287–291.

Skinner, B. F. (1953). *Science and human behavior.* New York: Macmillan.

Skinner, C. H., Belfiore, P. J., Mace, H. W., Williams-Wilson, S., & Johns, G. A. (1997). Altering response typography to increase response efficiency and learning rates. *School Psychology Quarterly, 12,* 54–64.

Skinner, C. H., Fletcher, P. A., & Henington, C. (1996). Increasing learning rates by increasing student responses rates: A summary of research. *School Psychology Quarterly, 11,* 313–325.

Skinner, C. H., Ford, J. M., & Yunker, B. D. (1991). A comparison of instructional response requirements on the multiplication performance of behaviorally disordered students. *Behavioral Disorders, 17,* 56–65.

Skinner, C. H., Neddenriep, C. E., Robinson, S. L., Ervin, R., & Jones, K. (2002). Altering educational environments through positive peer reporting: Prevention and remediation of social problems associated with behavioral disorders. *Psychology in the Schools, 39,* 191–202.

Skinner, C. H., & Shapiro, E. S. (1989). A comparison of taped-words and drill interventions on reading fluency in adolescents with behavior disorders. *Education and Treatment of Children, 12*, 123–133.

Skinner, C. H., Smith, E. S., & McLean, J. E. (1994). The effects of intertribal interval duration on sight-word learning rates in children with behavioral disorders. *Behavioral Disorders, 19*, 98–107.

Smith, A. (2003). Scientifically based research and evidence-based education: A federal policy context. *Research and Practice for Persons with Severe Disabilities, 28*, 126–132.

Smith, B.W., & Sugai, G. (2000). A self-management functional assessment-based behavior support plan for a middle school student with EBD. *Journal of Positive Behavior Interventions, 2*, 208–217.

Smith, R. G., & Iwata, B. A. (1997). Antecedent influences on behavioral disorders. *Journal of Applied Behavior Analysis, 30*, 343–375.

Snyder, J., & Stoolmiller, M. (2002). Reinforcement and coercion mechanisms in the development of antisocial behavior: The family. In J. Reid, G. Patterson, & J. Snyder (Eds.), *Antisocial behavior in children and adolescents: A developmental analysis and model for intervention* (pp. 65–100). Washington, DC: American Psychological Association.

Sprague, J., Walker, H., Golly, A., White, K., Myers, D. R., & Shannon, T. (2001). Translating research into effective practice: The effects of a universal staff and student intervention on indicators of discipline and school safety. *Education and Treatment of Children, 24*, 495–511.

Stahr, B., Cushing, D., Lane, K., & Fox, J. (2006). Efficacy of a function-based intervention in decreasing off-task behavior exhibited by a student with ADHD. *Journal of Positive Behavior Interventions, 8*, 201–211.

Stevens, V., De Bourdeaudhuij, I., & Van Oost, P. (2000). Bullying in Flemish schools: An evaluation of anti-bullying intervention in primary and secondary schools. *British Journal of Educational Psychology, 70*, 195–210.

Stokes, T. F., & Baer, D. M. (1977). An implicit technology of generalization. *Journal of Applied Behavior Analysis, 10*, 349–367.

Stokes, T. F., & Osnes, P. G. (1989). An operant pursuit of generalization. *Behavior Therapy, 20*, 337–355.

Stormont, M. A., Smith, S. C., & Lewis, T. J. (2007). Teacher implementation of precorrection and praise statements in Head Start classrooms as a component of a program-wide system of positive behavior support. *Journal of Behavior Education, 16*, 280–290.

Stouthamer-Loeber, M., & Loeber, R. (2002). Lost opportunities for intervention: Undetected markers for the development of serious juvenile delinquency. *Criminal Behaviour and Mental Health, 12*, 69–82.

Sugai, G., & Horner, R. H. (2002). The evolution of discipline practices: School-wide positive behavior supports. *Child & Family Behavior Therapy, 24*, 25–50.

Sugai, G., & Horner, R. H. (2006). A promising approach for expanding and sustaining school-wide positive behavior support. *School Psychology Review, 35*, 245–260.

Sugai, G., Horner, R., & Gresham, F. M. (2002). Behaviorally effective school environments. In M. Shinn, H. Walker, & G. Stoner (Eds.), *Interventions for academic and behavior problems* (2nd ed., pp. 315–350). Bethesda, MD: National Association of School Psychologists.

Sugai, G., Horner, R., & Todd, A. W. (2000). *Effective Behavior Support (EBS) Survey: Assessing and planning behavior support in schools.* Eugene: University of Oregon.

Sugai, G., Lewis-Palmer, T., Todd, A., & Horner, R. H. (2001). *School-wide evaluation tool.* Eugene, OR: University of Oregon.

Sutherland, K. S., Alder, N., & Gunter, P. L. (2003). The effect of increased rates of opportunities to respond on the classroom behavior of students with emotional/behavioral disorders. *Journal of Emotional and Behavioral Disorders, 11*, 239–248.

Sutherland, K. S., & Oswald, D. (2005). The relationship between teacher and student behavior in classrooms for students with emotional and behavioral disorders: Transactional processes. *Journal of Child and Family Studies, 14*, 1–14.

Sutherland, K. S., & Singh, N. N. (2004). Learned helplessness and students

with EBD: Deprivation in the classroom. *Behavioral Disorders, 29*, 169–181.

Sutherland, K. S., & Wehby, J. H. (2001). Exploring the relationship between increased opportunities to respond to academic requests and the academic and behavioral outcomes of students with emotional and behavioral disorders: A review. *Remedial and Special Education, 22*, 113–121.

Sutherland, K. S., Wehby, J. H., & Copeland, S. R. (2000). Effect of varying rates of behavior-specific praise on the on-task behavior of students with EBD. *Journal of Emotional & Behavioral Disorders, 8*(1), 2–8.

Sutherland, K. S., Wehby, J. H., & Yoder, P. J. (2002). Examination of the relationship between teacher praise and opportunities for students with EBD to respond to academic requests. *Journal of Emotional and Behavior Disorders, 10*(1), 5–13.

Tankersley, M., Harjusola-Webb, S., & Landrum, T. J. (2008). Using single-subject research to establish the evidence base of special education. *Intervention in School and Clinic, 44*, 83–90.

Taylor-Greene, S., Brown, D., Nelson, L. Longton, J., Gassman, T., Cohen, J., Swartz, J., Horner, R. H., Sugai, G., & Hall, S. (1997). School-wide behavioral support: Starting the year off right. *Journal of Behavioral Education, 7*, 99–112.

Taylor-Greene, S. J., & Kartub, D. T. (2000). Durable implementation of school-wide behavior support. *Journal of Positive Behavior Support, 2*, 233–235.

Templeton, J. (1990). Social skills training for behavior-problem adolescents: A review. *Journal of Partial Hospitalization, 6*, 49–60.

Thomas, J. D., Presland, I. E., Grant, M. D., & Glynn, T. (1978). Natural rates of teacher approval and disapproval in grade-7 classrooms. *Journal of Applied Behavior Analysis, 11*, 91–94.

Thompson, R. H., White, K. R., & Morgan, D. P. (1982). Teacher-student interactions patterns in classrooms with mainstreamed mildly handicapped students. *American Educational Research Journal, 19*, 220–236.

Tiger, J. H., Hanley, G. P., & Hernandez, E. (2006). An evaluation of the value of choice with preschool children. *Journal of Applied Behavior Analysis, 39,* 1–16.

Tincani, M., & Crozier, S. (2008). Comparing brief and extended wait-time during small group instruction for children with challenging behavior. *Journal of Behavioral Education, 17,* 79–92.

Tingstrom, D. H., Sterling-Turner, H. E., & Wilczynski, S. M. (2002). The Good Behavior Gamer: 1969-2002. *Behavior Modification, 30,* 225–253.

Todd, A., Haugen, L., Anderson, K., & Spriggs, M. (2002). Teaching recess: Low-cost efforts producing effective results. *Journal of Positive Behavior Interventions, 4,* 46–52.

Todd, A. W., Horner, R. H., & Sugai, G. (1999). Self-monitoring and self-recruited praise: Effects on problem behavior, academic engagement, and work completion in a typical classroom. *Journal of Positive Behavior Interventions, 1,* 66–76.

Treatment for Adolescents with Depression Study (TADS) Team. (2004). Fluoxetine, cognitive behavioral therapy, and their combination for adolescents with depression. *Journal of American Medical Association, 292,* 807–820.

Trussell, R. P., Lewis, T. J., & Stichter, J. P. (2008). The impact of targeted classroom inventerventions and function-based behavior interventions on problem with emotional/behavioral disorders. *Behavioral Disorders, 33,* 153-166.

Turnbull, A., Edmonson, H., Griggs, P, Wickham, D., Sailor, W., Freeman, R., Guess, D., Lassen, S., McCart, A., Park, J., Riffel, L., Turnbull, R., & Warren, J. (2002). A blueprint for school-wide positive behavior support: Implementation of three components. *Exceptional Children, 58,* 377–402.

Turnbull, H. R., III. (2005). Individuals with Disabilities Education Act Reauthorization: Accountability and personal responsibility. *Remedial and Special Education, 26,* 320–326.

Turton, A. M., Umbreit, J., Liaupsin, C. J., & Bartley, J. (2007). Function-based intervention for an adolescent with emotional and behavioral disorders in Bermuda. *Behavioral Disorders, 33,* 23–32.

Umbreit, J. (1995). Functional assessment and intervention in a regular classroom setting for the disruptive behavior of a student with attention deficit hyperactivity disorder. *Behavioral Disorders, 20,* 267–278.

Umbreit, J., & Blair, K. W. (1996). The effects of preference, choice, and attention on problem behavior at school. *Education and Training in Mental Retardation and Developmental Disabilities,* June, 151–161.

Umbreit, J., Ferro, J., Liaupsin, C., & Lane, K. (2007). *Functional behavioral assessment and function-based intervention: An effective, practical approach.* Upper Saddle River, NJ: Pearson.

Umbreit, J., Lane, K. L., & Dejud, C. (2004). Improving classroom behavior by modifying task difficulty: Effects of increasing the difficult of too-easy tasks. *Journal of Positive Behavior Interventions, 6,* 13–20.

Urdan, T., & Schoenfelder, E. (2006). Classroom effects on student motivation: Goal structures, social relationships, and competence beliefs. *Journal of School Psychology, 44,* 331–349.

Van Acker, R., Grant, S. H., & Henry, D. (1996). Teacher and student behavior as a function of risk for aggression. *Education and Treatment of Children, 19,* 316–334.

Varley, C., & McClellan, J. (1997). Case study: Additional sudden deaths with tricyclic antidepressants. *Journal of the American Academy of Child and Adolescent Psychiatry, 36,* 390–394.

Vaughn, B., & Horner, R. H. (1995). Effects of concrete versus verbal choice systems on problem behavior. *Augmentative and Alternative Communication, 11,* 89–92.

Vaughn, B., & Horner, R. H. (1997). Identifying instructional tasks that occasion problem behaviors and assessing the effects of student versus teacher choice among these tasks. *Journal of Applied Behavior Analysis, 30,* 299–312.

Velosa, J. F., & Riddle, M. A. (2000). Pharmacologic treatment of anxiety disorders in children and adolescents. *Pharmacology, 9,* 119–133.

von Mizener, B. H., & Williams, R. L. (2009). The effects of student choices on academic performance. *Journal of Positive Behavior Intervention, 11,* 110–128.

Wagner, M., Kutash, K., Duchnowski, A. J., Epstein, M. H., & Sumi, W. C. (2005). The children and youth we serve: A national picture of the characteristics of students with emotional disturbance receiving special education services. *Journal of Emotional and Behavioral Disorders, 13,* 79–96.

Wagner, M., Newman, L., Cameto, R., Levine, P., & Garza, N. (2006). An overview of findings from Wave 2 of the National Longitudinal Transition Study-2 (NLTS2). *National Center for Special Education Research.* (ERIC Document Reproduction Service No. ED495660)

Walker, B., Cheney, D., Stage, S., & Blum, C. (2005). Schoolwide screening and positive behavior supports: Identifying and supporting students at risk for school failure. *Journal of Positive Behavior Interventions, 7,* 194–204.

Walker, G. R. (1993). Noncompliant behavior of people with mental retardation. *Research in Developmental Disabilities, 14,* 87–105.

Walker, H. M. (2003, February 20). *Comments on accepting the Outstanding Leadership Award from the Midwest Symposium for Leadership in Behavior Disorders.* Kansas City, KS: Author.

Walker, H. M., Forness, S., Kauffman, J., Epstein, M., Gresham, F. M., Nelson, C. M., & Strain, P. (1998). Macro-social validation: Referencing outcomes in behavioral disorders to societal issues and problems. *Behavioral Disorders, 24,* 130–140.

Walker, H. M., Horner, R. H., Sugai, G., Bullis, M., Sprague, J. R., Bricker, D., & Kauffman, M. J. (1996). Integrated approaches to preventing antisocial behavior patterns among school-age children and youth. *Journal of Emotional and Behavioral Disorders, 4,* 193–256.

Walker, H. M, Irvin, L., Noell, J., & Singer, G. (1992). A construct score approach to the assessment of social competence: Rationale, technological considerations, and anticipated outcomes. *Behavior Modification, 16,* 448–474.

Walker, H. M., Kavanagh, K., Stiller, B., Golly, A., Severson, H. H., &

Feil, E. G. (1998). First Step to Success: An early intervention approach for preventing school antisocial behavior. *Journal of Emotional and Behavioral Disorders, 6*(2), 66–80.

Walker, H. M., & McConnell, S. (1995). *Walker-McConnell Scale of Social Competence and School Adjustment.* Florence, KY: Thomson Learning.

Walker, H. M., Ramsey, E., & Gresham, F. M. (2004). *Antisocial behavior at school: Evidence-based practices.* Belmont, CA: Wadsworth/Thomson Learning.

Walker, H. M., Seeley, J. R., Small, J., Severson, H. H., Graham, B., Feil, E. G., Serna, L., Golly, A. M., & Forness, S. R. (2009). A randomized controlled trial of the *First Step to Success* early intervention: Demonstration of program efficacy outcomes within a diverse, urban school district. *Journal of Emotional and Behavioral Disorders, 17,* 197–212.

Walker, H. M., & Severson, H. H. (1992). *Systematic screening for behavior disorders (SSBD): User's guide and technical manual.* Longmont, CO: Sopris West.

Walker, H. M., & Severson, H. H. (2002). Developmental prevention of at-risk outcomes for vulnerable antisocial children and youth. In K. L. Lane, F. M. Gresham, & T. E. O'Shaughnessy (Eds.), *Interventions for children with or at risk for emotional and behavioral disorders* (pp. 177–194). Boston, MA: Allyn & Bacon.

Walker, H. M., Severson, H. H., & Feil, E. G. (1994). *Early Screening Project (E.S.P.): A proven child find process.* Longmont, CO: Sopris West.

Walker, H. M., Severson, H., Todis, B. J., Block-Pedego, A. E., Williams, G. J., Haring, N. G., & Barckley, M. (1990). Systematic Screening for Behavior Disorders (SSBD): Further validation, replication, and normative data. *Remedial and Special Education, 11,* 32–46.

Walker, H. M., Sprague, J. R., Perkins-Rowe, K. A., Beard-Jordan, K. Y., Seibert, B. M., Golly, A. M., Severson, H. H., & Feil, E. G. (2005). The First Step to Success program: Achieving secondary prevention outcomes for behaviorally at-risk children through early intervention.

In M. H. Epstein, K. Kutash, & A. J. Duchnowski (Eds.), *Outcomes for children and youth with emotional and behavioral disorders and their families: Programs and evaluation best practices* (2nd ed., pp. 501–523). Austin, TX: Pro-Ed.

Walker, H. M., Stiller, B., Golly, A., Kavanagh, K., Severson, H., & Feil, E. (1997). *First Step to Success: Helping young children overcome antisocial behavior (an early intervention program for grades K–3).* Longmont, CO: Sopris West.

Walker, H. M., Stiller, B., Severson, H., Feil, E., & Golly, A. (1998). First Step to Success: Intervening at the point of school entry to prevent antisocial behavior patterns. *Psychology in the Schools, 35,* 259–269.

Watson, S. T., & Robinson, S. L. (1998). A behavior analytic approach to treating depression. In T. S. Watson & F. M. Gresham (Eds.), *Handbook of child behavior therapy: Issues in clinical child psychology* (pp. 393–411). New York: Plenum Press.

Webster-Stratton, C. (1998). Parent training with low-income clients: Promoting parental engagement through a collaborative approach. In Lutzker, J. R. (Ed.), *Child abuse: A handbook of theory, research and treatment* (pp. 183–210). New York: Plenum Press.

Webster-Stratton, C. (2006). *The Incredible Years: A trouble-shooting guide for parents of children aged 3–8.* Seattle, WA: Incredible Years Press.

Wehby, J. H., & Hollahan, M. S. (2000). Effects of high-probability requests on the latency to initiate academic tasks. *Journal of Applied Behavior Analysis, 33*(2), 259–262.

Wehby, J. H., Lane, K. L., & Falk, K. B. (2005). An inclusive approach to improving early literacy skills of students with emotional and behavioral disorders. *Behavior Disorders, 30,* 155–169.

Wehby, J. H., Symons, F. J., Canale, J. A., & Go, F. J. (1998). Teaching practices in classrooms for students with emotional and behavioral disorders: Discrepancies between recommendations and observations. *Behavioral Disorders, 24,* 51–56.

Wehmeyer, M. L., & Field, S. (2007). *Instructional and assessment strategies to promote the self-determination of*

students with disabilities. Thousand Oaks, CA: Corwin Press.

Weisz, J. R., Thurber, C. A., Sweeney, L., Proffitt, V. D., & LeGagnoux, G. L. (1997). Brief treatment of mild-moderate child depression using primary and secondary control enhancement training. *Journal of Counseling and Clinical Psychology, 65,* 703–707.

Wentzel, K. R. (1993). Does being good make the grade? Social behavior and academic competence in middle school. *Journal of Educational Psychology, 85,* 357–364.

West, R. P., & Sloane, H. N. (1986). Teacher presentation rate and point delivery rate: Effect on classroom disruption, performance accuracy, and response rate. *Behavior Modification, 10,* 267–286.

White, M. A. (1975). Natural rates of teacher approval and disapproval in the classroom. *Journal of Applied Behavior Analysis, 8,* 367–372.

Whittington, C. J., Kendall, T., Fonagy, P., Cottrell, D., Cotgrove, A., & Boddington, E. (2004). Selective serotonin reuptake inhibitors in childhood depression: Systematic review of published versus unpublished data. *The Lancet, 363,* 1341–1345.

Wigfield, A., & Karpathian, M. (1991). Who am I and what can I do? Children's self-concepts and motivation in achievement situations. *Educational Psychologist, 26,* 233–261.

Wilkinson, L. A. (2008). Self-management for children with high-functioning autism spectrum disorders. *Intervention in School and Clinic, 43,* 150–157.

Wilson, B. A. (2000). *Wilson reading system.* Oxford, MA: Wilson Language Training. with adolescent boys. *Journal of Counseling and Development, 70,* 600–605.

Witt, J. C., & Elliott, S. N. (1985). Acceptability of classroom intervention strategies. In T. R. Kratochwill (Ed.), *Advances in school psychology* (Vol. 4., pp. 251–288). Mahwah, NJ: Erlbaum.

Wolf, M. M. (1978). Social validity: The case for subjective measurement or how applied behavior analysis is finding its heart. *Journal of Applied Behavior Analysis, 11,* 203–214.

Wolery, M., & Gast, D. L. (1984). Effective and efficient procedures for the transfer of stimulus control. *Topics in Early Childhood Special Education, 4*, 55–77.

Wolraich, M. L. (2003). The use of psychotropic medications in children: An American view. *Journal of Child Psychology and Psychiatry, 44*, 159–168.

Wood, B. K., Umbreit, J., Liaupsin, C. J., & Gresham, F. M. (2007). A treatment integrity analysis of function-based interventions. *Education and Treatment of Children, 30*, 105–120.

Woodcock, R. W., McGrew, K. S., & Mather, N. (2001). *Woodcock-Johnson III Tests of Achievement.* Itasca, IL: Riverside.

Wright-Gallo, G. L., Higbee, T. S., Reagon, K. A., & Davey, B. J. (2006). Classroom-based functional analysis and intervention for students with emotional/behavioral disorders. *Education and Treatment of Children, 29*, 421–436.

Yeager, C., & McLaughlin, T. (1995). The use of a time-out ribbon and precision requests to improve child compliance in the classroom: A case study. *Child and Family Behavior Therapy, 17*(4), 1–9.

Yeaton, W., & Sechrest, L. (1981). Critical dimensions in the choice and maintenance of successful treatments: Strength, integrity, and effectiveness. *Journal of Consulting and Clinical Psychology, 49,* 156–167.

Yell, M. L., Meadows, N. B., Drasgow, E., & Shriner, J. G. (2009). *Evidence-based practices of educating students with emotional and behavioral disorders.* Upper Saddle River, NJ: Pearson.

Zaragoza, N., Vaughn, S., & McIntosh, R. (1991). Social skills interventions and children with behavior problems: A review. *Behavioral Disorders, 16,* 260–275.

Zarcone, J. R., Iwata, B. A., Hughes, C. E., & Vollmer, T. R. (1993). Momentum versus extinction effects in the treatment of self-injurious escape behavior. *Journal of Applied Behavior Analysis, 26*, 135–136.

Zarcone, J. R., Iwata, B. A., Mazaleski, J. L., & Smith, R. G. (1994). Momentum and extinction effects on self-injurious escape behavior and noncompliance. *Journal of Applied Behavior Analysis, 27*(4), 649–658.

Name Index

Subject Index